PRELUDE

When Swami Muktananda first visited the United States, he deplaned (as flight attendants are fond of saying) and walked directly into a large, modern terminal.

He stood for a while, looking around the enormous airport—so different from India, he might have been on another planet.

He saw a vast assortment of food, drinks, magazines and newspapers; padded, upholstered furniture was everywhere; the rest rooms cost nothing, and had hot and cold running water; everyone was properly dressed; the airport was clean, well-lit, and the whole place—the size of most *villages* in his homeland—was not only air-conditioned but *carpeted*.

Even so, he saw the passengers rushing by, hurrying to their planes, seemingly not appreciating any of it.

"They live in paradise," he observed, "I wonder if they'll ever know."

*The last thing
we decide in writing a book
is what to put first.*

BLAISE PASCAL

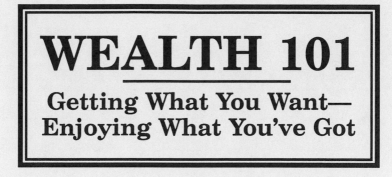

WEALTH 101

Getting What You Want— Enjoying What You've Got

by

John-Roger & Peter McWilliams

Prelude Press

8159 Santa Monica Boulevard
Los Angeles, California 90046

Published simultaneously in the United States and Canada
Printed in the United States of America

Editor: Jean Sedillos
Book and Cover Design: Paul LeBus
Back Cover Design: Paul LeBus, Michael Barba
Proofreaders: Julie Armstrong, Amy Bowman, Zachery Cook,
John Donohue, Erin Fairchild, Christopher McMullen,
Vanessa Graeber Meyer, Karen Maria Rufa, Perry Segal,
Bea Stangrover, Janet Stoakley, Carol Taylor, Paurvi Trivedi
Jacket Cover Photography: Betty Bennett
Desktop Publishing: Karen Maria Rufa

If your local bookstore is out,
please order additional copies by calling

1-800-LIFE-101

*Readers are of two sorts:
one who carefully
goes through a book,
and the other who as carefully
lets the book go through him.*

DOUGLAS JERROLD

CONTENTS

PART FOUR
GETTING MORE OF WHAT YOU WANT 385

PART FIVE

Seek wealth,
it's good.

IVAN BOESKY

WEALTH 101

**Getting What You Want—
Enjoying What You've Got**

Many are called
but few get up.

OLIVER HERFORD

1863–1935

INTRODUCTION

Welcome to *WEALTH 101*.

This is not your typical book about money.

First, we're going to suggest that you really don't need any more; that you can live your life fully and joyfully with what you already have; that after basic biological needs are met, enjoying life has very little to do with money; and that if you entirely let go of the pursuit of money for its own sake, you'll probably be a lot better off.

Then we'll tell you how to get more money.

Wealth is enjoying what we already have, not getting more of what we *think* will make us happy. We are wealthy when we have learned to live with ourselves, knowing that what we are and have is enough.

Ironically, when we are enjoying what we already have, getting more of what we want is easier—and, not surprisingly, more enjoyable.

When we're enjoying what we have, we are not lost in the myth—a monstrously popular myth, but a myth none-theless—that things and people *outside ourselves* make us happy.

When we know it's our *appreciation* of what we have—not *what* we have—that brings enjoyment, it's easier to choose what we really want. When we pursue what we really want, we stand a much better chance of not only getting it, but of enjoying the pursuit.

"Before I had a lot of money, I was really quite happy," said Oprah Winfrey. "And, I will tell you this—you may not believe it—I never would have gotten the money if I wasn't happy to begin with. I never would have gotten it."

In other words—enjoy what you've got to get what you want.

Not that we're against money, you understand. We like money. In fact, we *love* money. Money is a powerful symbol of energy, and energy is a great thing. As such, money is a

Annual income twenty pounds,
annual expenditure
nineteen nineteen six,
result happiness.
Annual income twenty pounds,
annual expenditure
twenty pounds ought and six,
result misery.

CHARLES DICKENS
DAVID COPPERFIELD

tool. It can be misused—and it can be splendidly used, too. Money doesn't care.

There are specific techniques for getting more money. We'll tell you what we know. There are also techniques for getting other forms of energy—some more valuable than mere money. We'll suggest a good many of those techniques, too. And then we'll come full circle and discuss enjoying the fruits of your harvest.

For some, that enjoyment is felt as jubilation, happiness, ecstasy. For others, it's contentment, fulfillment, a quiet sense of satisfaction for a job well done. However you experience enjoyment—delight, serenity, or any combination—we like to think you'll find something in these pages to enhance that.

Then we come to the shortest—but perhaps the most crucial—section of the book, "Balance."

Some people are too busy "earning a living" to live. Our advice to them? Slow down. At the very least, follow Bernard Barush's suggestion: "Always do one less thing than you think you can do." Or, if we were in a more caustic mood, we might quote George Bernard Shaw: "To be clever enough to get a great deal of money, one must be stupid enough to want it."

Other people are too poor to enjoy life. To these people we'd probably say, "Speed up!" Get going. Get enough wealth flowing through your life to follow your dream. And don't wait. Do it now. As Zero Mostel pointed out in Mel Brooks's *The Producers,* "He who hesitates is poor."

So, should you slow down, or speed up? There are no "right" answers. Balance is a highly personal thing—dynamic, and requiring great skill, like crossing a tightrope, with a heavy wind, in a thunderstorm, during an earthquake. The balance point always seems to be moving, shifting, and appears as elusive as love.

But, like love, when found, the balance point can be just as rewarding.

So, welcome to wealth. Enjoy.

*Unprovided
with original learning,
unformed
in the habits of thinking,
unskilled
in the arts of composition,
I resolved—
to write a book.*

EDWARD GIBBON

☆

A special meditation on wealth based on this book is available on audio cassette. It is designed to be listened to daily for thirty days, or you can play it in the background while reading *WEALTH 101*—or while doing almost anything else. It is available for $10, by calling 1-800-LIFE-101.

WEALTH 101 is also available—complete and unabridged—on audio cassette tapes. It's $22.95, and includes the above-mentioned meditation on wealth. So, if you were going to buy the meditation tape, you can get the rest of this book on tape for only $12.95 more. Please order by calling 1-800-LIFE-101.

Thank you.

☆

This book is part of THE *LIFE 101* SERIES, which includes

*LIFE 101: Everything We Wish We Had Learned
About Life In School—But Didn't*

*You Can't Afford the Luxury of a Negative Thought:
A Book for People with Any Life-Threatening Illness—
Including Life*

DO IT! Let's Get Off Our Buts

Although all the books in the series support each other, each stands independently and can be read separately.

If money is your hope
for independence
you will never have it.
The only real security that
a man can have in this world
is a reserve of knowledge,
experience and ability.

HENRY FORD

PART ONE

WEALTH

The way we see it, wealth is more than just money—much more. Most of what we consider wealth, in fact, has nothing to do with money.

We define wealth as health, happiness, abundance, prosperity, riches, loving, caring, sharing, learning, knowing what we want, opportunity, enjoying and balance.

Together, they form wealth. We consider these attributes of wealth to be *attitudes,* not things.

Wealth is a way of looking at life.

More on this later. First, let's take a closer look at each of the aspects of wealth.

*Beloved, I wish
above all things
that thou mayest prosper
and be in health,
even as thy soul prospereth.*

3 JOHN 1:2

Wealth Is Health

Perhaps more than anything else, wealth is good health. "The first wealth is health," Emerson said. It's hard to imagine any amount of material possessions making up for—or being enjoyed in—ill health. As Rabelais pointed out, "Without health, life is not life; it is only a state of languor and suffering." Or, this from Bacon: "A healthy body is a guest-chamber for the soul; a sick body is a prison."

"Look to your health; and if you have it, praise God, and value it next to a good conscience," wrote Izaak Walton in 1653, "for health is the second blessing that we mortals are capable of; a blessing that money cannot buy."

"O, health! health!" Ben Johnson wrote, "the blessings of the rich! the riches of the poor! who can buy thee at too dear a rate, since there is no enjoying the world without thee?"

When we speak of health, we are not just referring to a lack of illness. For many people, health is defined as not being sick—an absence of symptoms equals health. For us, however, health is much more. It is the *presence* of vitality, passion, loving and enthusiasm.

"Measure your health by your sympathy with morning and Spring," wrote Thoreau. "If there is no response in you to the awakening of nature, if the prospect of an early morning walk does not banish sleep, if the warble of the first bluebird does not thrill you, know that the morning and spring of your life are past. Thus may you feel your pulse."

In fact, when one is fully alive—filled with vitality, passion, loving and enthusiasm—then the presence of a few physical symptoms would probably not be enough to make one feel unhealthy—or unwealthy.

Many people declare themselves unhealthy at the first sign of a symptom—and, heaven knows, if one looks carefully, one can always find *something* that resembles a

When I had my operation,
the doctor gave me
a local anesthetic.
I couldn't afford
the imported kind.

"LAUGH-IN"

symptom. "There's lots of people in this world who spend so much time watching their health," Josh Billings pointed out, "that they haven't the time to enjoy it."

This anxious leap toward declaring oneself unhealthy is, well, not very healthy. The British scientist John Haldane observed, "I've never met a healthy person who worried much about his health, or a good person who worried much about his soul."

When illness does come, a healthy person looks upon it as a lesson. What does this illness have to teach me? What can I learn from it? If this sounds like New Age psychobabble, consider who said it some 2,500 years ago— Hippocrates: "A wise man should consider that health is the greatest of human blessings," wrote the Father of Medicine, "and learn how by his own thought to derive benefit from his illnesses."

Emerson echoed this in 1821: "We forget ourselves and our destinies in health, and the chief use of temporary sickness is to remind us of these concerns."

Healthy people do not postpone a healthy outlook or healthy activities for "later"—they embrace health here and now. A brilliant example of "I'll feel healthy when..." was written in 1888 by Anton Chekhov: "My holy of holies is the human body, health, intelligence, talent, inspiration, love, and the most absolute freedom imaginable, freedom from violence and lies, no matter what form the latter two take. Such is the program I would adhere to if I were a major artist."

Embracing health, using illness as a teacher, encouraging vitality, passion, loving and enthusiasm right now, no matter what else is going on—these, it seems to us, are the basis—and the attitude—of real wealth.

"Long life to you! Good health to you and your household! And good health to all that is yours!" (1 Samuel 25:6).

*When one door
of happiness closes,
another opens;
but often we look so long
at the closed door
that we do not see the one
that has been opened for us.*

HELEN KELLER

Wealth Is Happiness

Happiness is so easy—and yet, so difficult.

Happiness is looking at all the good and bad in any given moment—both within us and around us—and then *choosing* to focus upon the good. That's all. Simple to understand, easy to do (once we actually do it), and yet, so hard to remember to do. "The best advice on the art of being happy," Madame Swetchine reminds us, "is about as easy to follow as advice to be well when one is sick."

Happiness, contrary to popular belief, does not depend on what takes place outside ourselves. As William Cowper wrote in 1782, "Happiness depends, as Nature shows,/ Less on exterior things than most suppose."

"Some day people will learn that material things do not bring happiness," said Charles Steinmetz, "and are of little use in making people creative and powerful." John Dewey agreed: "[We look] for happiness in possession of the external—in money, a good time, somebody to lean on, and so on. We are impatient, hurried and fretful because we do not find happiness where we look for it."

Yes, we may be distracted into happiness by some fascinating object or person outside ourselves, but, as we have repeatedly (and painfully) learned, that kind of happiness is not lasting. Where do we find lasting happiness?

Aristotle said it most succinctly: "Happiness depends upon ourselves." Plato (naturally) agreed, although a little less succinctly: "The man who makes everything that leads to happiness depend on himself, and not upon other men, has adopted the very best plan for living happily."

Proverbs 15:15 tells us, "He that is of a merry heart hath a continual feast." La Rochefoucauld told us how to savor that feast: "Happiness is in the taste, and not in the things."

In other words, happiness is not what happens to us, but what, of all that happens to us, we choose to focus upon. This is of course, not news. Marcus Aurelius Antoninus

*Happiness lies in good health
and a bad memory.*

INGRID BERGMAN

told us long ago, "The happiness of your life depends on the quality of your thoughts." Whether you listen to the author of *Peter Pan,* James Barrie, ("It is not in doing what you like, but in liking what you do that is the secret of happiness") or Rabbi Hyman Schachtel ("Happiness is not having what you want, but wanting what you have"), the message remains the same.

Are we saying you must respond positively to everything that happens to you ("I dropped my mother's antique vase on my foot and I think I broke them both. What joy!")? No. We are saying that no matter what's happening, there's always *something* good to focus upon. ("I think I'll take a picture of the floor and call it 'Flowers and Vase Fragments—A Study in Randomnicity.'")

This positive refocusing, of course, takes no small degree of effort. "The Constitution of America only guarantees pursuit of happiness—you have to catch up with it yourself," reported Gill Robb Wilson. He continued, "Fortunately, happiness is something that depends not on position but on disposition, and life is what you make it."

What did the man who wrote "life, liberty and the pursuit of happiness" have to say about happiness? "Perfect happiness, I believe, was never intended by the Deity to be the lot of one of his creatures in this world," wrote Thomas Jefferson, "but that he has very much put in our power the nearness of our approaches to it is what I have steadfastly believed."

When and where do we seek happiness? "Today, this hour, this minute is the day, the hour, the minute for each of us to sense the fact that life is good," said Robert Updegraff, "with all its trials and troubles, and perhaps more interesting because of them."

My idea of heaven is eating <u>pâtés de foie gras</u> to the sound of trumpets.

SYDNEY SMITH

1771–1845

Wealth Is Abundance

The Italians have a word for it: *abbondanza*—more than enough, plenty, abundance. Naturally, the Italians apply it mostly to the discussion of food, but abundance covers more than food.

Abundance is having more than we need and want.

There are two ways to go about getting this, of course. One is to get all that we need and want, and then some more. The second is to reduce our level of needing and wanting. Or, perhaps, some balance between the two.

In seeking abundance, most people automatically go after the first option. Our cultural belief goes something like this: "Keep all you've got, protect it at all costs (even if you're no longer using it), and get more, more, more as quickly as possible, but certainly before almost everyone else. You can have it all! Go for it!"

There's one fundamental problem with this approach: it doesn't work. First, there's not enough time to get "it all"—there is simply too much "all" our overheated imaginations can desire, and not enough time. Second, by the time we're even close to getting something, our minds are usually off wanting something else.

This ability to want more than we can possibly get gives most people a feeling of perpetual longing—of not being abundant. "If you desire many things," said Ben Franklin, "many things will seem few."

This is, of course, not true just of our time. Two thousand years ago Tacitus observed, "many, amid great affluence, are utterly miserable." "Abundance consists not alone in material possession," said Charles Sheldon, "but in an uncovetous spirit."

Is the solution, then, to want nothing? Not necessarily. Desires can be powerful stimulants to genuine progress, worthwhile achievement and real satisfaction. As Samuel Johnson put it, "Some desire is necessary to keep life in motion."

*There is enough
in the world for everyone
to have plenty
to live on happily
and to be at peace
with his neighbors.*

HARRY S TRUMAN

When this idea is taken to an extreme, the critics of "desiring desirelessness" have said (as Jonathan Swift did say in 1711), "The stoical scheme of supplying our wants by lopping off our desires, is like cutting off our feet, when we want shoes." It's a lot less trouble, of course, to get a pair of shoes than to deal with the ramifications of being footless.

The workable approach to abundant living is twofold. First, we must realize that our physical needs are already provided for. Our needs are air, food, water, shelter, clothing, protection and television. When our needs are not met, we die. As we are all alive (one of the prime prerequisites for reading this book), our needs have been met—continuously—from the moment of our birth until now. That's need—keeping our physical bodies alive. Everything else is want.

Which brings us to the second part of the solution: what to do about our wants. If we choose what we *really* want from the many things that might be nice to have, and pursue those wants with a passion, we tend to feel abundant.

In an 1827 book with an interesting title, *Guesses at Truth,* Julius and Augustus Hare wrote, "How few our real wants! and how easy it is to satisfy them! Our imaginary ones are boundless and insatiable."

And the wants we choose can be some pretty big wants. "To have life more abundant, we must think in the limitless terms of abundance," explained Thomas Dreier. Somerset Maugham said it more simply: "If you refuse to accept anything but the best, you very often get it."

We say, you can have anything you want, but you can't have everything you want.

Wealth is having that "anything" you really want—and everything that goes with it—and letting the rest of the world (and its wants) go by.

I only want enough
to keep body and soul apart.

DOROTHY PARKER

Wealth Is Prosperity

Whenever we start talking about needs and wants—and say that all we really need are air, water, food, clothing, shelter, protection and television—some people get scared. Images of bag people dance in their heads. Surely wealth includes a *few* creature comforts—a VCR at least.

Even Aristotle would agree: "Happiness seems to require a modicum of external prosperity."

"It's no shame being poor," Sheldon Harnick wrote, "but it's no great honor, either." William Pitt and Sydney Smith, both writing in the late 1700s, agreed. "Poverty of course is no disgrace," said Pitt, "but it is damned annoying." "Poverty is no disgrace to a man," echoed Smith, "but it is confoundedly inconvenient." Similarly: "It's no disgrace to be poor, but it might as well be" (Elbert Hubbard). "Honest poverty is a gem that even a king might be proud to call his own, but I wish to sell out" (Mark Twain).

Yes, a certain degree of creature comfort seems to belong to any definition of wealth. But how much is enough, and how much is too much?

That depends on what we want—what we *really* want. As tools for obtaining and supporting the things we really want, prosperity is fine. When we begin to accumulate because, well, "that would be nice" or "everyone else seems to have one," then we might be inviting disaster.

If we squander our resources on this and that, we won't have enough resources left to accomplish the things we really want. Not having, doing and being what we *really* want is, to us, disaster.

Calvin Coolidge tried unsuccessfully to cool the heated race for prosperity. In 1928, only a year before the crash, he cautioned, "Prosperity is only an instrument to be used, not a deity to be worshiped."

I wish you
all sorts of prosperity
with a little more taste.

ALAIN RENÉ LESAGE

1735

When we worship that "strange god" of materialism—getting things simply because there are things to be gotten—we leave the course of our heart's desire.

How often have we seen someone (none of *us* has done it, of course) become prosperous, only to, as they say, blow it? "First he bought a '57 Biscayne and put it in a ditch," Joni Mitchell relates in a song about a friend's windfall; "He drank up all the rest, that sonofabitch."

It's called conspicuous consumption. It's an illness, and as rampant as the other consumption was a century ago. No wonder Mark Twain said, "Few of us can stand prosperity. Another man's, I mean."

The solution, once again, lies in balance. Listen to Roswell D. Hitchcock:

"Wealth is not of necessity a curse, nor poverty a blessing. Wholesome and easy abundance is better than either extreme; better that we have enough for daily comfort; enough for culture, for hospitality, for Christian charity. More than this may or may not be a blessing. Certainly it can be a blessing only by being accepted as a trust."

We have enough resources to do what we really want to do, but not enough to do everything we want to do. There is enough to gather the tools we need to build foundations under our castles in the air ("If you have built castles in the air...now put the foundations under them."—Thoreau), but not enough to build vacation castles around the globe.

Knowing this, and choosing well, is prosperity.

"Peace be within thy walls, and prosperity within thy palaces" (Psalm 122:7).

There are people who
have money
and people who
are rich.

COCO GABRIELLE CHANEL

Wealth Is Riches

Rich is a word that is, well, rich in meaning. It means magnificent, sumptuous, having an abundant supply, abounding, fertile, extremely productive, containing choice ingredients, pleasantly full and mellow, warm and strong in color, and amusing.

Most of these don't necessarily have anything to do with money, and yet, how often do we think of "being rich" as simply having a lot of money, expensive trinkets and an extravagant lifestyle?

The popular misconception is that *riches* refers to things that are scarce, things that only a few people can have. Not so. Many of the most magnificent, sumptuous, pleasantly full, mellow and amusing experiences in life are readily available—for little or no cost.

"In those vernal seasons of the year, when the air is calm and pleasant," Milton wrote, "it were an injury and sullenness against Nature not to go out, and see her riches, and partake in her rejoicing with heaven and earth."

In addition to nature there's the richness of friends, family, our work, a good film, books, museums, libraries. More than any other time in history, we have what Voltaire called an "embarrassment of riches."

We all have riches. Some have them in money, others in expensive things—but most have riches in talent, ideas, creativity, loving, caring, wisdom or beauty. "I have no riches but my thoughts," wrote Sara Teasdale, "Yet these are wealth enough for me."

The secret is to use the riches we have—and the ones we can obtain—to enjoy the moment more fully, and to achieve our heart's desire.

"It is not the rich man you should properly call happy," Horace wrote in 23 B.C., "but him who knows how to use with wisdom the blessings of the gods."

I care for riches, to make gifts
To friends, or lead
a sick man back to health
With ease and plenty.
Else small aid is wealth
For daily gladness;
once a man be done
With hunger, rich and poor
are all as one.

EURIPIDES

413 B.C.

But this teaching is even more ancient than that. In 2350 B.C., Ptahhotep instructed, "Follow your desire as long as you live...When riches are gained, follow desire, for riches will not profit if one is sluggish."

When we do not use our riches, they become a burden. "The use of riches is better than their possession," Fernando de Rojas (1465–1538) wrote. "Riches do not make one rich but busy." Or, as Bacon put it, "Riches are a good handmaid, but the worst mistress."

In terms of enjoying the moment, Thoreau tells us, "A man is rich in proportion to the number of things which he can afford to let alone." And this from Shakespeare: "Who is it that says most? which can say more / Than this rich praise—that you alone are you?"

This richness extends from us to our surroundings, our society, our culture. "If we are to achieve a richer culture, rich in contrasting values," Margaret Mead wrote, "we must recognize the whole gamut of human potentialities, and so weave a less arbitrary social fabric, one in which each diverse human gift will find a fitting place."

"Command them to do good, to be rich in good deeds, and to be generous and willing to share," Paul wrote in 1 Timothy 6:18–19. "In this way they will lay up treasure for themselves as a firm foundation for the coming age, so that they may take hold of the life that is truly life."

We're not so sure about the "command" part, but the rest of it sounds pretty good to us. To do good for others is one of the richest experiences we know.

"That's the state to live and die in!" wrote Charles Dickens, "R-r-rich!"

So, the All-Great,
were the All-Loving too.

ROBERT BROWNING

1855

Wealth Is Loving

You may think that we're going to get all gooey here when we talk about loving. We're not. Loving's not gooey. Loving is hard work.

Loving is not just a feeling—something we "fall into." Loving is a choice. We must choose—sometimes against seemingly impossible odds, with enormous evidence to the contrary—to love *whatever* we encounter.

First, we must learn to love ourselves. Heavens, is *that* difficult. Only we know all the nasty things we've done and all the wicked things we've thought. Only we know how often we've failed and how often we've done the right-appearing thing for the wrong reason. And, knowing all this, we are asked to love ourselves?

Yes. We wish we knew an alternative, but we don't. Loving ourselves is the only real foundation we've found for loving everyone and everything else in the world.

The good news, of course, is that we also know all the goodness within us—all the kind thoughts we've thought, all the compassionate things we've done, all the caring feelings we've had.

Like life, we are collections of both good and bad. Like happiness, loving is *choosing* to focus on the good. From the challenge of loving ourselves, it's relatively easy to move on to the challenge of loving everyone and everything else.

Do we have to love everyone and everything? No, only what's in front of us. If there's something we don't love, and can't seem to find *anything* positive about it to focus on, we can simply move away from it and place ourselves with something we can love. If we are thinking about something, and can't find *anything* to love about it, we can think about something else, something we can love.

Why do we practice loving? For the person or thing we love? Oh, a little. For ourselves? Absolutely. As La Rochefoucauld put it, "The pleasure of love is in loving.

The most common trait of all
primitive peoples is a reverence
for the lifegiving earth,
and the native American shared
this elemental ethic:
the land was alive to his loving touch,
and he, its son,
was brother to all creatures.
His feelings were made visible
in medicine bundles and
dance rhythms for rain,
and all of his religious rites
and land attitudes savored
the inseparable world of nature
and God, the master of Life.
During the long Indian tenure
the land remained undefiled
save for scars no deeper than
the scratches of cornfield clearings
or the farming canals of
the Hohokams on the Arizona desert.

STEWART LEE UDALL

arouse." And as another poet wrote, "The love I give you is secondhand. I feel it first." Or, another: "What do I get from loving you? Loving. You."

Our loving, of course, is not just for people. "I love it, I love it; and who shall dare," wrote Eliza Cook, "To chide me for loving that old armchair?" Loving things feels good, and there are a great many things these days in need of our loving. The planet Earth, for example. "Thank God," wrote Thoreau, "men cannot fly, and lay waste the sky as well as the earth."

The loving we are talking about expects nothing in return. The joy of loving is a reward in itself. "To love for the sake of being loved is human," said Alphonse de Lamartine, "but to love for the sake of loving is angelic."

So, be angelic. Sure it's hard work. The habit of loving only a few selected things and people is strong, but habits can be broken, and new behaviors learned. Let them say of you, as John Dryden said in 1680, "Large was his wealth, but larger was his heart."

More important, learn to say that of yourself long before anyone writes your epitaph.

*Be kind and considerate to others,
depending somewhat
upon who they are.*

DON HEROLD

Wealth Is Caring

Caring is very much like loving, except that it adds the elements of compassion, empathy and action to the loving.

Loving is unconditional. We find something good about someone or something, and we love it. There is no result required or desired. When we care, we look for a result. We become *slightly* attached to the outcome.

If we care for a sick animal, for example, we want the animal to get better. If we care about the environment, we want it to become cleaner. If we care for a wound, we want the wound to heal.

The trick is not to become *too* attached to the outcome. When we do, we bring out the second use of the word *care*, as in "Cast away care; he that loves sorrow / Lengthens not a day, nor can buy tomorrow," (Thomas Dekker, 1656). Here *care* becomes a synonym for worry. This is not being careful.

We must be careful that our caring does not become interference, or meddling—a form of thinking that what we want for others is more important than what they want for themselves. "I only did it because I care," has covered a multitude of intrusions. And yet, when a good friend is on a clear course of destruction, sometimes intervention is the caring thing to do.

The solution? Back to our old friend, balance. Somewhere between caring too much—which only makes one miserable, dominating and ineffective—and complete indifference—which may be the way of the saints, but we ain't saints yet—lies caring enough to make a positive difference, but not so much that it seriously affects our well-being.

Without caring, we become like Lily Tomlin's Ernestine: "We don't care. We don't have to. We're the phone company." With caring, we can all take part in Hippocrates's advice "...to superintend the sick to make them well, to care for the healthy to keep them well, also to care for one's own self."

If wisdom were offered me
with the proviso
that I should keep it shut up
and refrain from declaring it,
I should refuse.
There's no delight
in owning anything
unshared.

SENECA

FIRST CENTURY A.D.

Wealth Is Sharing

Imagine one morning you woke up and found yourself the only person in the world—everybody else simply gone. Yes, you would—in a sense—own everything, but imagine how dull it would be. You could have anything you wanted—except that there would be no one to share it with. If this wasn't one of those "Twilight Zone" episodes about what hell is like, it could have been.

When we talk about sharing what we have, we're talking about physical possessions, sure, but even more, we mean sharing who we *are*—our warmth, our humor, our ideas, our talents, our joys and, yes, our sorrows.

"Not what we give, but what we share," wrote James Russell Lowell in 1848, "For the gift without the giver is bare." "Even children followed with endearing wile," Oliver Goldsmith wrote in 1770, "And plucked his gown, to share the good man's smile." And Pythagoras, between theorems, said, "Friends share all things."

When we visit a friend's house for dinner, it's usually not the food we go for. "It isn't so much what's on the table that matters," W. S. Gilbert wrote, "as what's on the chairs."

"I think that, as life is action and passion," said Oliver Wendell Holmes, Jr., "it is required of a man that he should share the passion and action of his time."

When we are with those we care about, our ability to share rises from a wellspring deeper than we thought was in us. "Man discovers his own wealth," Rabindranath Tagore observed, "when God comes to ask gifts of him."

*Wealth is not
in making money,
but in making the man
while he is making money.*

JOHN WICKER

Wealth Is Learning

In the end, it's not what we have or do that matters—it is what we take from what we have and do, what we internalize, what we make our own. The process of making something our own is called learning.

Like the boy eagerly shoveling through the horse manure "because there's got to be a pony in here somewhere," so, no matter how manure-like life can get, there's got to be a lesson in there somewhere. "No matter what happens to me, I'm going to learn something useful from it," is a fundamental attitude of wealth.

Here we're not necessarily talking about the institutions of higher learning (which, alas, have become for more and more people a place to hide from what they need to know), but the learning we get in that greatest classroom of all—life.

"The entire object of true education," wrote John Ruskin, "is to make people not merely do the right thing, but to enjoy right things; not merely industrious, but to love industry; not merely learned, but to love knowledge."

Knowledge can be more powerful than money. It's interesting that among the meanings for the word *tip,* these two are included: first, extra money paid for a job well done, and, second, a bit of important information. If we're willing to learn from the latter (information), we can use it to make much more than the former (money).

Our willingness to learn and to apply what we've learned—in a word, *grow*—is a hallmark of wealth.

If this is coffee,
please bring me some tea;
but if this is tea,
please bring me some coffee.

ABRAHAM LINCOLN

Unhappiness is in
not knowing what we want
and killing ourselves to get it.

DON HEROLD

Wealth Is Knowing What You Want

Many people think wealth is *having* what you want. We have found, however, that a good many people already have what they want—or at least what they said they wanted at some former time—and *still* don't feel wealthy. They want more, but they're not sure what "more" is.

Yes, they have a shopping list—which usually begins with "a million dollars" and continues with this and this and this and this and this and a little of that, please, if you're not too tired. They—to quote one of the most absurd terms coined in the past century— "want it all."

As we said before—and will say again—there is simply too much "all" and not enough time this time around. We *can* have anything we want, but we can't have *everything* we want. (Even if it *were* practical, the concept of "having it all" is a strange one. As Maurice Sendak pointed out, "There must be more to life than having everything.")

Knowing what we truly want—not what other people think would be best for us, or what our family expects of us, or what our culture has programmed us for—but what *we* truly want, is a significant aspect of wealth.

To have our heart's desire clearly delineated and defined, and know that we're moving toward it every day, brings a sense of satisfaction and security that, as they say, even money can't buy.

Another nice thing about knowing what you want is that, when you get what you want, you know it—and can then celebrate. And celebration is certainly wealth.

America's best buy
is a telephone call
to the right man.

ILKA CHASE

Wealth Is Opportunity

Opportunities come in all shapes and sizes. Wealth is knowing opportunities when they come (unwealthy people often mislabel them "problems") and, if opportunities don't come often enough, knowing how to make them happen. "A wise man," wrote Bacon, "will make more opportunities than he finds."

Like wealth itself, opportunity is not a matter of things or events—it is an attitude, a way of seeing the world. Opportunity is saying, "No matter *what* happens to me, I will use it for my upliftment, learning and growth."

"A pessimist is one who makes difficulties of his opportunities," wrote Reginald B. Mansell; "an optimist is one who makes opportunities of his difficulties."

A popular myth about opportunity is that some people have more than others. Not so. Like oxygen, opportunity is available—in abundance—for all.

Alas, Mr. Dooley doesn't agree with us on this point. In 1901 he said of Andrew Carnegie: "Opporchunity knocks at ivry man's dure wanst. On some men's dures it hammers till it breaks down th' dure an' thin it goes in an' wakes him up if he's asleep, an' iver aftherward it wurruks f'r him as a night-watchman."

Another myth is that opportunity only knocks once. Opportunity will, in fact, knock you down. The gift is realizing that what knocked you down was an opportunity, not a bus.

It is true, however, that if opportunities are ignored, they *seem* to come fewer and farther between. "Opportunities multiply as they are seized," said John Wicker; "they die when neglected."

In fact, the opportunities keep coming as regularly as ever—we simply fall into the habit of ignoring them.

To be aware of opportunities one must be, well, *aware.* "The opportunity that God sends does not wake up him who

There is no security
in this life.
There is only opportunity.

DOUGLAS MACARTHUR

is asleep," says the Senegalese proverb. (Now, really, when was the last time you read a book that quoted a Senegalese proverb?)

"Many do with opportunities as children do at the seashore," wrote Thomas Jones, "they fill their little hands with sand, and then let the grains fall through, one by one, till all are gone."

When we learn to see the wealth of opportunities all around us, all the time, we realize that we can't possibly make use of them all. So, we choose those opportunities we want to pursue—as we do at a banquet—and let the rest go on to someone else.

Ecclesiasticus (4:20) reminds us, "Observe the opportunity."

"On with the dance,
let the joy be unconfined!"
is my motto,
whether there's
any dance to dance or
any joy to unconfine.

MARK TWAIN

Wealth Is Enjoying

We consider enjoyment such an important part of wealth that we have devoted an entire section—and by far the largest section—of this book to it. (Part Three: "Enjoying What You've Got.")

Enjoyment, we have found, is composed of two elements, *appreciation* and *gratitude*. Although we'll explore each in elaborate detail later, let us speak briefly about them here.

Appreciation is finding something to like about a given person, place, thing or experience. Sometimes it happens spontaneously, sometimes we have to work to find it. Appreciating—valuing, relishing, cherishing, liking—is, well, *fun*. We all seem to want it, to seek it. And yet, over time, that alone is not enough.

Something is missing.

To this, then, we add *gratitude*. Feeling thankful for whatever it is we're appreciating—and for the feeling of appreciation itself—rounds out the experience of enjoyment. Gratitude adds warmth, depth and a sumptuous quality to appreciation. Gratitude also, interestingly, paves the way for the next round of appreciation.

The ability to enjoy what we have—both inside and outside ourselves—is one of the cornerstones of wealth.

*Fortunate, indeed, is the man
who takes exactly
the right measure of himself,
and holds a just balance
between what he can acquire
and what he can use.*

PETER MERE LATHAM

1789–1875

Wealth Is Balance

In this admittedly contradictory, paradoxical and conflict-filled world, there is one last element of wealth to consider: balance.

Is health gained through dynamic activity or deep rest? Answer? Balance.

Shall we accept things as they are, or change things to how we would like them to be? Answer? Balance.

Shall we increase what we have, or decrease what we want? Answer? Balance.

Shall we work to get more of what we want, or slow down and enjoy more of what we already have? Answer? Balance.

And so it goes with all the dilemmas of life. It's not a matter of which side is right and which is wrong. Each is usually both right and wrong, depending on all the other elements of one's life. That's where balance comes in— weighing all sides and choosing the direction that would be the best at that moment.

Balance is dynamic, ever moving, ever changing. Think of a tightrope walker holding a balance pole. One moment it's steady, the next moment it swings wildly to the right. Then it dips violently to the left. Then it's steady again. There is no "right" place for the pole to be— the only "right" thing to do is stay on the tightrope.

Balance is an intensely personal thing. What is balance for one person may be utter boredom to a second and extreme bravery to a third.

Balance is so important a concept to the understanding and obtaining of wealth that we've devoted the entire last section of this book to it. Much more on balance, then, later.

Wealth to us
is not mere material for vain glory
but an opportunity for achievement;
and poverty we think
it no disgrace to acknowledge
but a real degradation
to make no effort to overcome.

THUCYDIDES
413 B.C.

That must be wonderful;
I don't understand it at all.

MOLIERE
1622

And there we have our definition of wealth—health, happiness, abundance, prosperity, riches, loving, caring, sharing, learning, knowing what we want, opportunity, enjoying and balance.

Do these sound familiar? Of course they do—to one degree or another, they describe a portion of you and your life.

You already *are* wealthy.

Oh, sure, we'd like to have more wealth—that's what the rest of this book is about. Realize, however, that in seeking more, you are going from *wealthy* to *wealthier*, not from poor to wealthy.

It's easier to go from wealthy to wealthier than to go from poor to wealthy—and a lot more fun, too.

Begin to notice the health, happiness, abundance, prosperity, riches, loving, caring, sharing, learning, knowing what you want, opportunity, enjoying and balance you already have. Remind yourself, over and over:

"I am wealthy."

My friends, money is not all.
It is not money that will
mend a broken heart
or reassemble the fragments
of a dream.
Money cannot brighten
the hearth nor repair the
portals of a shattered home.
I refer, of course,
to Confederate money.

ARTEMUS WARD

PART TWO

MONEY

Let's take a look at that thing most people associate with the word *wealth*—money.

This will be a brief look, a few chapters at most. In Part Four, "Getting More of What You Want," we'll look at getting more money if, after Part Three, "Enjoying What You've Got," more money is what you choose to get.

*Money is the representative
of a certain quantity
of corn or other commodity.
It is so much warmth,
so much bread.*

EMERSON

What Is Money?

Money is a symbol of energy.

If we were, say, chicken farmers, money would represent so many chickens. We can exchange our chickens for a symbol of the energy chickens represent (money), take the symbol to the pig farmer, and exchange it for pigs. We can also trade the symbol of our chicken energy (money) for other services or commodities, from political favors to fax machines.

This system of "money" saves us lugging chickens all over town. It also allows us to trade with people who have no interest in our commodity. The pig farmer might not want chickens—he wants pomegranates. In order to get pigs, we would have to find a pomegranate grower who wanted chickens, trade him chickens for pomegranates, then trade the pig farmer pomegranates for pigs.

The "money" system also helps us know the value of things. Rather than an elaborate system detailing how many chickens every other known item is worth, we simply have to know how much "money" chickens are worth, and how much "money" other things are.

Money as a symbol also allows the pig farmer to buy a smaller portion of pomegranates than the amount he could obtain for a whole pig. ("For one pig you get 128 pomegranates and two chickens." "But I don't *want* any chickens!") Money, quite simply, helps keep things simple.

In addition to all this, money is often used as a way of keeping score—especially in the game of business. It's not the *only* way of keeping score, of course, but it's a way that's very popular. Even so, money is still a symbol.

That's all money is. Just a symbol. Why, then, is money so powerful? Because, as a symbol, it is more universally recognized than Coca Cola.

But how important is money *really?* In the next chapter we'll explore this oft-debated question.

*The chief value of money
lies in the fact
that one lives in a world
in which it is overestimated.*

H. L. MENCKEN

Point/Counterpoint: How Important Is Money?

MODERATOR: Welcome, ladies and gentlemen, to "Point/Counterpoint." Tonight's question, "How important is money?" Taking the position that money is the most important thing in the world is Gunther Moneylove. Taking the counterposition that money is not very important at all is Felicity Lovelife. Your opening statements, please. First, Mr. Moneylove.

MONEYLOVE: It's clear that money is the most important thing in the world. It is the most agreed-upon symbol of energy in the world, hence, the most powerful thing in the world. "Money speaks sense in a language all nations understand," wrote Aphra Behn in 1680. More recently, J. R. Ewing agreed: "money speaks all languages."

MODERATOR: Ms. Lovelife.

LOVELIFE: Money is just a symbol. We want what the money can buy, not the money itself. Money is just paper and plastic and metal. For the most part, money itself is not very engaging. Some of the pictures on money might be amusing—like the 1920s car on the back of the U.S. $20 bill, or the holograms on the credit cards, but that's about it. Even George Washington—whose face is on more money than almost anyone—once wrote, "It is not a custom with me to keep money to look at."

MONEYLOVE: Hardly anyone loves money for *itself*, of course, but for what it represents.

LOVELIFE: I thought this debate was about money. Money is paper, plastic and metal. If you agree money is not that important, then I've won the debate and we can spend the rest of the program talking about something more interesting.

MONEYLOVE: Nothing is more interesting than money. Electricity may not be interesting, but what it can do is. It's what money can do that makes it the most important—and interesting—thing in the world.

A friend, I am told,
is worth more
than pure gold.

POPEYE

LOVELIFE: The most important things in the world are things that money can't buy.

MONEYLOVE: Such as?

LOVELIFE: Such as love. *[Sings]* "I don't care too much for money, money can't buy me love."

MONEYLOVE: Who wrote that?

LOVELIFE: Paul McCartney.

MONEYLOVE: I rest my case. There's one man who knows the power of an English pound. As Henry Ward Beecher said, "Poverty is very good in poems but very bad in the house; very good in maxims and sermons but very bad in practical life."

LOVELIFE: *[Still singing]* "Everybody knows it's true. Can't buy me lo-o-o-o-ve, no, no, no, no-o-o-o-o!"

MONEYLOVE: Money can buy your loved one flowers and candy and trips to Paris and Lexuses and life-saving operations and head starts in careers and romantic poetry on greeting cards. With all these tokens of appreciation, you don't think someone will eventually love you?

LOVELIFE: Having money is no guarantee that someone will love you.

MONEYLOVE: And being poor is? Two thousand years ago, in *The Art of Love,* Ovid wrote, "Gold will buy the highest honors; and gold will purchase love."

LOVELIFE: Ibsen said, "Money brings you food, but not appetite; medicine, but not health; acquaintances, but not friends."

MONEYLOVE: "I'm tired of love, I'm tired of rhyme, but money gives me pleasure all the time." Hilaire Belloc.

LOVELIFE: "Money is like love" wrote Kahlil Gibran; "it kills slowly and painfully the one who withholds it, and it enlivens the other who turns it upon his fellow man."

MONEYLOVE: As the Yiddish proverb explains, "With money in your pocket, you are wise and you are handsome and you sing well too."

My life is a bubble;
but how much
solid cash it costs
to keep that bubble floating!

LOGAN PEARSALL SMITH

LOVELIFE: Here's another Yiddish proverb: "Pearls around the neck—stones upon the heart."

MONEYLOVE: Speaking of proverbs, how about this from Proverbs 19:4: "Wealth brings many friends, but a poor man's friend deserts him."

LOVELIFE: "The love of money is the root of all evil." 1 Timothy 6:10.

MONEYLOVE: "A feast is made for laughter, and wine maketh merry: but money answereth all things." Ecclesiastes 10:19.

LOVELIFE: "Watching for riches consumeth the flesh, and the care thereof driveth away sleep." Ecclesiasticus 31:1.

MODERATOR: Can we agree that the Bible disagrees on this point? And, for the same reason, can we avoid quoting Shakespeare?

MONEYLOVE: I had some really nice Shakespeare quotes.

LOVELIFE: Me, too.

MODERATOR: Can we just move on, please.

LOVELIFE: I'd like to continue with Thoreau.

MONEYLOVE: Oh, no. Thoreau.

LOVELIFE: Thoreau wrote, "Money is not required to buy one necessity of the soul."

MONEYLOVE: Give me a break. Camus countered that pretention best: "It's a kind of spiritual snobbery that makes people think they can be happy without money."

LOVELIFE: "Banks are failing all over the country," wrote Thoreau, "but not the sand banks, solid and warm and streaked with bloody blackberry vines. You may run on them as much as you please, even as the crickets do..."

MONEYLOVE: I think I'm going to Thoreau up.

LOVELIFE: "In these banks, too, and such as these, are my funds deposited, funds of health and enjoyment. Invest in these country banks. Let your capital be simplicity and contentment."

*Money doesn't always
bring happiness.
People with ten million
dollars are no happier
than people with
nine million dollars.*

HOBART BROWN

MONEYLOVE: If he had bought Walden Pond with real money, not "simplicity and contentment," and put it in a solid trust, not "health and enjoyment," maybe they wouldn't be trying to turn Walden Pond into Walden Condo City.

LOVELIFE: And, finally, this too from Thoreau: "Good for the body is the work of the body, good for the soul the work of the soul, and good for either is the work of the other."

MONEYLOVE: What does that mean?

LOVELIFE: I'm not sure, but Thoreau said it, and he's been on my side so far.

MONEYLOVE: Okay, you want the Transcendentalists? How about Emerson: "Money, which represents the prose of life, and which is hardly spoken of in parlors without an apology, is, in its effects and laws, as beautiful as roses."

LOVELIFE: Emerson also said, "If a man own land, the land owns him."

MONEYLOVE: "The world is his, who has money to go over it."

LOVELIFE: "My cow milks me."

MONEYLOVE: I'd like to see that.

LOVELIFE: Emerson also said, "Money often costs too much." He, of course, was referring to the transcendental qualities of life—friendship, nature, happiness—which one must often sacrifice in pursuit of mere money.

MONEYLOVE: Or maybe he just didn't like the interest rate he was getting on his farm loan.

LOVELIFE: You're bordering on the sacrilegious, you know.

MONEYLOVE: Nonsense! Look what's written on money: "In God We Trust."

LOVELIFE: Oh, so now money is more important than God!

*Actually, I have
no regard for money.
Aside from its
purchasing power,
it's completely useless
as far as I'm concerned.*

ALFRED HITCHCOCK

MONEYLOVE: Money is *worshiped* by more people than God. I'm not saying that's right or wrong—I'm simply saying what *is*. "Some men worship rank, some worship heroes, some worship power, some worship God, and over these ideals they dispute—" wrote Mark Twain, "but they all worship money."

LOVELIFE: "Money wasn't that important," said George Foreman. "Money doesn't help you sleep. Money doesn't help your mother be well, money doesn't help your brother stay interested in his studies. Money don't help nothing. Money is only good when you've got something else to do with it. A man can lose everything, family, all your dreams, and still have a pocketful of money."

MONEYLOVE: Touching, but off the point. "Money is indeed the most important thing in the world," wrote Shaw; "and all sound and successful personal and national morality should have this fact for its basis." *That* is the point.

LOVELIFE: The point was made 2,100 years ago by Publilius Syrus in one of his maxims: "A good reputation is more valuable than money." It is a point you obviously have ignored.

MONEYLOVE: Which maxim is that?

LOVELIFE: 108.

MONEYLOVE: Ah-ha! By Maxim 656 he had come to his senses: "Money alone sets all the world in motion." And, while we're on the ancients, here's one from Euripides: "Money's the wise man's religion."

LOVELIFE: When did he write that?

MONEYLOVE: 425 B.C.

LOVELIFE: Ah-ha! Twelve years later he discovered the truth and wrote, "only our characters are steadfast, not our gold."

MODERATOR: Please, please. Haven't we had enough quotations? I hate quotations. Tell me what you know.

MONEYLOVE: Who said that?

Money, it turned out,
was exactly like sex,
you thought of nothing else
if you didn't have it
and thought of other things
if you did.

JAMES BALDWIN

MODERATOR: Emerson. At any rate, our program is nearing its end; time for your closing statements. Mr. Moneylove.

MONEYLOVE: Thank you. I leave you with this from John Kenneth Galbraith: "Wealth is not without its advantages and the case to the contrary, although it has often been made, has never proved widely persuasive."

MODERATOR: Ms. Lovelife.

LOVELIFE: "How could there be any question of acquiring or possessing," wrote Saint-Exupéry, "when the one thing needful for a man is to become—to be at last, and to die in the fullness of his being." I thank you.

MODERATOR: And thank you all for joining us for another stimulating installment of "Point/Counterpoint."

*Much work is merely
a way to make money;
much leisure is merely
a way to spend it.*

C. WRIGHT MILLS

So Which Is True?

Both.

Each point of view represents an end—an extreme—of a continuum. It's a continuum we all live within.

At times, money is the most important thing in our lives. At other times, it's the least. Most of the time it plays a part, as do other things.

How much more should we want, and how much should we learn to enjoy what we already have? It's our choice. It's a matter of finding our personal balance between the two.

That's what the remainder of this book will explore.

The next section, "Enjoying What You've Got," gives suggestions on, if not one *end* of the continuum, at least one *endish* of the continuum.

The section after that, "Getting More of What You Want," focuses on the other end. (There, by the way, is where we'll explore all those practical suggestions on how to get more money.)

The final section of the book, "Balance," tells how to discover, use and maintain a personal equilibrium between the two extremes. (This, by the way, can produce some wonderful, unknown results.)

MONEYLOVE: Sounds good to me.

LOVELIFE: Let's go.

MODERATOR: As Shakespeare said, "Once more unto the breach, dear friends, once more."

ORSON WELLES: Now we sit through Shakespeare in order to recognize the quotations.

MONEYLOVE: *[aside]* How did he get in here?

LOVELIFE: *[aside]* I don't know.

There are two things
to aim at in life:
first, to get what you want;
and, after that, to enjoy it.
Only the wisest of mankind
achieve the second.

LOGAN PEARSALL SMITH

PART THREE

ENJOYING WHAT YOU'VE GOT

While reading through our definition of wealth—health, happiness, abundance, prosperity, riches, loving, caring, sharing, learning, knowing what you want, opportunity, enjoying, and balance—you probably had the thought, "I already have some of those."

Indeed you have.

It isn't that we aren't already wealthy in many respects—we are—it's that we often forget, take things for granted and overlook enjoying what we already have.

This section—by far the longest in this book—is designed to enhance our appreciation of and gratitude for the wealth we already have.

It is abundant.

But make no mistake about it: making the changes necessary to enjoy more is hard work. Change may not be hard physical work, but, when the habit of nonenjoyment is strong, it is hard emotional and mental work.

In other words, when we're miserable, we're being lazy. Most people won't do the work.

This section of the book outlines the work that is cut out for us. It's full of ideas, concepts, suggestions and exercises, all designed to enhance appreciation of the moment and gratitude for what already is.

*Joy is the feeling
of grinning inside.*

DR. MELBA COLGROVE

What Is Enjoyment?

As we mentioned earlier, we consider enjoyment to have two primary components—appreciation and gratitude. To fully enjoy something, we must first appreciate it, like it, savor it. This is fun, of course, but when we add the second element—gratitude—we add thankfulness to the appreciation and have full, rounded, heartfelt enjoyment.

"All of the animals except man," wrote Samuel Butler, "know that the principal business of life is to enjoy it." "There is no such thing as the pursuit of happiness," observed Joyce Grenfell, "but there is the discovery of joy." And, as it states in the Chinese proverb (which is a nice way of saying we probably got it from a fortune cookie), "One joy scatters a hundred griefs."

No amount of material possession produces wealth. *Enjoying* what we have—no matter how much or how little it may be—is what makes us wealthy. "Wealth is not his that has it," wrote Benjamin Franklin, "but his that enjoys it."

The endless pursuit of things at the expense of enjoying what we already have is often referred to as being caught "on the treadmill." Fred Allen called it "the treadmill to oblivion." "If your capacity to acquire has outstripped your capacity to enjoy," observed Glen Buck, "you are on the way to the scrap-heap."

The things to enjoy are the things that are in front of—and within—us. The time to enjoy them is now. "We may lay in a stock of pleasures, as we would lay in a stock of wine," wrote Charles Colton in 1825; "but if we defer tasting them too long, we shall find that both are soured with age."

Too many people postpone the enjoyment of life until some vaguely specified "later," when some goal or person or ability has been obtained. "May we never let the things we can't have, or don't have, or shouldn't have, spoil our enjoyment of the things we do have and can

*Gratitude is not only
the greatest of virtues,
but the parent of all the others.*

CICERO

have," cautioned Richard Evans. "As we value our happiness let us not forget it, for one of the greatest lessons in life is learning to be happy without the things we cannot or should not have."

Enjoyment not only erases past hurts; it is easily stored, ready to dissolve future disappointments before they are even felt. "No enjoyment, however inconsiderable, is confined to the present moment," said Sydney Smith. "A man is the happier for life from having made once an agreeable tour, or lived for any length of time with pleasant people, or enjoyed any considerable interval of innocent pleasure."

The element of enjoyment that seems to make it linger the longest is gratitude. As the French say, "Gratitude is the heart's memory."

Enjoyment is not just found in stopping and observing, but also in action, in doing. "There is the true joy of life:" wrote George Bernard Shaw, "to be used by a purpose recognized by yourself as a mighty one; to be thoroughly worn out before being thrown on the scrap heap; to be a force of nature instead of a feverish, selfish little clod of ailments and grievances complaining that life will not devote itself to making you happy."

Life will not devote itself to making you happy—or making you joyful. *You* must devote yourself to that. "Enjoyment is *not* a goal," wrote Paul Goodman; "it is a feeling that accompanies important ongoing activity." Who decides what is "important"? You, of course.

Being involved in the worthwhile cause of spreading joy to others seems to rub off on the giver. "The very society of joy redoubles it," wrote Robert South; "so that, while it lights upon my friend, it rebounds upon myself, and the brighter his candle burns, the more easily will it light mine."

Of course, our best advice is: light your own fire, discover the appreciation and gratitude for whatever is around and within yourself *right now.*

*I wish I knew
how customs like this
get started;
it would make them
easier to stamp out.*

MARTIN LANE
"THE PATTY DUKE SHOW"

Why It's Amazing
We Ever Enjoy Anything

Since enjoyment is so healing, nurturing and, well, *enjoyable*—why don't we feel it all the time? Answer: we have a lot of strikes against us—deep-seated biological, cultural and psychological programming—that are as real as gravity, and as limiting to enjoyment as gravity is to levitation.

As we explore each, do your best not to get *too* depressed. Knowing what we're up against in our journey toward more enjoyment is, in fact, a positive thing.

Our Filtering Brains

Although our five senses deliver to our brains billions of bits of information each second, we are unaware of most of them. This is because the brain automatically filters them from our conscious awareness. What is and is not allowed to pass into conscious awareness is a matter of programming. Much of the programming is biological— our brains just came that way. Some of the programming is cultural—our parents, teachers and society that shaped us. A bit of it is of our own doing.

The biological programming of our brain filters out everything that's not changing, not moving, not new. In the days of wild beasts, this biological programming made sense—in a landscape worthy of an impressionist canvas, the only thing our ancestors wanted to know was, "Where's the meat?" The meat tended to be on the move (as compared to, say, trees), so what moved was more important than what stood still. In addition, when our ancestors stood the risk of *becoming* the meat (dinner), the threat was usually in the form of something moving—this time toward our forebears. Filtering out all but the moving, the changing and the new helped our ancestors survive.

The major problem with this biological programming today is that (A) we don't need it (meat these days just lies there in packages in the supermarket, and wild

*Our memories
are card indexes
consulted, and then
put back in disorder
by authorities
whom we do not control.*

CYRIL CONNOLLY

*A good memory
is one trained
to forget the trivial.*

CLIFTON FADIMAN

beasts are for the most part confined to nature documentaries), and (B) we take much of the good in our lives for granted.

When we consider all that is good in our lives, we notice that—for the most part—it is not changing, moving or new. Sure, some of the good is doing at least one of those, but most of it has been steadily there for a while.

Take our bodies, for example. If we have a pain in our arm and the pain stops, our arm feels good. After a while, however, the arm feels pretty much like all the other parts of our body that are not in pain, and is again ignored. When we're not in pain, we're seldom aware that our body is free from pain. That our body is free from pain is, of course, a good thing, but a good thing that we, most of the time, take for granted.

Why? Because the brain is filtering from our conscious awareness signals from our body saying, "A-OK." We don't need to consciously know 10,000 times a second that our middle toe is not hurting, so the information is filtered out. Unfortunately, we also are filtering out the "good" contained in a pain-free middle toe.

This taking things for granted applies to all the functioning of the body, from digestion to vision to the process of thinking itself—when working OK, we're not aware that it's working OK, and therefore not aware of the goodness inherent in that.

It's also true for things outside ourselves. The new car is so wonderful when it's new. After a few weeks, however, it becomes "the car." It's the same car; we've just become accustomed to it. The same is true of most relationships. At first it's "some enchanted evening," and eventually it's "your week to take out the garbage." It's not that the car or the relationship (or anything else you care to name) is not still good, or that we wouldn't miss it if it were no longer in our life. It's just that we've filtered out all that wasn't changing, moving or new about it.

We simply aren't *aware* of the good that is around—or within—us for any length of time. If we're not aware of it,

Dad worked hard for us,
he provided for us,
and he certainly didn't want
to have to talk to us
on top of that.

KEVIN ARNOLD

"THE WONDER YEARS"

we don't appreciate it, and if we don't appreciate it, we're not likely to feel grateful for it—hence enjoyment is not.

Childhood Programming

Our minds are also programmed by our parents, teachers, society and all those influences that are generally called "the environment." Some of this programming is intentional—there are certain things the environment *wants* us to know—and some of it is unintentional—the environment doesn't exactly *want* us to know it, but it gets programmed into us just the same.

Some common examples of the intentional programming: walk on your feet, speak a certain language, wear clothes, the potty's over here, and so on. Some of the unintentional programming includes—for most people—stay average, fit in, you can't truly be happy until you love someone who loves you back, don't rock the boat and so on.

Some of the childhood programming robs us of enjoyment because, after all, "you're getting to be big now and you can't enjoy yourself all the time." We are directly trained to stop enjoying and start behaving. If it's a choice between enjoying ourselves and doing what some authority figure wants, guess what we're programmed to do? Good-bye to *lots* of enjoyment.

Some of the childhood programming robs us of enjoyment because, when we want to do something enjoyable, we've been taught it's not right, not natural, not normal—which is a way of saying "not average," or, "if you don't conform, we won't know what to do with you, and we want to know what to do with you all the time, so knock it off." And, as there is no such thing as an "average person," we, sooner or later, want to do something unaverage; therefore we can't enjoy it to the full because, after all, "something inside tells me this just isn't right." That something was not "you"; it was just cultural programming.

***Ben Cartwright:** I'm not
in the habit of giving lectures,
and if I do,
it's because they're needed.
Might have been
a good idea if your father
had given you a few.*

***Candy Canaday:** Oh, he did.*

***Ben:** Obviously they
didn't have much effect.*

***Candy:** Oh, yes they did;
I left home.*

"BONANZA"

Our Own Programming

As we go through life, in addition to what we are taught—intentionally or unintentionally—by the outer environment, we also do our own programming. We make decisions about what's going on. Sometimes these decisions are conscious and sometimes they're not, but decisions are made and, through them, we program ourselves.

As a child we might, for example, feel let down or betrayed, so we decide, "Nobody can be trusted. I'm not going to trust anymore." Or, we might tell the truth about something, and get punished for it. "The truth hurts," we decide. "I'm not going to tell the truth anymore." We can program those decisions deep in our minds.

Most of these decisions are made based upon the relative helplessness and powerlessness of a child. When we grow to adulthood—with far more ability to help ourselves and considerably more power than children—we still abide by these rules. We don't even know they're rules, usually; we don't see them as decisions we made and programming we did on ourselves long ago. It's "just the way I am."

One of the most insidious decisions most of us make about ourselves to one degree or another is that we're not good enough, undeserving, *unworthy*.

Children are, for the most part, raised on the "don't" system. They do whatever they do, and when they do something "wrong," they are corrected. All the "right" things they do are usually not praised as much as the "wrong" things are criticized, so the child can easily conclude, "I can't do anything right," or "I can never get what I want." Eventually a decision is made, "If I can't do anything right and I can't get what I want, I guess I must not be good enough. I'm not worthy."

This unworthiness is such a fundamental destroyer of enjoyment that it has chapters of its own in this section. For now, however, we'll just include unworthiness as one of the many reasons why it's amazing that we ever enjoy ourselves—*ever.*

*The latter part
of a wise man's life
is taken up in curing
the follies, prejudices,
and false opinions
he had contracted
in the former.*

JONATHAN SWIFT

The Fight or Flight Response

In addition to the brain automatically filtering out almost all of the ongoing good, the body also has a mechanism that almost always overreacts to any perceived "bad." This mechanism is known as the fight or flight response.

When we perceive danger, the body automatically prepares to battle the intruding evil (fight), or to run away from it (flight). Although this response can be triggered casually, the body does not respond in a casual way. The fight or flight response prepares the body to fight or flee *for its life.*

In days past, this reaction was essential to survival. Our ancestors lived in hostile environments, with carnivorous beasts far more physically powerful than humans. We, as a species, needed an extra edge, and that edge was constantly being *on* edge—ever on the lookout for danger; responding instantly to danger with a full-scale rallying of our biological might.

Today—in the Western world, at least—this need to fight or flee *for our lives* has become both unnecessary and damaging. The very response that kept us alive as a species for millions of years is now killing us. Any number of life-threatening illnesses are caused or assisted in their progress by the repeated triggering of the fight or flight response. (For a further study of this, please see our book *You Can't Afford the Luxury of a Negative Thought: A Book for People with Any Life-Threatening Illness— Including Life.* 1-800-LIFE-101)

More to the purpose of this chapter, however, are not the long-term effects of the fight or flight response on our mortality, but the short-term, daily, almost continual effects the response has upon our well-being—upon our enjoyment of life.

Almost any perceived negative occurrence—either real or imagined, within us or outside us, involving us or not involving us, actually happening or merely a possibility—triggers the fight or flight response. We feel one or both of the

Mr. Spock: *May I point out that I had an opportunity to observe your counterparts quite closely. They were brutal, savage, unprincipled, uncivilized, treacherous— in every way, splendid examples of Homo sapiens. The very flower of humanity. I found them quite refreshing.*

Captain Kirk [to Dr. McCoy]: *I'm not sure, but I think we've been insulted.*

"STAR TREK"

emotions most closely associated with the response—anger, the energy to fight; and fear, the energy to flee.

For the most part, fear and anger are not considered "enjoyable" emotions, although some people have certainly learned to enjoy the "rush" of them—the feeling of "being alive." When we think of enjoyable emotions, however, anger and fear are usually not at the top of our list.

When the fight or flight response is triggered, the mind begins looking for additional danger, additional things "wrong" with the situation. More so than usual, it filters out any "good" in the environment. It's looking for *wild beasts,* for heaven's sake, not beautiful sunsets. Remember, our lives depend upon finding the wild beasts long before they find us.

This, being life, is far from perfect (at least insofar as "perfect" is created in our imaginations), so there's always *something* that's not right; some portion of our plan is always in danger. Hence, some people live much of their lives in an almost continual angry or fearful (fight/flight) condition. Hardly a conducive condition to enjoying the moment.

The Negativity around Us

The fight or flight response feels right at home in the world created by what is broadly called "the media." Newspapers and newscasts give us news of what? Mostly fresh disasters. It's not really, "What's new?" but "What's new *and bad?*" that sells papers and gets ratings. Even if it means leaving out facts, or slanting a story, the bad side of any occurrence (or person) is what sells.

In the more admittedly fictional world, things are not much better—in many cases, in fact, they are worse. By the time a child is ten, he or she has witnessed 100,000 acts of violence and 8,000 murders on television. How many murders does one see in real life? Not that many, probably. And yet, we have the image that people would just as soon kill each other as eat together. For a while, in movies it was difficult to see even a romantic comedy that didn't have murder as part of the plot.

*Creative minds
always have been known
to survive
any kind of bad training.*

ANNA FREUD

Then there are all the horror films, slash-and-gash films, psychotic-on-the-loose films, your-babysitter-is-really-a-mutant-serial-killer-robotic-assassin-from-Mars films, and so on.

Then there are the *people* around us. Gossip, limitation and "Oh, what a cruel, cruel, unfair world this is" seem to be the primary subjects of many people's conversation. In fact, the Ain't-It-Awful Club meets every weekday afternoon from 5:00 till 7:00 in cocktail lounges and bars all over the country. For the price of a drink (and from 5:00 to 7:00 they're two-for-one), you can tell another how terrible your life is—providing you are willing to give the listener equal time to try and top your tragedies with examples of his or her own. For some unknown reason, this period of time is known as The Happy Hour.

All of this environmental negativity is bound to affect us. It's easy to believe that the world is a much worse place than it actually is. Enjoying ourselves doesn't fit into a world of such profound negativity. We can easily feel when we're enjoying something that (A) we're taking more than our share, as there obviously isn't much enjoyment to go around, so we should feel guilty and somehow "put some back"; or (B) our present-moment enjoyment is just a fluke, a moment of luck, a passing flash of fortune, and cannot possibly last; therefore we shouldn't enjoy it too much, because it will be gone soon and the more we enjoy it now, the more we'll miss it later—and the later is coming real soon. Not very enjoyable.

Entropy

Here's a law, like gravity. Although the name of this law is less common, its effects are generally as well known as gravity's. In an oversimplified way, the law of entropy goes like this: if you're not putting energy into something to make it better, it's going to get worse. Nothing stays the same. If we're not actively involved in building something up, it's being torn down.

In life we see this all around: paint peels, metal rusts (or tarnishes), wood rots, cement crumbles, unattended

Granny: *Why don' y' just shoot me like an ol' horse an' sell m' body fer glue?*

Jed Clampett: *Now, Granny, that's ridiculous.*

Jethro Bodine: *Yeah, you wouldn't make enough glue fer a—*

Jed: *Don't help me, boy!*

"THE BEVERLY HILLBILLIES"

businesses deteriorate, and people, well, people we leave alone find other people.

This law, obviously, tells us that we have to work hard just to keep in place. No time to enjoy! While I'm enjoying this, that is falling apart. Excuse me, I must run and take care of that.

We're Always Recovering from Something

Most people are trained to postpone enjoyment until everything is taken care of, handled, all better. That's a perfectly rational-sounding idea. In practice, however, it happens to be just another of those "rational lies" we tell ourselves that rob us of enjoyment.

The fact is, we're always recovering from something. We stub our toe, and just as that's almost better we suffer an emotional loss, and about the time we're over that, the car gets a flat tire, and when the tire's almost fixed, the mechanic tells us we need a brake job, and when we have the money for the brake job, we get a cold, and just as the cold is almost gone, we discover we gained back seven of the five pounds we lost the last time we dieted, and just as we're about to lose the last pound on the new diet...

In other words, it seems as though we always have *something* to be genuinely worried about. The difficulty is the persuasive cultural myth that tells us: until there's nothing to worry about, we can't (or at least shouldn't) enjoy ourselves.

The Glamour Trap

Glamour is a cultural conditioning that says simply because something is new, improved, desired by others, popular or in demand, we should want it—*desperately*. Glamour basically tells us that we shouldn't want what *we* want, we should want what we *should* want.

Who decides what we should want? Madison Avenue, fashion mavens, the media. Who decides whether their "should" is a genuine should? Popular opinion. If something is successful, it must be good; therefore we should all want it.

*Natural wealth is limited
and easily obtained;
the wealth defined
by vain fancies
is always beyond reach.*

EPICURUS

THIRD CENTURY B.C.

Glamour makes fertile ground for at least six of the Seven Deadly Sins. (A sin, by the way, is simply missing the mark, a mistake. We are punished *by* our sins, not *for* them.)

Glamour makes us overly *proud* of what we have that others don't, while we feel *envy, lust* and *avarice* over other people's possessions (including their relationships). We're *angry* when we don't get all we want when we want it. We're *gluttonous* in our consumption—taking in far more than we need.

About the only Deadly Sin glamour does not directly incite is *sloth*. (Actually, it does invite a slothful attitude toward the pursuit of our own goals—the ones that come from our heart—so maybe it's seven out of seven.)

With glamour, what we have is never enough. Who has time to enjoy what we've got when there's so much new, improved and popular yet to get?

The Upward Mobility Treadmill

A close cousin to glamour (perhaps even an offspring) is upward mobility. Most of us are trained from early childhood that nothing is ever enough—there is always more to get, more to do, and we must, therefore, get it and do it.

Humans have a natural desire to always want to do more, become better at what we really love doing and grow more as people.

Upward mobility, however, says we should want more! better! faster! about not just what we love and are naturally drawn toward, but about *everything*.

We're trained to keep up with the Joneses. Why? Don't ask questions! There isn't time! The Browns are gaining on us! Wanting more for the sake of more is a great eliminator of joy. "There's no time to enjoy this success—I must immediately move on to the next!"

*The moral flabbiness
born of the
bitch-goddess SUCCESS.
That—with the squalid
cash interpretation
put on the word success—
is our national disease.*

WILLIAM JAMES

1906

☆

All of these influences—our filtering brains, childhood programming, our own programming, the fight or flight response, the negativity around us, entropy, always recovering from something, the glamour trap, and the upward mobility treadmill—press on us, creating the antithesis of enjoyment: anxiety and depression.

Sob, heavy world,
Sob as you spin,
Mantled in mist,
remote from the happy.

W. H. AUDEN
THE AGE OF ANXIETY
1947

This is, I think,
very much the Age of Anxiety.

LOUIS KRONENBERGER

1954

Anxiety and Depression

Anxiety is a form of fear. "Anxiety is the space between the 'now' and the 'then,'" explained Fritz Perls. Anxiety is an upward-thrusting energy. It demands we do something *right now* about closing the gap between "now" and "then." The fight or flight response is triggered, and the body wants to take action—productive, physical action—*right away*. "Getting an idea should be like sitting down on a pin," said E. L. Simpson; "it should make you jump up and do something."

Alas, we live in the land of "wait," the time of "later." We are ready to meet and conquer the beast *here and now,* and what do we hear? "Mr. Johnson won't be in until Tuesday." "Our office hours are from nine to five, Monday through Friday. Please call back then. This is a recording." "Your application is being processed. You should hear from us in three to four weeks." "Don't call us, we'll call you."

We can't *do* anything about the thing we want to do, but the energy to do remains. We can't do anything about it because, for the most part, *they won't let us.* Grrrrr.

Along comes the anger side of the fight or flight response. It comes in the form of depression. Depression is a downward-pushing energy. It meets the upward-thrusting anxiety. Our own fight (anger/depression) or flight (fear/anxiety) response has a pushing match inside us. The energies wrestle each other to a standstill. The result is inaction. It's an uneasy peace, but it keeps us from tearing phones off walls, "making a scene," or in some other way "killing the messenger."

In our swift progression as a species from running from beasts to standing in line at banks, from hunting to hunt and peck (a few centuries of culture thinly layered over millions of years of biological evolution), our inner reactions have not yet caught up with outer realities. Result: anxiety and depression.

If lawyers are disbarred
and clergymen defrocked,
doesn't it follow
that electricians can be delighted;
musicians denoted;
cowboys deranged;
models deposed;
tree surgeons debarked
and dry cleaners depressed?

VIRGINIA OSTMAN

"Is not man himself the most unsettled of all the creatures of the earth?" asked Ugo Betti. "What is this trembling sensation that is intensified with each ascending step in the natural order?"

We remain animals, but are cut off from nature. We lose our joy, our wonder, our awe. "Joy, interrupted now and again by pain and terminated ultimately by death, seems the normal course of life in Nature," observed Joseph Krutch. "Anxiety and distress, interrupted occasionally by pleasure, is the normal course of man's existence."

To quote the Japanese proverb: "Every little yielding to anxiety is a step away from the natural heart of man."

In addition to this, we are trained as children to get good grades, get a good job, get a good spouse, get children, get ahead. In all this getting we get something else: anxiety and depression.

"He worked like hell in the country so he could live in the city," observed Don Marquis, "where he worked like hell so he could live in the country." This is typical of the hamster wheel on which many people spin their lives.

We ask ourselves the wrong questions. "How can I get this new and desirable thing?" rather than "How can I more fully enjoy what I already have?" Anxiety-producing questions produce anxiety-producing answers.

Then the cultural programming that says "Be nice" enters. We use depression to keep the anxiety in check. We postpone action to a more "appropriate" time. This causes more anxiety, which causes...

It's the fight or flight response as experienced in modern, daily life. In its extreme, it's a clinical illness called manic-depression. The extreme elation and severe depression of a manic-depressive are painful to watch.

Equally painful is the mirror a manic-depressive holds up to our own lives. We may not have the extremes of mania and depression, but we recognize all too well the anxiety-depression struggle: impatience and resignation, overcommitment, spending more than we make, excess

Mrs. Bakerman: *Dr. Hartley,*
if you're looking
for a new member
of our group,
I know a nice schizophrenic.

Mr. Peterson: *Or how about*
a manic-depressive?
At least you know
they'll be fun half the time.

"THE BOB NEWHART SHOW"

and abstinence—it has many forms. It is also referred to as bi-polar behavior.

One thing's for sure: swinging radically between the pole of anxiety and the pole of depression is not enjoyable. As Seneca pointed out, "The mind that is anxious about the future is miserable." Or this from Ecclesiasticus 30:24: "Jealousy and anger shorten life, and anxiety brings on old age too soon."

Adam was human;
he didn't want the apple
for the apple's sake;
he wanted it
because it was forbidden.

MARK TWAIN

The Original Sin

Where did all this come from? Where did we break from the rest of nature? When did we leave the garden? When did we fall? What was the first mistake we humans made—the first sin? *(Sin* comes from a Roman archery term meaning "to miss the mark.") How did humanity blow it?

An answer can be found in the story of Adam and Eve. Taken either literally or metaphorically, it does provide an explanation to the age-old question, *"What happened?!"*

In the beginning all was well. God made heaven and earth, planted a garden called Eden, made man from the dust of the earth and took him to the garden to tend it. This was Adam. The birds and the beasts were to eat all the green plants, and Adam was given all the seed-bearing plants and seed-bearing fruits as food.

In the middle of the garden were two trees: "the tree of life and the tree of the knowledge of good and evil" (Genesis 2:9). (All the following chapter and verse references will be from Genesis.)

In the midst of all this abundance and joy there was only one stipulation: "You are free to eat from any tree of the garden," God told Adam; "but you must not eat from the tree of the knowledge of good and evil, for when you eat of it you will surely die" (2:16–17).

All the creatures were brought to Adam, and he named them. But among them, no suitable helper for Adam was found. So God put Adam to sleep, took a rib from him, and made Eve.

Everything went along swimmingly until the serpent started talking to Eve. "Did God really say, 'You must not eat from any tree in the garden?' " (3:1).

Eve answered, "We may eat fruit from the trees in the garden, but God did say, 'You must not eat fruit from the tree that is in the middle of the garden, and you must not touch it, or you will die.' " (3:2–3).

Art is a collaboration
between God
and the artist,
and the less the artist does
the better.

ANDRÉ GIDE

Ah! The first Communication Breakdown. Either Adam in the telling, or Eve in the listening, or both, got the information not quite right. God was misquoted for the first—and certainly not the last—time.

First, there were *two* trees in the middle of the garden, "the tree of life and the tree of the knowledge of good and evil" (2:9). Second, God never said the humans couldn't *touch* the fruit of the knowledge of good and evil, God said they couldn't *eat* it (2:17).

Back to our story. "You will not surely die," the serpent told Eve, "For God knows that when you eat of it your eyes will be opened, and you will be like God, knowing good and evil" (3:4–5).

So, Eve took a stroll to the middle of the garden. When she "saw that the fruit of the tree was good for food and pleasing to the eye, and also desirable for gaining wisdom, she took some and ate it" (3:6).

Here we come to the first popular misunderstanding concerning the story. Almost any school child, when asked "What fruit did Eve eat?" will answer, "An apple." The child, in almost any school, would be told, "Correct." And yet, it is not.

The fruit was almost certainly not an apple—or any other fruit we know today. Genesis 1:29: "Then God said, 'I give you every seed-bearing plant on the face of the whole earth and every tree that has fruit with seed in it. They will be yours for food.' "

As an apple is a "fruit with seed in it," it was OK to eat. The fruit of the tree of the knowledge of good and evil must have been a seedless variety.

We mention this because there's a great deal of information people *think* came from the Bible—and other sources of wisdom, inspiration or authority—that simply did not come from there. The truth is often the opposite of popular belief. Our suggestion on this—as in all things—is: check it out for yourself.

He was not made
for climbing
the tree of knowledge.

SIGRID UNDSET

Back again to our story. Adam, who happened to be with Eve, also ate of the fruit of the tree of the knowledge of good and evil. "Then the eyes of both of them were opened, and they realized they were naked" (3:7).

They, of course, had been naked all along—or perhaps we should say they were *nude* or *au natural*. Eden was, after all, a clothing-optional garden. What happened was that Adam and Eve *realized* they were nude, and put the judgment of "good and evil" on it (in this case, "evil") and called themselves *naked*.

They *realized*. It was the first of many "real-lies" that "the knowledge of good and evil" has brought to humanity. Without the "real-lies-ation" that this is good and that is evil, everything simply *is*. Both this and that can be enjoyed equally. We are not *pushing for* this and *fighting against* that. Hence, no anxiety. No depression.

Sure, there's fear and there's pain—but there's no *fear* of fear, or *fear* of pain. There's no "I shouldn't feel pain" or "I mustn't feel fear." Should, must, have-to, ought-to, got-to—perhaps these are the true fruits of the tree of the knowledge of good and evil. They certainly are its by-products.

Having "realized" nakedness was evil, Adam and Eve did what they could to cover themselves by sewing fig leaves together. This must not have worked very well, because when God came strolling through the garden, they hid.

"Where are you?" asked God (3:9).

"I heard you in the garden," answered Adam, "and I was afraid because I was naked; so I hid" (3:10).

"Who told you that you were naked?" asked God (3:11). At this point it's hard not to add human qualities to God. One can almost see Him reacting to Adam as a parent might when asked by his child, "If the cat happened to get in the washing machine, would putting it in the drier dry it off again?" or, when the child is older, a phone call that begins, "Is the car insurance paid up?" The whole picture of what happened—and all the ramifications of it—come together in a sudden, painful flash.

Criminal: *You made a mistake, and I'm not going to pay for it.*

Sgt. Joe Friday: *You going to use a credit card?*

"DRAGNET"

"Have you been eating of the tree that I commanded you not to eat from?" (3:11). (Yes, apparently God does occasionally end a sentence with a preposition, at least in the New International Version.)

Adam answers, proving he has mastered blame and irresponsibility: "The woman you put here with me—she gave me some fruit from the tree, and I ate it" (3:12). Not only was it the woman's fault; it was also God's, because, after all, "you put [her] here with me."

God turned to Eve and asked, "What is this you have done?" and Eve—taking her cue from Adam—blamed the snake. "The serpent deceived me, and I ate" (3:13).

So God passed out punishments—which might have been punishments, or might have been reasonable predictions to a couple of humans who now have the knowledge of good and evil, right and wrong, should and should not, must and must not.

Adam and Eve were forced to leave the garden because, as God explained to either Himself or some other heavenly beings who might have been with Him, "The man has now become like one of us, knowing good from evil." (Who *was* He talking to???) "He must not be allowed to reach out his hand and take also from the tree of life and eat, and live forever" (3:22).

We like to interpret this to mean that, knowing good from evil and *not* being a god is tough enough, but to be caught in that position *forever* is torture beyond belief. (It's interesting to note that God never forbade them from eating of the tree of life. Living forever without judging everything as either good or evil wouldn't be so bad. They just ate of the wrong tree.)

Knowing good from evil is the original sin—the original mistake—of humanity. It brought the bitter fruit of should, must, have-to and all the others into the world. Shall we blame God? Adam? Eve? The serpent? Or shall we just accept it as the way things are, as what is?

*You're really letting me down
as a boyfriend,
not being able to control
the weather and all.*

STEPHANIE VANDERKELLAN
"NEWHART"

The Myth of the Ideal

The human imagination is a wonder of creation. In an instant it can transport us from the Eiffel Tower to the Statue of Liberty to the Grand Canyon to a lunar landing vehicle go-carting on the surface of the moon—all while we're sitting and reading a book.

The imagination is also responsible for all the progress made by humanity. It can see a house where there is no house, a light bulb where there is a kerosene lamp, a radio where there is a music box, a television where there is a radio, health where there is illness, peace where there is discord.

Humans can imagine an improvement for almost every situation or activity they touch, and, with action to back it up, can often make that imagined improvement real. For humanity, the imagination is a powerful source of health, strength, safety, comfort, progress, success, wealth and life itself.

Alas, it is also the source of most of our miseries.

Because the imagination can make an improvement on almost anything, it never quite knows when to stop and enjoy the improvements that have already been made.

Seeing how something can be improved to perfection is often called *the ideal*. The Germans call it *verstang*. When our imagination projects its ideal view of what we and others *must, should,* and *ought to* be, enjoyment is nowhere to be found. We can't enjoy anything until it's *improved:* brighter, cleaner, newer—*better.*

What is, is never enough.

When what is gets close to the ideal, the ideal changes—it improves again; it becomes greater, higher, finer, better. As Josh Billings pointed out, "It ain't so much trouble to get rich as it is to tell when we have got rich." Enough is somehow never enough.

Now, in a selected area of life—our specialty, our big dream, our heart's desire—this striving for an ideal may

*We need
some imaginative stimulus,
some not impossible ideal
such as may shape
vague hope,
and transform it
into effective desire,
to carry us year after year,
without disgust,
through the routine work
which is so large a part of life.*

WALTER PATER

1885

help bring out the best in us. The problem is that we have an ideal about almost *every* part of life. We think that in career, relationships, romance, religion, social, political, environmental and just about all other areas of life, that just because we imagine how something *could* be better, it *should* be better.

And we suffer for it. At the very least, we don't enjoy what we already have because we're attached to how it should be improved. "Castles in the air cost a vast deal to keep up," Baron Lytton pointed out. Included in the cost is the emotional torment we suffer when we demand that our "should" should be met.

This "should" is often called *expectation*. It's another word for the original sin of knowing good from evil. We *expect* the world to live up to our ideals; we place an emotionally backed *demand* that it *must*. When the world doesn't live up to it (which, of course, is most of the time), we're not happy.

Somerset Maugham explained, "American women expect to find in their husbands a perfection that English women only hope to find in their butlers."

All of this gets worse, of course, when we apply our ideals to *ourselves*. We seem to be constantly compiling an ideal of how we should be—how we should look, what we should accomplish, what we should say, how we should feel and what we should think. We seem to take the best from the best—the greatest attributes of our greatest heroes, both real and fictional—and strive to make it our own.

That it can't be done seldom enters our mind. It *must* be done, and done *now!* Or else! Or else what? Anxiety and depression. "It is not materialism that is the chief curse of the world," wrote H. L. Mencken, "but idealism. Men get into trouble by taking their visions and hallucinations too seriously."

Another problem with the ideal is that some ideals are so high, some people might never even begin. The gap between where we are and the best that's been done

The music teacher
came twice each week
to bridge the awful gap
between Dorothy and Chopin.

GEORGE ADE

thus far is so great, we can become discouraged from the start.

Let's say we wanted to write a poem. Here's what Coleridge had to say in 1817 about the ideal that we, as potential poets, should strive for:

"The poet, described in ideal perfection, brings the whole soul of man into activity, with the subordination of its faculties to each other, according to their relative worth and dignity. He diffuses a tone and spirit of unity, that blends, and (as it were) fuses, each into each, by that synthetic and magical power...imagination."

If a poet is expected to do all *that,* why bother trying?

Ideals rob us of doing things simply for the fun of it. We must do something well at first, and then strive to get better and better. This attitude is not only unenjoyable; it's also exhausting.

At root, the demands we place against reality are lies. They are not the truth. They are an ideal—what *could* be, not what *must* be. "Don't use that foreign word 'ideals,'" wrote Henrik Ibsen in 1884. "We have that excellent native word 'lies.'" Most of the harm is done when we believe the lies to be true. "The visionary denies the truth to himself," explained Nietzsche in 1879, "the liar only to others." "The truth is what is," said Lenny Bruce, "what should be is a dirty lie."

The solution? We'll be discussing that in great detail later. For now, be consoled and, perhaps, re-idealized by this from H. F. Hedge: "What we need most, is not so much to realize the ideal as to idealize the real."

"The true ideal is not opposed to the real," explained James Russell Lowell, "but lies in it; and blessed are the eyes that find it."

There are joys
which long to be ours.
God sends ten thousand truths,
which come about us
like birds seeking inlet;
but we are shut up to them,
and so they bring us nothing,
but sit and sing awhile
upon the roof,
and then fly away.

HENRY WARD BEECHER

The Two Primary Barriers to Enjoyment

We have found that all of this programming—both biological and social—reflects itself in two primary barriers to enjoyment. These are *unworthiness* and *ingratitude*.

Unworthiness tells us we're not good enough for what we want, so we don't pursue it, so we don't get it. Further, unworthiness tells us we're not good enough for what we already *have*. This causes a low-level guilt that permeates our lives. Unworthiness causes our lives to be self-fulfilled prophecies of doom and gloom. "She not only expects the worst," Michael Arlen described it, "but makes the worst of it when it happens."

Ingratitude takes the opposite position: what we have is not good enough for *us*. Why be grateful for a one-bedroom apartment when we want a four-bedroom house? "Life is a hospital," Baudelaire observed, "in which every patient is possessed by the desire to change his bed." There's always something to find wrong with anything, and as long as something's wrong, why be thankful? "There was never a banquet so sumptuous," says the French proverb, "but someone dined poorly at it."

Unworthiness and ingratitude effectively destroy enjoyment and all other forms of wealth in our lives.

*To avoid criticism,
do nothing,
say nothing,
be nothing.*

ELBERT HUBBARD

Unworthiness

One of the most unfortunate—and probably the most destructive—decisions children can make about themselves is that they are undeserving, not good enough, unworthy.

It is, however, easy to see how this decision can be made—even in the best-raised children.

Childhood is a time of discovery; of unparalleled, intensive learning. All that distinguishes a gooing, gaaing almost totally helpless infant from a walking, talking, remarkably self-sufficient almost-adult of, say, ten must be learned.

From birth to two years old, in fact, is the most intense learning period of our lives. *Everything* must be learned. The learning process goes on every waking hour. No wonder infants sleep so much. All that learning is exhausting!

Children learn, for the most part, by trial-and-error. They have an insatiable curiosity and an innate ability to imitate. If it's in their environment, they want to see it, touch it, fondle it, put it in their mouths and explore it in any way in order to learn about it.

When children are seeing, touching, fondling, mouthing and exploring things that are all right for them to see, touch, fondle, mouth and explore, the parents stand by and let the process happen. Food and toys seem to be particularly acceptable areas of exploration. (Hence our cultural preoccupation with eating and playthings, perhaps?)

When children want to see, touch, fondle, mouth and explore things that are *not* acceptable, they hear about it—often in no uncertain terms. "No." "Stop." "Don't do that." Making something forbidden, of course, only arouses curiosity, and the child tries again with even more determination. The no's get stronger until (A) the object is removed, (B) the child is removed, or (C) a suitable substitute of exploration is offered.

School Principal: *I'm sure your children will be very happy here.*

Gomez: *If we'd wanted them to be happy, we would've let them stay at home.*

"THE ADDAMS FAMILY"

In a typical day of exploration, the praise for successful learning is usually far outweighed by the "no," "don't," "stop that," "shame," "bad," and "wrong" of correction. Over time, what is remembered is (A) long periods of noninteraction with The Adults; (B) a few moments of praise, and (C) a lot of "don'ts"—supported, perhaps, by some sort of punishment.

As a child grows, the successfully learned behavior that once garnered praise soon becomes expected. "Six months ago I got praise for taking one step; now I'm walking all over the place and they don't even notice." In fact, the very things that were once the cause of praise can become the source of correction. Drawing a picture on paper is great; drawing an even better picture on a wall is not.

While repeated successful behavior becomes expected and is soon no longer praised, repeated unsuccessful ("bad") behavior receives ever-increasing scorn. "I do all this stuff right and nothing; then I do this one thing wrong and BOOM!"

In this environment, it's easy for children to conclude that they are simply unable to do right, that there must be something wrong with them, that they just aren't good enough.

This set of circumstances usually gets worse when the child starts school. "Mastered printing the alphabet? Now let's try cursive writing." "Got addition down? Let's tackle subtraction. (And wait till we get to long division!)"

In addition to the learn-everything-fast treadmill, school also exposes children to organized competition and world-class comparisons. "Why aren't you as well-behaved as Suzie? Why can't you spell as well as John? Why don't you excel in history like Janet?" and on and on. We are expected to be as good in each subject as the best person in the class.

Then there are the taunts and harsh comparisons children make about each other, the "in" groups one is on the out with, the bullies, the gossips, the tattletales, the

Ferdinand:
Wherefore weep you?

Miranda: *At mine
unworthiness,
that dare not offer
What I desire to give;
and much less take
What I shall die to want.*

SHAKESPEARE

THE TEMPEST

teacher's pets—the world, it seems, supports our original decision that we somehow aren't good enough.

This unworthiness limits our enjoyment in two ways. First, it prevents us from getting the things we truly want. We don't feel deserving of our dream, so we accept the programming of another—or the culture—and pursue some goal not our own. Naturally, we do this without the full enthusiasm we would have for a goal of our own choosing, so we don't even achieve the programmed goal too well. We end up without what we want, and with only a part of what "they" wanted us to have. This is not a joyful situation.

Second, the good that does come our way is suspect. "If you love me, an unworthy person, there must be something wrong with you," or, as Stephen Sondheim wrote, "Thank you for the present, but what's wrong with the stuff?" or, as Groucho Marx said, "I refuse to join any club that would have me as a member." Unworthiness always has us looking for the catch, the angle, the small print.

When told of good news, what's the first thing many people say? "Oh, no!" or, "I can't believe it!" Unworthiness won't let us believe it. We even feel guilty that goodness is in the hands of an unworthy being such as ourselves.

Rather than deal with the underlying unworthiness, many people cover their low self-worth with overconfidence—a bravado and a self-assurance that is overwhelming.

A sure sign of this false confidence is ingratitude.

*I think our parents
got together in 1946 and said,
"Let's have lots of kids
and give them
everything they want,
so that they can grow up
and be totally messed up
and unable to cope with life."*

HOPE STEADMAN
"THIRTYSOMETHING"

Ingratitude

We have found that almost all our difficulty with other people comes down to one of the following:

1. People don't do what we want them to do.

2. When they do what we want them to do, they don't do it in the way we want it done.

3. When they do what we want, the way we want it done, they don't do it *when* we want it.

When we get what we want, in the way we want it, when we want it, then we are the nicest people in the world. Nobody's nicer. Some may be *equally* nice, but none nicer.

Let's face it. We're spoiled.

When we have too much unshared milk of human kindness, it tends to spoil. Being spoiled is another way of saying we're ungrateful. As far as we can tell, ingratitude comes from three sources.

First, it seems to be the natural result of a brain that filters out everything that isn't changing. The "good" in our lives is often not changing as rapidly as the "bad." We seem to be biologically programmed to lack appreciation.

Second, the cultural programming of "more is better" makes what we have only a single step on a long staircase to Utopia. "Don't enjoy each step," we are taught, "save it for one big, eternal enjoyment when you get to the top!"

Third, ingratitude is a clever cover for unworthiness. In a bold, rebellious reaction to the decision "I can't have anything," the slightly older child decides "I want it all!" Until one has "all," why bother enjoying any of it? There's still so much more "all" to get.

Whatever the reasons—be it one of these, a combination of them, or some reasons we've yet to discover—the habit of ingratitude is a primary inhibitor to enjoyment and wealth.

Blow, blow, thou winter wind,
Thou art not so unkind
As man's ingratitude.

SHAKESPEARE
AS YOU LIKE IT

I hate ingratitude
more in a man
Than lying, vainness,
babbling, drunkenness,
Or any taint of vice
whose strong corruption
Inhabits our frail blood.

SHAKESPEARE
TWELFTH NIGHT

Most of us grew up in a time when more was better, and more was inevitable. There may have been gaps in the steadily upward path of progress, but the gaps—however deep—were always understood to be temporary.

During the depression of the 1930s, prosperity was always "just around the corner." During World War II, when creature comforts grew scarce, people knew they only had to sacrifice "for the duration." The idea that our material abundance will stay the same—or worse, get worse—with no end in sight is not one we've entertained in the twentieth century.

We take for granted such basic things as central heating, indoor plumbing, electricity, potable water, uncontaminated food, a certain level of health care, refrigeration, transportation, "free" entertainment from radio, television and libraries, and much more.

> PETER: While writing this chapter, I lost my electricity for a day. I complained to my mother that I couldn't get any writing done because my computer didn't work. She asked, "Why don't you use pencil and paper?" It had never occurred to me! Although I've written twenty books "by hand," the twelve years I've used a computer have spoiled me utterly.

We take things for granted and, therefore, don't feel grateful for them. If it's granted, why should we? That's the norm, that's expected, that's what we're entitled to.*

What we've mentioned thus far are, of course, external things we often fail to be grateful for. How about our bodies? Of all the things the average, healthy person takes most for granted, his or her body is high on the list. Motion, speech, hearing, seeing, tasting, touch, digestion, assimilation—even relative freedom from pain—how often are we grateful for these?

---

*The temptation at this point is to look not at our own lives, but at the lives of those "less fortunate"—either people we know personally, people we've heard about, or fictional characters from books, movies, television and newspapers. It's easy to ask, "What about *them?*" rather than seeing how ingratitude applies to our own lives.

Ralph Kramden: *I promise you this, Norton. I'm gonna learn. I'm gonna learn from here on in how to swallow my pride.*

Ed Norton: *That ought not to be too hard. You've learned how to swallow everything else.*

"THE HONEYMOONERS"

Then there are the thoughts we think without having to think about thinking them, memory, intelligence, wisdom, intuition, our personalities and all the treasures contained therein—a sense of humor, kindness, compassion, caring, loving.

Then there's the gift of life itself.

Unless one of these bodily functions is taken from us or is severely threatened, we seldom notice it, much less take the time to be grateful for it.

And what does all this ingrained ingratitude cost us?

First, it keeps us from enjoying what we've got. We are not *aware* of the wealth in each moment. Not even being aware of the wealth, how can we be grateful for it?

Second, ingratitude keeps us from getting more of what we want. Whom do you prefer giving things to—the person who doesn't even bother to acknowledge your gift, or the person who expresses genuine gratitude? Why should the Universe respond any differently? Yes, the squeaky wheel may be the first one greased, but it's also the first one replaced.

Ingratitude places a barrier on what we receive—the greater the ingratitude, the greater the barrier.

Some people say, "I hate my life. I hate everything about my life. I need to change." What these people need to change is their *attitude* of ingratitude. They need to learn to appreciate and be grateful for the life they already have, *then* work on changing it.

If they somehow rally all their strength and make the changes they think will make them happy, within a short time they'll hate the new life as much as they hated the old—probably more. After all, they worked *so hard* for the new life. They no doubt worked to change the outer, but they did little to change the inner.

This is a recurring theme in this book, and we'll look at it from many angles: if we're not enjoying what we've got, it's going to be difficult to get the "more" we want—and even if we do get "more," we won't enjoy that either.

*Hope is the feeling you have
that the feeling you have
isn't permanent.*

JEAN KERR

Is It Hopeless?

So, here we have our brains filtering out all the good stuff, our external childhood programming telling us to be normal and fit in, our internal decisions from the past telling us we're not good enough, the fight or flight response keeping us fearful and/or angry most of the time, the media and gossip telling us how horrible everything is even in the most remote corner of the Universe; things are falling apart all around us; we're always recovering from something; glamour tempts us with the new and improved; upward mobility demands that we get more whether we want more or not—all of which leads to feelings of unworthiness and ingratitude.

And with all these strikes against us, we're asked to enjoy life? *Enjoy life?* With all this going on, just staying alive is a major achievement. Enjoy life? Is it hopeless?

Well, we hope so.

Hope, so often, is what people use in place of *action*. They know something isn't right, they know something must change, and instead of *doing something about it,* they merely *hope it will get better.*

Hope as a spark plug—a vision of something better to get us going—is fine. Hope as a substitute for action—for changing what needs to be changed, either inner, outer or both—is, as W. Burton Baldry called it, "disappointment deferred."

What do your intrepid co-authors think? Do we think life can be enjoyed more fully, year after year? Absolutely. Do we think merely hoping will achieve it? No. Greater enjoyment requires change. We need to change our attitudes (mostly) and our environment (less mostly), and change requires action, not hope.

"Hope is the most treacherous of human fancies," wrote James Fenimore Cooper (1789–1851). "There is nothing so well known as that we should not expect some-

It is natural to man
to indulge
in the illusion of hope.
We are apt to shut our eyes
against a painful truth,
and listen to the song
of that siren,
till she transforms us
into beasts.

PATRICK HENRY

1775

thing for nothing," observed Edgar Watson Howe in 1911, "but we all do and call it Hope."

"Just as dumb animals are snared by food," said Petronius two thousand years ago, "human beings would not be caught unless they had a nibble of hope."

Caught in what? Caught in the idea that they are powerless, and that hope alone will bring them deliverance from the trap of complacency.

Earlier, we looked at original sin from the viewpoint of the Bible. Now, let's look at hope from the perspective of Greek mythology. It's the story of Pandora's Box. It fits right in with Adam and Eve as, in Greek mythology, Pandora was the first woman. (We *know* you bought this book to find out how to get more money and we keep telling you *stories*—patience, dear reader, patience.)

Pandora, you will recall, against the will of the gods, gave fire (not the knowledge of good and evil) to humanity. She also found a jar that contained all the evils of the world. (Again, popular belief is that it was a box, but it was, in fact, a jar. Why doesn't "60 Minutes" *do something* about all these misconceptions?)

Pandora was cautioned not to open the jar, but, curiosity being what it is, this warning only tantalized her. She opened the jar, and all the so-called evils of the world escaped.

We say "so-called evils" because in one popular telling, the jar actually contained not evils, but blessings. This version fits right into our way of thinking, as we think all the so-called negative aspects of life can be turned into positives by a simple adjustment of attitude. Much, *much* more on this later.

After Pandora opened the jar, and all the evils flew into the world, what was the last thing in the jar? Hope.

The popular interpretation of this story is, "Isn't it nice that the gods put hope in the bottom of the jar, because we have hope that all the evils of the world will, hopefully, all be cleaned up."

Well, isn't life a picnic?
I get to be miserable forever.
I'm just going to have to mope
and be unhappy
and then one day I'll die.

STEPHANIE VANDERKELLAN

"NEWHART"

Nonsense. We think that hope—in the form of complacency—is one of the greatest evils. Without hope, humanity would have gotten busy and cleaned up all the other evils long ago. Hope provides the environment in which the other evils can flourish. As Nietzsche wrote in 1878, "Hope in reality is the worst of all evils, because it prolongs the torments of man."

Just as discouragement is the biggest obstacle in successfully pursuing our dreams, so hope is the biggest barrier to eliminating evil from the world.

What is evil? Evil is *live* spelled backwards. Evil is unnecessary life experience. If cutting off a dog's tail is necessary, so be it. Cutting the tail off an inch at a time is unnecessary, however, and thus evil. If we have to burn our hand once to know that the stove is hot, thus is life. If we fail to learn our lesson and burn our hand over and over again, that's evil.

"I suppose it can be truthfully said," said Robert G. Ingersoll in 1892, "that Hope is the only universal liar who never loses his reputation for veracity." Robert Frost put it this way: "A man will sometimes devote all his life to the development of one part of his body—the wishbone."

Yes, the handmaiden of Hope is Wish. As Alexander Woollcott said, "Many of us spend half of our time wishing for things we could have if we didn't spend half our time wishing."

Hope has a good reputation in some circles because it has been confused with what we would call "goals" or "inspiration." As long as something—*anything*—is combined with *action,* we're in favor of it. To the degree action is postponed for some vague mystical intervention, well, that's not our style—or our suggested method of gaining wealth.

Alexander Pope is often quoted as a supporter of hope: "Hope springs eternal in the human breast." In fact, Pope was not for hope. The next line in his *Essay on Man* continued, "Man never is, but always to be blest." It's that

*In the factory
we make cosmetics;
in the store
we sell hope.*

CHARLES REVSON

"to be blest" that bothers us. Enough "to be." Let's get on with the blessings by remembering "God helps those who help themselves."

So often we use hope to avoid or postpone the difficult actions we know we must take. "The illusions of hope," wrote Harry F. Banks, "are apt to close one's eyes to the painful truth." If our eyes are closed, we don't act. It's not that we don't *need* to act, it's just that we don't act.

Yes, there is a happy medium between hope as a stimulant for change—a way of seeing that success is a possibility for the change we contemplate—and the stagnating "I hope, I hope, now I'll wait for success to be brought to me," version of almost-certain failure. "This wonder we find in hope, that she is both a flatterer and a true friend," wrote Owen Feltham (1602–1668). "How many would die did not hope sustain them; how many have died by hoping too much!"

The spark of hope, if not sustained by successful and satisfying results, will not motivate one for long. "Men cannot for long live hopefully unless they are embarked upon some great unifying enterprise," wrote C. A. Dykstra, "one for which they may pledge their lives, their fortunes and their honor."

"The man who lives only by hope," says the Italian proverb, "will die with despair." And our own Benjamin Franklin, drawing on a gastronomical analogy, wrote in his *The Way to Wealth,* "He that lives upon hope, dies fasting." (The prestigious *Harper Book of American Quotations* had one of the most amusing typos we've discovered. It quoted Mr. Franklin as saying, "He that lives upon Hope, dies farting.")

According to Dante, the gates of hell are emblazoned with the motto, "Abandon hope, all ye who enter here."

Could it be that the gates of paradise are festooned with the same slogan?

*Statistically, the probability
of any one of us being here
is so small that you'd think
the mere fact of existing
would keep us all in
a contented dazzlement
of surprise.*

LEWIS THOMAS

The Blessings Already Are

When we stop taking life for granted, we begin to see life as a gift. All that we have, all that we are, the very fact that we're alive is a blessing.

The word *blessing* is often used in a religious context. We do not *necessarily* mean it in a religious sense here (although it certainly *can* be, if that is the way you choose to see it).* We'll use the word *blessing* to mean "a gift." Whom or what the gift—the blessing—is from we'll let you determine.

Even the sometime cynic Voltaire recognized that life is a blessing: "All is a miracle. The order of nature, the revolution of a hundred million of worlds around a million of suns, the activity of light, the life of animals, all are grand and perpetual miracles."

> JOHN-ROGER: For more than twenty-five years, I have ended almost every lecture I've given, every seminar I've taught and every Discourse I've written with the same ancient phrase—*Barush Bashan*. It means, "The blessings already are."

Our basic needs—air, food, water, clothing, shelter, protection—have obviously been met, consistently, for as many years as we have been alive. These are blessings.

Further, we have enjoyed having any number of wants satisfied along the way. Consider your life. Observe all the blessings beyond the basic needs that surround you. Almost everything in your life is a blessing you desired at some earlier point—and now you have it.

Truly, the blessings already are.

Have we received all the blessings we are to receive in this lifetime? Well, unless you breathe your last breath before

---

*In THE *LIFE 101* SERIES, we place religious, spiritual, agnostic, atheistic and all other beliefs into a category we call The Gap. What you choose to fill your Gap with—or what you discover within your Gap—is entirely between you and the contents of your Gap. It's your choice. What we discuss in these books works regardless of what you put—or have found—in your Gap.

If we had no winter,
the spring would not
be so pleasant:
if we did not sometimes
taste of adversity,
prosperity would not
be so welcome.

ANNE BRADSTREET

1664

you finish reading this sentence, the answer to that question is obviously no.

The insanity of humanity is that, just because more blessings are on the way, we fail to appreciate the blessings already at hand. It's insanity because, if we wait until all the blessings for this lifetime are present and accounted for, we can't enjoy them until the moment of our death.

There are blessings we obviously acknowledge as blessings, but forget about (for those all-too-human reasons we've already discussed). And then there are blessings that we never quite see as blessings, but are blessings nonetheless.

We might even venture a radical comment here: *everything* that happens to us is a blessing.

If that's *too* radical for you, then let's modify it to: a great deal of what we initially *think* are curses become, eventually, blessings ("blessings in disguise").

There are two primary ways in which seeming-curses are, in fact, blessings.

First, we need to occasionally experience the polar opposite of what we want in order to appreciate the pole we *want* to enjoy. Without darkness there is no light, without cold there is no warmth, without pain there is no pleasure.

"A man is insensible to the relish of prosperity," said Sa'Id in 1258, "till he has tasted adversity." Knowing how bad life can be allows us to appreciate how good life is. In this way, even the so-called negative experiences are blessings, because they give us the ability to appreciate the so-called positive.

Second, within each seeming-adversity is a lesson. Naturally, we *want* good, but when bad comes along, we can use it to learn—turn it into a blessing, "make stumbling blocks into stepping stones" as the proverb goes.

This is, of course, ancient wisdom. "When times are good, be happy," encourages Ecclesiastes 7:14, "but when

*In the depth of winter,
I finally learned that
within me there lay
an invincible summer.*

ALBERT CAMUS

times are bad, consider: God has made the one as well as the other."

Things were still the same in the first century, when Seneca wrote, "The good things which belong to prosperity are to be wished, but good things that belong to adversity are to be admired."

And so they seem to be the same today. "When life gives you oranges, enjoy. When life gives you lemons, make lemonade." Enjoy the good in your life, and make blessings from the rest by learning.

If nothing else, the "slings and arrows" of semi-outrageous fortune keep us from becoming utterly bored. "A reasonable amount of fleas is good for a dog," wrote Edward Westcott; "it keeps him from brooding over being a dog." And Francis Galton had this take: "Well-washed and well-combed domestic pets grow dull; they miss the stimulus of fleas."

Realizing that the blessings already are is such a relief— it gives us permission to enjoy life *right now*. We don't have to wait until this list of blessings and that list of desires are fulfilled. We can relax, slow down, take it easy. This in itself is a blessing. "Haste, haste," says the Swahili proverb, "has no blessing."

"He is richest who is content with the least," said Socrates, "for content is the wealth of nature." Thoreau, of course, agreed: "That man is the richest whose pleasures are the cheapest."

So much depends on how we see things: some people see the treasures in the chest; others measure how much more room there is in the chest for additional treasures.

For the former, life is charmed. For the latter, they're never happy until the chest is overflowing. (Then, of course, they complain because they need a bigger chest.)

Some see the glass half full; others see the glass half empty; and still others see the glass ninety percent full, and worry that someone's going to tip it over.

*Pat and I have the satisfaction
that every dime that we've got
is honestly ours.
I should say this, that Pat
doesn't have a mink coat.
But she does have a respectable
Republican cloth coat,
and I always tell her that
she would look good in anything.*

RICHARD M. NIXON
1952

Here's an example of seeing blessings as already existing vs. blessings still to be found. It was written in 1933 by Luther Standing Bear:

> Only to the white man was nature a "wilderness" and only to him was the land "infested" with "wild" animals and "savage" people. To us it was tame. Earth was bountiful and we were surrounded with the blessings of the Great Mystery. Not until the hairy man from the east came and with brutal frenzy heaped injustices upon us and the families that we loved was it "wild" for us. When the very animals of the forest began fleeing from his approach, then it was that for us the "Wild West" began.

What we did to the western United States, we are doing to the entire planet—but first we have done it to ourselves. We see blessings as something to come, not something that surrounds us, always has surrounded us, and always will surround us.

"There's so much speculating going on that a lot of us never get around to living," observed Russell Baker. "Life is always walking up to us and saying, 'Come on in, the living's fine,' and what do we do? Back off and take its picture."

We have lost track of ourselves. We have lost track of the moment. We have lost track of the precious present.

How did this come to be? And, more importantly, what can we do about it?

No time like the present.

MARY DE LA RIVIÈRE MANLEY

1696

The Present

The problem is a well-documented one: we spend so much time regretting the past (depression) and fearing the future (anxiety) that we have no time for the present. Or, perhaps, it's because we spend so little time in the present, we regret the past and fear the future. Whatever the cause, it's a common complaint.

"No mind is much employed upon the present," Samuel Johnson wrote in 1759; "recollection and anticipation fill up almost all our moments."

"If a man carefully examine his thoughts he will be surprised to find how much he lives in the future," Emerson observed in 1827. "His well-being is always ahead. Such a creature is probably immortal."

One can hear the edge of sarcasm in Emerson's last sentence. To constantly live our lives in the past and future assumes we have an infinite amount of time to spend, well, *daydreaming*. Of course, we don't. We're all going to die someday; therefore our time here is finite.

"We are, perhaps, uniquely among the earth's creatures, the worrying animal," wrote Lewis Thomas. "We worry away our lives, fearing the future, discontent with the present, unable to take in the idea of dying, unable to sit still."

We postpone our enjoyment of the present. We'll enjoy the moment later, when things are better. We ransom our present happiness to the future. "We are never present with, but always beyond ourselves," observed Montaigne in 1580; "fear, desire, hope still push us on toward the future."

Ah, the future! "That period of time," wrote Ambrose Bierce, "in which our affairs prosper, our friends are true and our happiness is assured."

"The supreme value is not the future but the present. The future is a deceitful time that always says to us, 'Not yet,' and thus denies us," wrote Octavio Paz. "The future is not the time of love: what man truly wants he wants

They were upon their great theme:
"When I get to be a man!"
Being human, though boys,
they considered
their present estate
too commonplace
to be dwelt upon.
So, when the old men gather,
they say: "When I was a boy!"
It really is the land of nowadays
that we never discover.

BOOTH TARKINGTON
1914

now. Whoever builds a house for future happiness builds a prison for the present."

"Those who talk about the future are scoundrels," said Louis Ferdinand Céline. "It is the present that matters." And Longfellow, using a full year's quota of exclamation marks, agreed:

> Trust no Future, howe'er pleasant!
> Let the dead Past bury its dead!
> Act,—act in the living Present!
> Heart within, and God o'erhead!

We are so frightened of the present. "The word 'now' is like a bomb through the window," wrote Arthur Miller, "and it ticks." Another great playwright, Shakespeare, put it thus: "Past and to come seem best; things present worst."

"Philosophy triumphs easily over past evils and future evils," said La Rochefoucauld, "but present evils triumph over it."

This has been a problem for some time. "It is not the weight of the future or the past that is pressing upon you, but ever that of the present alone," counseled Marcus Aurelius in the second century. "Remember that the sole life which a man can lose is that which he is living at the moment."

Where did all of this postponement of present pleasures start?

We've already looked at two stories of Creation and the early days of humanity. Allow us to tell you a third.

When the Earth was almost complete, God gathered the best and the brightest of God's helpers to make one very important decision. Something needed to be hidden until humanity was mature enough to appreciate it and use it properly.

It was the greatest treasure of humankind, the greatest gift, the greatest blessing: it was humanity's true Self—the Self that was undeniably and experientially linked to the Source of all creation, a direct connection to God and all of Nature.

*So, if you have not
been trustworthy
in handling worldly wealth,
who will trust you
with true riches?*

LUKE 16:11

But where to hide it? Humans had a peculiar characteristic: if they didn't earn what they got, they didn't much appreciate it, and if they didn't appreciate it, they didn't take very good care of it. Immaturity 101. But when humans appreciated something, they took very good care of it, indeed.

But how does one "earn" a gift? This Self was a gift from God, not something to be earned. It was decided that this gift would be hidden, and humanity's "earning" of it would be the finding of it.

"But where to hide it?" God asked the helpers.

"Let's hide it on the highest mountain," suggested one of God's helpers.

"No," said God; "eventually humanity will climb the highest mountain."

"Then let's hide it in the depths of the ocean," suggested another.

"Humanity will someday plumb the depths of the ocean," said God. "Besides, neither of these hiding places gives all of humanity the same opportunity to find it. The poor and the weak must have the same opportunity as the rich and the strong."

This caused something of a pause.

"*Where* are we allowed to hide it?" asked an astute helper.

"As with most things," answered God, "you can hide it in space and in time."

More thinking in the firmament.

After what seemed an eternity (and it could well have been), one of the helpers finally spoke: "The last space humans would think to look for such a gift would be within themselves."

"Yes," agreed another, "we can hide it within each of them, equally."

Pete: Have you ever thought
about death? Do you realize
that we each must die?

Dud: Of course we must die,
but not yet. It's only half past four
of a Wednesday afternoon.

Pete: No one knows when God in
His Almighty Wisdom
will choose to vouch-safe
His precious gift of Death.

Dud: Granted. But chances are
He won't be making a pounce
at this time of day.

PETER COOK AND DUDLEY MOORE

"That's the last place they'll look," exclaimed another, enthused about the idea.

"You've found an excellent place to hide it," smiled God, "but *when* should they be able to find it?"

"Four A.M. on Tuesday mornings..."

"...but only if Tuesday falls on a leap year..."

"...and they have to have fasted and prayed for three days and nights before..."

"We're making up rules for life," said God, "not a Nintendo Samurai Warrior game."

A thoughtful silence again settled upon God's Council.

"If we're going to hide it in the most obvious place—within each of them," said a helper, "why not make the finding of it most possible at the most obvious time—right now."

"Here and now..." considered another. "Yes. That would do it."

"Humans are so seldom where they are when they are," agreed a third. "We'll put the gift in the most obvious place—inside each of them; and we'll place it in the most available possible time—right now, the moment."

"And to make matters even more obscure," smiled one helper, "we'll name the gift, and the time when the gift can be found, by the same name."

"The present," another smiled.

"Yes, the present." There was a consensus in heaven.

"Well done," said God. "Now, let's work on The Commandments. How many do we have so far?"

"Three thousand, eight hundred and seventy-four."

"Do you think we can work on shortening these a bit?"

☆

Every situation
—nay, every moment—
is of infinite worth;
for it is the representative
of a whole eternity.

GOETHE

The truth of this story remains unverified—and certainly our telling of it veered on the fanciful. Yet, from what we've been able to discover about the present, it's *as if* it happened that way.

Our greatest gift is always with us, always here, always now.

> The Present, the Present is all that thou hast
> For thy sure possessing;
> Like the patriarch's angel hold it fast
> Till it gives its blessing.

So wrote Whittier in 1847. Thoreau made it a commandment: "You must live in the present, launch yourself on every wave, find your eternity in each moment." Alexander Martin made it a suggestion: "Take time to enjoy the present."

"With the Past, as past, I have nothing to do; nor with the Future as future," wrote Emerson. "I live now, and will verify all past history in my own moments."

"The passing moment is all we can be sure of," observed Somerset Maugham; "it is only common sense to extract its utmost value from it; the future will one day be present and will seem as unimportant as the present does now."

The present is the only time in which we can do anything, feel anything, be anything.

"For present joys are more to flesh and blood," wrote John Dryden in 1687, "Than a dull prospect of a distant good."

"The present time has one advantage over every other—" wrote Charles Caleb Colton in 1825, "it is our own." And Longfellow, in 1839: "Look not mournfully into the Past. It comes not back again. Wisely improve the Present. It is thine."

And yet, with all the "good press" the poets, philosophers and sages of old have given the present, why don't we see it? Why don't we spend more time there? (Here?) Why is the present so elusive?

I am in the present.
I cannot know what
tomorrow will bring forth.
I can know only what
the truth is for me today.
That is what I am
called upon to serve,
and I serve it in all lucidity.

IGOR STRAVINSKY

1936

"Let anyone try, I will not say to arrest, but to notice or to attend to, the present moment of time," wrote William James a hundred years ago. "One of the most baffling experiences occurs. Where is it, this present? It has melted in our grasp, fled ere we could touch it, gone in the instant of becoming."

Emerson, one hundred and fifty years ago, observed the same phenomenon: "We can see well into the past; we can guess shrewdly into the future; but that which is rolled up and muffled in impenetrable folds is today."

A clue on living more in the present might be found in this from Jean de la Bruyère: "Children enjoy the present because they have neither a past nor a future."

As Jesus said, "Let the little children come to me, and do not hinder them, for the kingdom of God belongs to such as these." (This quote is found in three books of the New Testament: Luke 18:16, Mark 10:14 and Matthew 19:14, although Matthew quotes Jesus as saying "the kingdom of heaven" rather than "the kingdom of God." Jesus seems to use the two phrases interchangeably.)

"I tell you the truth," said Jesus (Matthew 18:3); "unless you change and become like little children, you will never enter the kingdom of heaven."

And where is the kingdom of heaven and the kingdom of God? "The kingdom of God is within you" (Luke 17:21).

So why aren't we "like little children"? Practical people have a fear that, although children have a good time, they don't seem to *accomplish* much. Humans always seem to want more, more and more. At a certain point, in order to get more, we learn to defer gratification.

The habit of deferring gratification, however, has become too strong—we're deferring it, seemingly, forever. Hence, we seldom enjoy what is.

The solution? Back to our old friend, balance. First, we must admit we're out of balance. As a culture, we have gone too far in the direction of deferring. It's time to get

I scarcely remember
counting upon happiness—
I look not for it
if it be not in the present hour—
nothing startles me
beyond the moment.
The setting sun will always
set me to rights—
or if a sparrow come
before my window
I will take part in its existence
and pick about the gravel.

JOHN KEATS

back into balance. The irony is that living more in the present allows us to accomplish *more* in the future.

"Real generosity toward the future," wrote Camus, "lies in giving all to the present."

"There is no moment like the present," said Marie Edgeworth. "The man who will not execute his resolutions when they are fresh upon him can have no hope from them afterwards; they will be dissipated, lost, and perish in the hurry and scurry of the world, or sunk in the slough of indolence."

"Every tomorrow has two handles," observed Henry Ward Beecher. "We can take hold of it with the handle of anxiety or the handle of faith. We should live for the future, and yet should find our life in the fidelities of the present; the last is only the method of the first."

When in balance, the past and future become part of a joyful present. "We live in the present, we dream of the future and we learn eternal truths from the past," said Madame Chiang Kai-shek. And Charles Lamb wrote, "My motto is, 'Contented with little, yet wishing for more.'"

When we learn to enjoy the present, we know that we will also enjoy the future, for the future inevitably becomes the present without our doing anything about it. "As for the Future," observed Saint-Exupery, "your task is not to foresee but to enable it."

Besides, living in the present makes pursuing the future more fun. In the third century B.C., Epicurus noted, "The man least dependent upon the morrow," that is, the person living in and enjoying the moment, "goes to meet the morrow most cheerfully."

So where do we start? Where do we find this all-important yet seemingly elusive present?

Where we are right now, of course. And it all starts with a breath.

Take a deep breath. Let it out. Relax. When we breathe, we consciously take control of a bodily process which is usually unconscious—breathing. We begin to take dominion

There is no time
like the pleasant.

OLIVER HERFORD

over our bodies. We give ourselves the message: "Relax. Take it easy. It's OK to enjoy the moment."

Take another deep breath—slower this time, and deeper. Hold it for a moment; then let it go. Relax. Then take another. Focus on the air going in, and the air going out. Let go of the past. Let go of the future. "Be here now," as Ram Dass suggested.

Three deep breaths may not make you fully enlightened (and then again, it may). You might notice, however, a bit more awareness of the moment than you had before. It's a start. Take your time. Be patient.

The present's not going anywhere. It will always be here.

To the dull mind
all of nature is leaden.
To the illumined mind
the whole world sparkles
with light.

EMERSON

Light, Highest Good

Light is one of the most enjoyable, practical and accessible blessings found in the present. Light is a concept that has permeated just about every religion, spiritual practice, growth philosophy and much of literature throughout history.

In the Bible, light is all over the place. In the Old Testament (the foundation of the teachings of Judaism), there are 137 references to light. Light appears as early as the third verse of the Old Testament: "God said, 'Let there be light,' and there was light. God saw that the light was good, and he separated the light from the darkness" (Genesis 1:3–4).

Of this, Francis Bacon wrote, "The first creature of God, in the works of the days, was the light of the sense: the last was the light of reason." John Milton called light "the prime work of God."

The New Testament (the foundation of the teachings of Christianity), has 93 references to light, including: "Then spake Jesus again unto them, saying, I am the light of the world: he that followeth me shall not walk in darkness, but shall have the light of life" (John 8:12).

Hinduism, the oldest and currently the religion with the most followers (2.5 billion), equates light to both reality and immortality. Here's a portion of the *Brhadaranyka Upanisad* (1.3.28):

> Lead me from the unreal to the real!
> Lead me from darkness to light!
> Lead me from death to immortality!

When Siddhartha Gautama became Buddha, the En*light*ened One, Buddhism was born. Buddha is often referred to as "the Light of Asia."

The holy text of Islam and the Moslems is the Koran. Here is one of the many references in the Koran (this one 24:35) to light: "God is the light of the heavens and the earth...light upon light."

*Great men are instruments
by which the Highest One
works out his designs;
light-radiators
to give guidance and blessing
to the travelers of time.*

MOSES HARVEY

Reasonable thinkers liked light. "Reason is the light and lamp of life," wrote Cicero around 100 B.C. Seventeen centuries later, John Locke picked up the torch: "Reason is a natural revelation, whereby the eternal Father of light communicates to mankind that portion of truth which he has laid within the reach of their natural faculties."

A half-century later, Louis Brandeis cautioned, "If we would be guided by the light of reason, we must let our minds be bold." Jesus, too, suggested the bold use of the light: "You are going to have the light just a little while longer. Walk while you have the light, before darkness overtakes you" (John 12:35).

More on the use of the light later. For now, let's look at what some great minds of literature had to say about light.

Literature itself Samuel Johnson called "a kind of intellectual light which, like the light of the sun, may sometimes enable us to see what we do not like." Emerson, on the other hand, thought, "There is no object so foul that intense light will not make it beautiful." James Thurber reconciled the two: "There are two kinds of light—the glow that illumines, and the glare that obscures."

"Light is the symbol of truth," stated James Russell Lowell. Rabindranath Tagore agreed: "Knowledge is nothing but the continually burning up of error to set free the light of truth." T. H. Huxley defined happiness as "the sense of having worked according to one's capacity and light to make things clear and get rid of cant and shams."

Oliver Wendell Holmes said that to do right was to be "faithful to the light within." Benjamin Disraeli thought that, ideally, a university should be "a place of light, of liberty, and of learning." It seems we're still working on that one.

An English proverb defines *zeal* as "fire without light." Woodrow Wilson suggested that, in life, "the thing to do is supply light and not heat."

George Santayana said that consciousness itself is "the inner light kindled in the soul; a music, strident or sweet,

Angels fly because they take themselves lightly.

G. K. CHESTERTON

made by the friction of existence." Jules Renard described dreaming as "to think by moonlight by the light of an inner moon."

Then there are those who praised light in verse— Longfellow, for example:

> Out of the shadows of night
> The world rolls into light.

Or, this from Dylan Thomas:

> Light breaks where no sun shines;
> Where no sea runs, the waters of the heart
> Push in their tides.

Even the existentialists gave an occasional nod toward light, after their own fashion. Camus, for example, said, "Fortunately there is gin, the sole glimmer of light in this darkness."

And let's not forget hard science. The hardest sciences of all—math and physics—honor light in Einstein's famous quote: "$E=mc^2$." He never *intended* it to become a quote, of course, but it became one just the same—everyone quotes it; very few people understand it, but everyone quotes it. In that, Einstein is something like Shakespeare—who said a great deal about light, but we're not going to quote any of it here, because it's time to move on to How to Focus Upon and Use Light.

The first thing to remember about light is just that—all we have to do is to *remember* about light. We're not bringing it in from somewhere else, we're simply acknowledging its presence in the moment. If the light weren't already here, we wouldn't be, either.

The same is true of "sending" the light. We don't really send it. It's already there. Sending light is as silly as sending air. All we do when we "send" light is acknowledge its presence where it already is.

We make a choice, a selection, a focus. "Everywhere the human soul," wrote Thomas Carlyle, "stands between a hemisphere of light and another of darkness." That's a grander way of saying what we've said many times: each

I simply haven't the nerve
to imagine a being,
a force, a cause
which keeps the planets
revolving in their orbits,
and then suddenly stops
in order to give me
a bicycle with three speeds.

QUENTIN CRISP

moment contains both good and bad, light and dark, positive and negative.

We can choose to focus upon either the negative or the positive. Why not focus on the positive? Focusing on the light that's already present in any situation is an option we always have.

The best news about this light—other than its existence—is that it seems to respond to human requests. No, the light is not some cosmic bellhop, as the quote on the facing page from Quentin Crisp explains nicely. The light does, however, seem to make a difference—if it's in our best interest that a difference be made.

That's where "the highest good" comes in. We can ask for the light to be somewhere or do something *for our highest good and the highest good of all concerned*. That way we know that our highest good and the highest good of everyone else is always foremost—even if it means that we don't get "our way" in every situation, every time.

As Samuel Butler explained, "The highest good; towards this all government, all social conventions, all art, literature, and science should directly or indirectly tend. Holy men and holy women are those who keep this unconsciously in view at all times whether of work or pastime."

Asking for our highest good and the highest good of all concerned keeps us from becoming sorcerer's apprentices—setting things in motion we have no idea how to control. "If a man could have half his wishes," said Benjamin Franklin, "he would double his troubles." Or, as Oscar Wilde observed, "When the gods choose to punish us, they merely answer our prayers."

We don't always know what's for our highest good and the highest good of all concerned—nor should we. How dull it would be if we knew *everything* that was going to happen to us and everyone else for all time. Life would become not just "Gilligan's Island," but "Gilligan's Island" *reruns*. Reruns of reruns, in fact. Ugh.

So, the highest good is our safety net, our insurance policy. If we ask for something and it comes to pass, we

Thunder is good,
thunder is impressive;
but it is lightning
that does the work.

MARK TWAIN

know it's for our highest good and the highest good of all concerned. If we ask for something and it doesn't come to pass, we know we got an answer—the answer was "no." Or, at least, "not just yet."

Or, perhaps our desire changes to accept—or even appreciate—what already is. That's the light working, too. Either way, we can relax and enjoy the moment. *This* moment.

Worrying about things does no good—we simply lose the enjoyment of the moment and kid ourselves into thinking that worrying has somehow been helpful.

Doing is helpful. If there's something we can *do* about a situation—and the outcome of the situation is important enough to us—then *do it*. If it's not important enough, or, if there's nothing we can do, send the light for everyone's highest good, and move on with what can be done.

Sending the light takes so little time—a few seconds at most. It's such a small expenditure—and the potential returns are so great—that we consider it an excellent investment in personal wealth.

I am large,
I contain multitudes.

WALT WHITMAN

Create a Container to Receive

PETER: When I first visited Los Angeles in the early 1970s, I was warned not to drink the water. In the parking lot of a supermarket was a water-vending machine. "Twenty-five cents a gallon," it read. I thought this was a fair price, so I put in my quarter and pushed the button. The machine hummed, buzzed and chugged. Then a gallon of water splattered on my feet. Why didn't they tell me I had to bring my own container? Welcome to L.A.!

Imagine yourself at a small but abundant waterfall. What would limit your ability to take from that waterfall your wealth of water? The size of your container, right? If you had a cup, you'd have a cup's worth of wealth (water). If you had a gallon jug, you'd have a gallon's worth of wealth. If you had a barrel, you'd have a barrel of wealth. If you had a tank-truck, well, you could supply all those twenty-five-cent water-vending machines in Los Angeles.

What if the same were true of all the attributes of wealth? What if your ability to experience health, happiness, abundance, prosperity, riches, loving, caring, sharing, learning, knowing what you want, opportunity, enjoying and balance were limited only by your ability to receive? What if each of these qualities were available to you in infinite supply, and the only thing limiting you were the size of your container?

We know it doesn't *seem* that way. It seems as though, if we have a cup, only a cup's worth of water *ever* dribbles over the falls. That is, however, an illusion—a highly convincing illusion, granted, but an illusion nonetheless.

If we want to expand our ability to experience health, happiness, abundance, prosperity, riches, loving, caring, sharing, learning, knowing what we want, opportunity, enjoying and balance, we must expand the size of our health, happiness, abundance, prosperity, riches, loving,

You can't win any game
unless
you are ready to win.

CONNIE MACK

caring, sharing, learning, knowing what we want, opportunity, enjoying and balance containers.

This is done through affirmations. An affirmation is a positive statement about something. With it, we *make firm* the truth of something, even if the truth is hidden in illusion. You can affirm wealth, even though the current illusion is one of poverty.

Affirmations are always stated in the present. "I am..." not "I'm going to be..."; "I have..." not "I want...." If we affirm what we're *going* to have and *going* to be, what are we affirming? That we're *going* to have and be that. We want to affirm that we *have* it and we *are* that.

Affirmations gain strength through repetition. With each repetition, we slightly increase the size of our container to receive and hold that which we affirm. Each repetition might only be a drop in a swimming pool, but, if we keep dripping, one of these days we'll be swimming.

The problem most people have with affirmations is that they stop long before obtaining any noticeable result. Then they say, "See? I told you it wouldn't work."

Why do people stop? It usually comes down to one reason: discomfort. Enlarging one's container for wealth is uncomfortable. Count on it.

To accept the idea that we already *are* healthy, happy, abundant, prosperous, rich, loving, caring, sharing, learning, knowing what we want, opportunity-rich, enjoying and balanced, we must challenge a great many limiting beliefs we hold about ourselves. Limiting beliefs, when challenged, create discomfort.

Saying an affirmation is like sending clear water, under pressure, into a clogged pipe. All the gunk that's clogging up the pipe surfaces. When we say an affirmation, over and over ("over and over" creates the pressure), all the gunk that's been clogging our pipes (our pipeline to wealth?) surfaces.

This gunk includes unworthiness, hurt feelings, anger, guilt and fear—all the emotions that make up what we call

I know that I am an artist.
LUDWIG VAN BEETHOVEN

I am the resurrection and the life.
JESUS

*I am not a member of any
organized political party.
I am a Democrat.*
WILL ROGERS

*I am by temperament
a conquistador.*
SIGMUND FREUD

I am that I am.
GOD

*I am indeed rich,
since my income is
superior to my expense,
and my expense is
equal to my wishes.*
EDWARD GIBBON

I am the state!
LOUIS XIV

the comfort zone. Who wants to feel all that? Nobody. We become distracted by something that's less uncomfortable than the gunk. We're off on some other line of thinking (often negative because, after all, most of us are more comfortable thinking negatively than positively). The next thing we know, five minutes have gone by and...what were we supposed to be thinking about?

A good way to overcome distractions is to say the affirmation out loud. No matter what we're thinking, at least a *part* of us is saying the affirmation.

How many times should we say an affirmation?

To really get it going, to charge it with our energy, to make the enlargement of our wealth container a major priority in our consciousness, we suggest saying it, initially, at least one thousand times. This may seem like a lot, but repeating a short affirmation one thousand times should take less than half an hour.

You can use toothpicks to keep count. Have one bundle of 100 toothpicks, and one bundle of 10. Hold the bunch of 100 toothpicks in your hand. Place the ten toothpicks in front of you. With each repetition, place one of the toothpicks in your hand into a new pile. When no toothpicks remain in your hand, you have said your affirmation 100 times. Move one of the ten toothpicks into a separate "marker" pile. Then pick up the 100 toothpicks and continue. When all 10 "marker" toothpicks are in the "marker" pile, you have said your affirmation 1,000 times. (When doing money affirmations, you can use cash in place of toothpicks.)

Another method is to count how many times you say the affirmation in one minute, then figure out how many minutes it will take you to reach 1,000.

Whatever the method, please give it a try. The affirmation will probably lose all its meaning for a while; the words themselves may lose meaning—it may all be just a lot of silly sounds. That's OK. Persevere. By the end of 1,000, you may find a new energy, power and meaning permeating the affirmation.

*A short saying
oft contains
much wisdom.*

SOPHOCLES

What are some affirmations? We've already suggested one—a sort-of "master affirmation" for this book—"I am wealthy." As we go along, we'll be suggesting more. Feel free to create your own, of course. Here are some to get started:

"I am healthy."

"I am happy."

"I am abundant."

"I am prosperous."

"I am rich."

"I am loving."

"I am caring."

"I am sharing."

"I am learning."

"I know what I want."

"I have abundant opportunities."

"I am enjoying my life."

"I am balanced."

Create the container to receive. Enlarge the container at every possible opportunity (the next line you stand in, think of it as affirmation time). As the container is enlarged, the process of living will fill it to brimming.

*As my Great Aunt Maude
always said,
to own a priceless treasure
one must first be worthy of it.*

ARTEMUS GORDON

"THE WILD, WILD WEST"

Worthy to Be Wealthy

To have wealth—and especially to *enjoy* wealth—one must feel worthy of wealth. We may have 100,000 reasons why we're not worthy. Our job is to forget those reasons—they're not doing us any good.

When we feel worthy of wealth, wealth comes to us. When we feel worthy of wealth, we can enjoy the wealth we already have. Worthiness is a key to wealth.

Worthiness is a given. If we have something—a relationship, a car, a career, life itself—we are worthy of it. If we don't have it, we're not worthy. If we want it, we must work on our worthiness.

Let's make the distinction between *worthiness* and *self-esteem*. Worthiness is a statement of what we are and have. Self-esteem is how we *feel* about what we are and have.

People often confuse the two terms. Becoming more and getting more is a process of enhancing our worthiness. Enjoying what we already have is a process of enhancing our self-esteem.

We'll work on self-esteem in a later chapter ("Remember the Good"). The technique of self-esteem is simply: do good things, and remember that you've done them. In this chapter, we'll work on worthiness, on enlarging the container of worthiness within ourselves.

The first thing to realize is how large the container already is. All that you are, all that you have, all that you do is an indicator of your present worth.

Reflect on the health, happiness, abundance, prosperity, riches, loving, caring, sharing, learning, knowing what you want, opportunity, enjoying and balance you already have in your life. That's how worthy you already are. Remember: if you weren't worth all these things, you wouldn't have them.

To make room for more wealth in our life, we must enlarge the "worthiness container." This we do through affirmations.

Worth begets
in base minds, envy;
in great souls, emulation.

HENRY FIELDING

1707–1754

Please don't think using affirmations is some mystical woo-woo process. We all use affirmations all the time, we just may not call it that.

In daily life, the process of getting what we want goes something like this: We have an idea: "It might be nice to have...," and we think more and more positively about it—an affirmation. Then we decide, "I want it," and think still more positively about having it—more affirmations. Eventually, when the container of our worthiness has been expanded sufficiently, we take action and get the thing we have been thinking about.

The same is true of *negative* affirmations. We want something, tell ourselves we *can't* have it, explain all the reasons *why* we can't have it and, sure enough, we don't get it. We *affirmed* that our container of worthiness was not large enough to hold the new desire, and, sure enough, it wasn't.

The master worthiness affirmation, of course, is simply, "I am worthy." In working with wealth, we can include

"I am worthy of wealth."

"I am worthy of health."

"I am worthy of happiness."

"I am worthy of abundance."

"I am worthy of prosperity."

"I am worthy of riches."

"I am worthy of loving."

"I am worthy of caring."

"I am worthy of sharing."

"I am worthy of learning."

"I am worthy of knowing what I want."

"I am worthy of opportunity."

"I am worthy of enjoying."

"I am worthy of balance."

Get out those toothpicks!

*I would rather
be able to appreciate things
I can not have
than to have things
I am not able to appreciate.*

ELBERT HUBBARD

Appreciation

As we mentioned earlier, we consider appreciation one of the two primary components of enjoyment. Appreciation is *liking* something—admiring it, being fond of it, having affection for it, perhaps even adoring it.

The key to appreciation is *time.*

"The present is burdened too much with the past," wrote Nathaniel Hawthorne. "We have not time, in our earthly existence, to appreciate what is warm with life, and immediately around us."

The essence of appreciation is to *make* the time. Time is a precious commodity. Appreciation requires us to spend some of that preciousness on the object of our appreciation.

Try an experiment. Find something ordinary in your present environment, something you can hold in your hand. Anything will do. Pick it up. Now spend five full minutes (by the clock) looking at it, feeling it, smelling it, exploring it. Please do that now.

For those who aren't doing it and are reading on, this must mean you (A) think you already know what the outcome of doing it will be; (B) are reading for information only and not for experience; or (C) are so fascinated by our prose style that you just can't seem to stop reading. If you're in category A, we suggest you try the experiment anyway. If nothing else, you'll find out you were right. If you're in category B, you can turn the page; that's where the information continues.

And, if you're in category C (God bless you!), here's a quote from Lord David Cecil to tide you over while we're waiting for those who are exploring their objects to return: "The primary object of a student of literature is to be delighted. His duty is to enjoy himself: his efforts should be directed to developing his faculty of appreciation." There. Everybody seems to be back now.

*Next to excellence
is the appreciation of it.*

WILLIAM MAKEPEACE THACKERAY

1811–1863

*I know only two tunes;
one of them is "Yankee Doodle,"
and the other isn't.*

U. S. GRANT

There. How was that? Did you peek (or peak) after two minutes with your object and think, "I've explored all there is to explore"? Did you get lost for ten minutes? Did you begin to notice things not directly connected to the object? Your hands, for example, or the senses (sight, touch, smell) used to perceive the object.

Do you *appreciate* the object more? Notice we never asked you to appreciate it. We merely asked you to spend time with it, to explore it. The natural result of spending time is appreciation.

Nowhere is this more true than with people. People love to be appreciated, and it's so much fun to appreciate. "The deepest principle in human nature," wrote William James, "is the craving to be appreciated."

When we crave other people's appreciation too much, we're asking for trouble. "Lean too much upon the approval of people," Tehyi Hsieh observed, "and it becomes a bed of thorns."

The answer is not to find others who appreciate us, but to learn to appreciate ourselves more. How? Simple. Spend time on ourselves, spend time *with* ourselves. Get to know the person we're going to be sleeping with every night for the rest of our lives.

To appreciate is an act of positive selection. We *choose* to spend time finding the good in something or someone. It requires discipline and focus. We must look for the good, even through the apparent bad. Our conditioned response might be, "I'm bored with this," or "I don't like it." Through work, we can move beyond the conditioned response to one that's more pleasing, more enjoyable, and, well, wealthier.

"The sorrow of knowing that there is evil in the best," said Dr. Austen Fox Riggs, "is far out-balanced by the joy of discovering that there is good in the worst."

How to increase our ability to appreciate? Practice, practice, practice. And what is *always* around for us to practice on? Why, ourselves, of course. "He only is a great man who can neglect the applause of the multitude,"

*Wise men appreciate all men,
for they see the good in each
and know how hard it is
to make anything good.*

BALTASAR GRACIÁN

1647

wrote Joseph Addison in 1712, "and enjoy himself independent of its favor."

As we look more toward ourselves rather than others for appreciation, the most amazing thing happens: others seem to appreciate us more. Not *all* others, of course—some will find us "vain, self-centered and conceited." Oh well, we'd probably never get their appreciation anyway. Simply tell these people, "Sackcloth and ashes are simply not my style anymore."

Those who are, well, *aware* appreciate self-appreciation. These are the people we'll be getting more appreciation from as we appreciate ourselves more.

Another way to enhance appreciation is—you guessed it—affirmations. Try some of these on for size:

"I appreciate my life."
"I appreciate myself."
"I appreciate my wealth."
"I appreciate my health."
"I appreciate my happiness."
"I appreciate my abundance."
"I appreciate my prosperity."
"I appreciate my riches."
"I appreciate my loving."
"I appreciate my caring."
"I appreciate my sharing."
"I appreciate my learning."
"I appreciate knowing what I want."
"I appreciate my opportunity."
"I appreciate my enjoying."
"I appreciate my balance."

Most of what's around us we take for granted. We ignore it. Appreciation—spending time looking for the good—helps us overcome one of the primary limitations to enjoying the wealth we already have: ignore-ance.

*Why, the greatest invention
in history is the safety pin.
The second greatest
is perforated toilet paper.*

TINY TIM

The Attitude of Gratitude

Our appreciation of something ripens into true enjoyment when we apply gratitude. Without gratitude, it's so easy to lose track of the goodness in our life.

An eighteenth-century suicide note read: "All this buttoning and unbuttoning." Granted, life before zippers and Velcro was far more tedious, but whoever unbuttoned his or her life over buttoning and unbuttoning forgot to feel grateful for buttons—and the clothes they went on.

If this eighteenth-century person had only learned from the writings of fellow-eighteenth-centurion, Sir Walter Scott: "Many of our cares are but a morbid way of looking at our privileges." The way out of such morbidity and into enjoyment is appreciation and gratitude.

What is the latitude of gratitude?

"Gratitude is not only the greatest of virtues," observed Cicero, "but the parent of all others." "Gratitude is the fruit of great cultivation," said Samuel Johnson; "you do not find it among gross people."

"Gratitude is a blessing we give to one another," wrote Robert Raynolds, and Ottokar Prohaszka continued: "Gratitude is to thank God for all His infinite goodness with all our heart."

Not all have such a holy view of gratitude. "I feel a very unusual sensation," said Benjamin Disraeli, "if it is not indigestion, I think it must be gratitude."

Unfortunately, too many people practice the *platitude* of gratitude. Gratitude for many has become yet another "should"; for others, it's just another form of manipulation.

It's easy to see how gratitude became a "should":

"Have you written your aunt to thank her for your birthday present yet?"

"No."

"When are you going to?"

Thank-you,
music-lovers.

SPIKE JONES

"Soon."

"Do you want me to take the present away until you finish the note?"

"No."

"Then get busy!"

The "good advice" about how important it is to be grateful seems to be everywhere—from Chinese proverbs ("When eating bamboo sprouts, remember the man who planted them.") to the Apocrypha ("Let not thine hand be stretched out to receive and shut when thou shouldst repay.")

"Do not refuse a wing to the person who gave you the whole chicken," R. G. H. Siu reminds us, and the English take it several steps further: "Don't drown the man who taught you to swim."

Good advice, all. It becomes mired, however, in the mists of childhood shoulds, musts and have-tos. Thankfulness is for some a solemn duty rather than a pleasurable sensation.

"There are minds so impatient of inferiority that their gratitude is a species of revenge," explained Samuel Johnson, "and they return benefits, not because recompense is a pleasure, but because obligation is a pain."

We do not recommend gratitude because we *should* be grateful, because we're somehow *nobler* or *better humans* for expressing gratitude—we recommend it because *it feels good.* "There is as much greatness of mind in acknowledging a good turn," observed Seneca, "as in doing it." It's not just due to greatness of mind that we express our thanks; it feels great, too.

For those who threw out the baby of gratitude with the bath water of childhood, recapturing that spirit of thankfulness is relatively easy. For those who have learned to use gratitude to manipulate others, the task may be more difficult.

Got no check books, got no banks.
Still I'd like to express my thanks—
I got the sun in the mornin'
and the moon at night.

IRVING BERLIN

I got the son in the mornin'
and the father at night.

RUSTY WARREN

People like to be thanked. "I can live for two months on a good compliment," said Mark Twain. Maybe people enjoy compliments because they are so scarce. As Kin Hubbard pointed out, "Some people pay a compliment as if they expected a receipt."

A few people have learned that others enjoy being thanked so much, that the thanks-giver often gets something in return.

It begins innocently enough. "Do not neglect gratitude," advised Princess Jackson Smith, "Say thank you." Fine. "Better still, say it in writing." Still fine. "A simple note of thanks is money in the bank and you will be remembered." Oops. Off the deep end. As soon as we look for some reward for our thankfulness other than the warm feeling of gratitude we feel inside, we are skating on thin ice up a creek without a paddle. (Aren't you grateful that *you* don't mix your metaphors as miserably as *we* do?)

This manipulative use of gratitude has given it, in some circles, a bad name. "In most of mankind gratitude is merely a secret hope for greater favors," said La Rochefoucauld, who was obviously in one of those circles.

When we use gratitude for manipulation, we may get what we want, but we sacrifice the cordial feeling of gratitude in the process. Some are finding that this is too great a price to pay.

In order to regain the feeling of gratitude, however, we must risk not getting the thing we want. That's scary. What if this "cordial feeling of gratitude" thing isn't worth it? We won't know till we try, will we?

Some people (often the *same* people) fall into the reverse trap: when they do something good, they *expect* gratitude—heaps and heaps of it. Like most expectations, this is not a good idea—certainly not a good idea if enjoyment is the goal.

Good advice on this habit comes from that master of good advice: "When befriended, remember it," advised Benjamin Franklin; "when you befriend, forget it."

Jed Clampett: *Pearl,*
what d'ya think?
Think I oughta move?

Cousin Pearl: *Jed,*
how can ya even ask?
Look around ya.
You're eight miles from yore
nearest neighbor.
Yore overrun with skunks,
possums, coyotes, bobcats.
You use kerosene lamps fer light
and you cook on a wood stove
summer and winter.
Yore drinkin' homemade
moonshine and washin' with
homemade lye soap.
And yore bathroom is fifty feet
from the house and you ask
"should I move?"

Jed: *I reckon yore right.*
A man'd be a dang fool
to leave all this!

"THE BEVERLY HILLBILLIES"

Even when people we do things for *feel* grateful, they often have trouble expressing it. "Gratitude is one of the least articulate of the emotions," explained Felix Frankfurter, "especially when it is deep." It's hard to express gratitude. It's easy to let fear stand in the way.

An interesting aspect of gratitude is that we can feel it when others do for us, *and* when we do for others. "There are two kinds of gratitude," observed E. A. Robinson, "the sudden kind we feel for what we take; and the larger kind we feel for what we give."

It feels so good to give—to do good for others—that we are grateful they accepted our gift. This certainly goes counter to the "get yours while the getting's good and get out" programming of our culture. It is, nonetheless, true—we are so grateful to be able to give.

If we're having trouble feeling grateful for what we have, maybe a good place to start is feeling grateful for what we *don't* have: all the miseries and sorrows that—for the moment—have passed us by.

"A man should always consider how much he has more than he wants, and how much more unhappy he might be than he really is." said Joseph Addison long after the idea had already become a cliché.

Even Joyce Carol Oates gives the popular version: "Things could be a lot worse."

This notion has, of course, been challenged. "Every time we tell anybody to cheer up, things might be worse," wrote Franklin P. Adams, "we run away for fear we might be asked to specify how."

And this penetrating dialogue from "Starsky and Hutch":

HUTCH: At least she's alive.

STARSKY: Hey, I've had it up to here with optimistic views of life.

*Let us be thankful
for the fools;
but for them
the rest of us
could not succeed.*

MARK TWAIN

Nonetheless, we can begin our journey to greater gratitude by being thankful for the evils we've missed. "Every misery I miss is a new blessing," said Izaak Walton, a philosophy that saw him safely to ninety back when the average life span was about forty-five years (1593–1683).

"The best medicine I know for rheumatism," said Josh Billings, "is to thank the Lord it ain't the gout." "Some people are always grumbling because roses have thorns," observed Alphonse Karr; "I am thankful that thorns have roses."

One of the surest signs of gratitude is laughter. Humor is a great way to turn gratings into gratitude. "A humorist," said Don Herold, "is a man who feels bad but who feels good about it." When you can give the simple twist of fate one more turn, it's often quite funny.

"Alas, she married another; they frequently do," sighed Artemus Ward; "I hope she is happy—because I am." "You put up with a few inconveniences," Reverend Jim Ignatowski from "Taxi" observed, "when you live in a condemned building."

Of course, it's fine to be grateful for all the *genuine* good in our lives—to be grateful for our current wealth. It's pleasant to take some time each day and reflect on the good around us. An interlude of gratitude—especially for those things we tend to take for granted—can do wonders for peace, contentment and well-being.

Naturally, our capacity for gratitude can be increased through affirmations.

"I am grateful for my life."

"I am grateful for myself."

"I am grateful for my wealth."

"I am grateful for my health."

"I am grateful for my happiness."

"I am grateful for my abundance."

"I am grateful for my prosperity."

"I am grateful for my riches."

The sheer beauty
of our planet surprised me.
It was a huge pearl,
set in spangled ebony.
It was nacreous, it was opal.
No, it was far more lovely
than any jewel.
Its patterned coloring was
more subtle, more ethereal.
It displayed the delicacy
and brilliance,
the intricacy and harmony
of a live thing.

OLAF STAPLEDON

"I am grateful for my loving."

"I am grateful for my caring."

"I am grateful for my sharing."

"I am grateful for my learning."

"I am grateful for knowing what I want."

"I am grateful for my opportunity."

"I am grateful for my enjoying."

"I am grateful for my balance."

And let's not forget to feel grateful for spontaneous gratitude. As Joseph Wood Krutch observed, "Happiness is itself a kind of gratitude."

When we are joyful, be grateful.

When we are grateful, we are joyful.

Believe nothing,
no matter where you read it,
or who said it
—even if I have said it—
unless it agrees
with your own reason
and your own common sense.

THE BUDDHA

Rules as Tools

Rules are fun. We use rules to live (RULE: Keep breathing!), we use rules to rebel against, we use rules to get what we want, we use rules to keep other people from getting what they want (especially if we want to keep it), we use rules to justify not getting what we want, and so much more. Rules are fun.

"Most of us, by the time we're up on the rules," lamented Pappy Maverick, "are generally too old to play." That's what this chapter is about—getting up on the rules before we're too old to play.

Fundamentally, rules are tools. As with all tools, they can be used for us or against us, used well or used poorly, used to create or to destroy.

Rules are generally given either (A) to control or (B) to help. Sometimes it's hard to tell one motivation from another; often it depends on which side of the rule we happen to fall.

The use of rules to control is best summed up by Thoreau: "Any fool can make a rule, and every fool will mind it." The use of rules to impart wisdom was explained by Kin Hubbard: "There's no secret about success. Did you ever know a successful man that didn't tell you all about it?" The trick, of course, is to separate which rules are written by fools for fools and which are written by the wise for the guidance of the wise.

The key is our personal experience. "The rules which experience suggests," commented R. S. Storrs, "are better than those which theorists elaborate in their libraries." "Laws are not invented," observed Azarias; "they grow out of circumstances."

What truly works for us becomes a part of us—we use it and forget it's a rule. We break it at our peril, and are "punished" *by* breaking it, not *for* breaking it. "His face was filled with broken commandments," observed John Masefield. The rules that don't work we abandon. (We

In reading and writing,
you cannot lay down rules
until you have learnt
to obey them.
Much more so in life.

MARCUS AURELIUS

SECOND CENTURY A.D.

may *tell* ourselves and others that we follow rules we've really abandoned, but our actions speak volumes.)

The world is full of rules, and we can't possibly follow them all. The trick is in giving a rule a chance. It might not *seem* as though it will work, but—surprise!—it does. Or, a rule may sound wonderful and yet not work at all. Once we know whether a given rule works or does not work based upon our personal experience, then we can use it or lose it.

"Life is like music, it must be composed by ear, feeling and instinct, not by rule," wrote Samuel Butler. "Nevertheless one had better know the rules, for they sometimes guide in doubtful cases, though not often."

"You got to know the rules before you can break 'em," said Sonny Crockett on "Miami Vice." "Otherwise, it's no fun." "It's a good idea to obey all the rules when you're young," Mark Twain advised, "just so you'll have the strength to break them when you're old."

Of course, as Thomas Fuller pointed out, "There is no useful rule without an exception." We must be flexible, or we find ourselves like the man described by Charles Lamb: "His life was formal; his actions seemed ruled with a ruler."

On the other hand, we can't be completely—albeit cleverly—undisciplined. "There are those whose sole claim to profundity," observed Paul Eldridge, "is the discovery of exceptions to rules." Do we hear the counsel of our old friend *balance* in here?

Before we give you the rules we suggest you explore (we only have three), we thought it would be fun to look at some of the rules other people have suggested.

In making lists of rules, ten seems to be the favorite number. This is no doubt in tribute to the original list of rules, the Ten Commandments. (Ah, for the simpler days when there was only one rule: don't eat of the tree of the knowledge of good and evil.)

*I know a fellow
who's as broke
as the Ten Commandments.*

JOHN MARQUAND

*Say what you will about
the Ten Commandments,
you must always come back
to the pleasant fact
that there are
only ten of them.*

H. L. MENCKEN

As the world seems to like lists of ten, and we seem to like lists of three, we'll compromise: Here are three lists of ten rules.

Mental Health Rules

1. HAVE A HOBBY: Acquire pursuits which absorb your interest; sports and "nature" are best.

2. DEVELOP A PHILOSOPHY: Adapt yourself to social and spiritual surroundings.

3. SHARE YOUR THOUGHTS: Cultivate companionship in thought and in feeling. Confide, confess, consult.

4. FACE YOUR FEARS: Analyze them; daylight dismisses ghosts.

5. BALANCE FANTASY WITH FACT: Dream but also do; wish but build; imagine but ever face reality.

6. BEWARE ALLURING ESCAPES: Alcohol, opiates and barbitals may prove faithless friends.

7. EXERCISE: Walk, swim, golf—muscles need activity.

8. LOVE, BUT LOVE WISELY: Sex is a flame which uncontrolled may scorch; properly guided, it will light the torch of eternity.

9. DON'T BECOME ENGULFED IN A WHIRLPOOL OF WORRIES: Call early for help. The doctor is ready for your rescue.

10. TRUST IN TIME: Be patient and hopeful, time is a great therapist.

—*Dr. Joseph Fetterman*

*The best rules
to form a young man are:
to talk a little, to hear much,
to reflect alone upon what
has passed in company,
to distrust one's own opinions,
and value others'
that deserve it.*

SIR WILLIAM TEMPLE

Ten Success Rules

1. Put success before amusement.
2. Learn something every day.
3. Cut free from routine.
4. Concentrate on net profits.
5. Make your services known.
6. Never worry over trifles.
7. Shape your decisions quickly.
8. Acquire skill and technique.
9. Deserve loyalty and co-operation.
10. Value character above all.

—Herbert N. Casson

Ten Pointers

1. Be yourself. Cultivate desirable qualities.
2. Be alert. Look for opportunities to express yourself.
3. Be positive. Determine your goal and the route to it.
4. Be systematic. Take one step at a time.
5. Be persistent. Hold to your course.
6. Be a worker. Work your brain more than your body.
7. Be a student. Know your job.
8. Be fair. Treat the other man as you would be treated.
9. Be temperate. Avoid excess in anything.
10. Be confident. Have faith that cannot be weakened.

—Everett W. Lord

There are two golden rules
for an orchestra:
start together
and finish together.
The public doesn't give a damn
what goes on in between.

SIR THOMAS BEECHAM

Some people work hard, but only come up with lists of nine:

1. Be so strong that nothing can disturb your peace of mind.
2. Talk health, happiness and prosperity.
3. Make your friends feel that there is something in them.
4. Look on the sunny side of everything.
5. Think only of the best.
6. Be just as enthusiastic about the success of others as you are about your own.
7. Forget the mistakes of the past and profit by them.
8. Wear a cheerful countenance and give a smile to everyone you meet.
9. Be too large for worry, too noble for anger, too strong for fear, and too happy to permit the presence of trouble.

—*Christian Larson*

The Six Laws of Work

1. A man must drive his energy, not be driven by it.
2. A man must be master of his hours and days, not their servant.
3. The way to push things through to a finish effectively must be learned.
4. A man must earnestly want.
5. Never permit failure to become a habit.
6. Learn to adjust yourself to the conditions you have to endure, but make a point of trying to alter or correct conditions so that they are most favorable to you.

—*William Frederick Book*

We started off
trying to set up
a small anarchist community,
but people wouldn't
obey the rules.

ALAN BENNETT

Of course, many people only make one rule at a time. We've compiled a list of those.

1. The golden rule is that there are no golden rules. Do not do unto others as you would they should do unto you; their tastes may not be the same.
    —*George Bernard Shaw*

2. Never call a man a fool; borrow from him.
    —*Addison Mizner*

3. If it might break, don't go near it.
    —*Herbert Stein*

4. The great rule is not to talk about money with people who have much more or much less than you.
    —*Katharine Whitehorn*

5. It is a good idea to "shop around" before you settle on a doctor. Ask about the condition of his Mercedes. Ask about the competence of his mechanic. Don't be shy! After all, you're paying for it.
    —*Dave Barry*

6. This warning from the New York City Department of Health Fraud: Be suspicious of any doctor who tries to take your temperature with his finger.
    —*David Letterman*

7. Go through the motions anyway; you might get lucky.
    —*Thomas Magnum*

8. When you handle yourself, use your head; when you handle others, use your heart.
    —*Donna Reed*

9. Worries go down better with soup than without.
    —*Yiddish proverb*

10. When the telephone rings, it is against the law not to answer it.
    —*Ring Lardner*

*Never burn
an uninteresting letter
is the first rule
of British aristocracy.*

FRANK MOORE COLBY

And, just before giving you our rules, we thought we'd give you these Unhelpful Rules for Foreign Travel:

1. Comments from the public are always welcome in courts of law. When you start speaking, an usher will call "Silence in court" to ensure that you are heard without interruption.

   —Peter Alexander

2. London barbers are delighted to shave patrons' armpits.

   —General Knowledge

3. Most foreign tourists know that in London they are encouraged to take a piece of fruit, free of charge, from any open-air stall or display.

   —Michael Lipton

4. Women are not allowed upstairs on buses; if you see a woman there ask her politely to descend.

   —David Gordon

5. Try the famous echo in the British Museum Reading Room.

   —Gerard Hoffnung

6. On first entering an Underground train, it is customary to shake hands with every passenger.

   —R. J. Phillips

OK, ready for *our* rules? Here they are:

1. **Don't hurt yourself and don't hurt others.**

1. **Take care of yourself so that you may help take care of others.**

1. **Use everything for your upliftment, learning and growth.**

(It's hard for us to decide which is most important. So who said a list can't have more than one #1?)

All of our rules boil down to these two simple phrases: Work and serve. Learn and grow.

And have fun along the way.

*I have seen you
in the sanctuary
and beheld your power
and your glory.*

PSALM 63:2

The Sanctuary

The imagination is a powerful tool. When used against us by creating unrealistic shoulds, musts, have-tos and other judgments, it can destroy our wealth utterly. When used for us, however, it can be one of the most vigorous creators of wealth—both inner and outer—in our lives.

The sanctuary is an inner structure that helps direct the imagination in wealthy ways. (If you have built a sanctuary while reading one of the other books in THE LIFE 101 SERIES, you can use this chapter to review, renew and perhaps add to the sanctuary you already have.)

We call it a sanctuary. Some call it a workshop, or an inner classroom. You can call it whatever word gives you the sense of asylum, harbor, haven, oasis, shelter—a place you can go to learn your lessons in peace and harmony.

There are absolutely no limits to your sanctuary, although it's a good idea to put some limits on it. In this way, the sanctuary is a transitional point between the limitations of our physical existence and unlimitedness.

The sanctuary can be any size, shape or dimension you choose—large and elaborate or small and cozy. It can be located anywhere—floating in space, on a mountain top, by an ocean, in a valley, anywhere. (You are welcome to combine all those, if you like.) The nice thing about the sanctuary: you can change it or move it anytime —instantly.

The sanctuary can contain anything you choose. We'll suggest some things here, but consider this just the beginning of your shopping list. Before giving our design tips (you can consider us interior designers—with an emphasis on the word *interior*), we'll talk about ways in which you might want to build your sanctuary.

Some people will build theirs by simply reading the suggestions: as they read each, it's there. Others might read them over now for information, and then put on

What if everything is
an illusion and
nothing exists?
In that case,
I definitely overpaid
for my carpet.

WOODY ALLEN

some soft music, close their eyes and let the construction begin. Still others may want to make this an *active* process. With their eyes closed (and being careful not to bump into too much furniture), they might physically move as each area of the sanctuary is built and used. All—or any combination—of these are, of course, fine.

While reading through our suggestions, you will probably get ideas for additions or alterations. By all means make notes of these, or simply incorporate them as you go. Have we gotten across the idea that this is *your* sanctuary? OK, let's go.

Entryway. This is a door or some device that responds only to you and lets only you enter. (We'll suggest a way to bring others into your sanctuary in a moment.)

Light. Each time you enter your sanctuary, a pure, white light cascades over you, surrounding, filling, protecting, blessing and healing you—for your highest good, and the highest good of all concerned.

Main Room. Like the living room of a house or the lobby of a hotel, this is the central area. From here, there are many directions to go and many things to explore.

People Mover. This is a device to move people in and out of your sanctuary. No one ever enters without your express permission and invitation. You can use an elevator, conveyor belt, *Star Trek* beam-me-up device, or anything else that moves people. Let there be a white light at the entry of the mover as well, so that as people enter and leave your sanctuary, they are automatically surrounded, filled, protected and healed by that white light, and only that which is for their highest good and the highest good of all concerned is taking place.

Information Retrieval System. This is a method of getting any kind of information—providing, of course, it's for your highest good (and the highest good of all concerned) that you have it. The information retrieval system can be a computer screen, a staff of librarians, a telephone, or any other device from which you feel comfortable asking questions and getting answers.

He partitioned off
twenty cubits
at the rear of the temple
with cedar boards
from the floor to ceiling
to form within the temple
an inner sanctuary,
the Most Holy Place.

1 KINGS 6:16

Video Screen. This is a video (or movie, if you like) screen in which you can view various parts of your life—past, present or future. The screen has a white light around it. When you see images you don't like or don't want to encourage, the light is off. When the screen displays images you want to affirm, the light glows. (Those who are old enough to remember Sylvania's Halo of Light television know just what we mean.)

Ability Suits. This is a closet of costumes that, when worn, give you the instant ability to do anything you want to do—great actor, successful writer, perfect lover, eager learner, Master of your Universe; any and all are available to you. When you're done with an ability suit, just throw it on the floor in front of the closet—ability suits have the ability to hang themselves up.

Ability Suit Practice Area. This is a place you can try new skills—or improve upon old ones—while wearing your ability suits. Leave lots of room, because there's an ability suit for flying and another for space travel. In your sanctuary, not even the sky's a limit.

Health Center. Here the healing arts of all the ages—past, present, future; traditional and alternative—are gathered in one place. All are devoted to your greater health. The health center is staffed with the most competent health practitioners visualization can buy. Who is the most healing being you can imagine? That's who runs your center.

Playroom. Here, all the toys you ever wanted—as a child or as an adult—are gathered. There's lots of room—and time—to play with each. As with ability suits, you never have to worry about "putting your toys away." They put themselves away.

Sacred Room. This is a special sanctuary within your sanctuary. You can go there for meditation, contemplation or special inner work.

Master Teacher. This is your ideal teacher, the being with whom you are the perfect student. The Master Teacher (or MT for short) knows everything about you

*Then have them
make a sanctuary for me,
and I will dwell among them.*

EXODUS 25:8

(has always been with you, in fact). The MT also knows all you need to learn, the perfect timing for your learning it, and the ideal way of teaching it to you. You don't *create* a Master Teacher—that's already been done. You *discover* your Master Teacher. To meet your Master Teacher, simply walk over to your people mover, ask for your Master Teacher to come forth, and from the pure, white light of your people mover comes your Master Teacher.

(We'll leave you two alone for a while. More uses for the sanctuary later. See you both in the next chapter!)

*In no other period of history
were the learned
so mistrustful of the
divine possibilities in man
as they are now.*

GOPI KRISHNA

Using Your Sanctuary for Creating Wealth

You can use your sanctuary any time, any place. It need not be used in a "formal" session with incense, candles and closed eyes (although that's fun, too).

Going to your sanctuary can be as simple and natural as remembering the melody for the words "Oh, say can you see, by the dawn's early light..." or the color of a banana or the smell of a rose or the taste of an orange. We usually don't have to *concentrate* to remember the things we know—we just know them.

So it is with the sanctuary: once we get to know it and get in the habit of using it, it always seems to be there. We can be in our sanctuary while standing in line, waiting for someone to stop talking, or reading the dull passages of a book. ("When *are* they going to tell me how to get more money?") In other words, when something else fascinating isn't going on (and, let's face it, that's most of the time), we can be in our sanctuary doing wealth work.

Here's where your personal creativity comes in. How can your experience of wealth (health, happiness, abundance, prosperity, riches, loving, caring, sharing, learning, knowing what you want, opportunity, enjoying and balance) be enhanced by the various tools within your sanctuary? We'll suggest a few ways here, but consider this listing as just a start. The possibilities are as infinite and varied as the experience of wealth itself.

Always pass through the white light as you enter the sanctuary (it only takes a split second), knowing that only that which is for your highest good and the highest good of all concerned is taking place.

Also, feel free to invite your Master Teacher along for any or all of these explorations.

People Mover. What person or persons can give you advice, counsel, guidance or assistance in gaining greater health, happiness, abundance, prosperity, riches, loving,

*Educational television should
be absolutely forbidden.
It can only lead
to unreasonable expectations
and eventual disappointment
when your child discovers that
the letters of the alphabet
do not leap out of books and
dance around the room
with royal-blue chickens.*

FRAN LEBOWITZ

caring, sharing, learning, knowledge of what you want, opportunity, enjoying and balance? This can be anyone—past present, future, even fictional. (Sometimes there's a question about wealth that only Yoda or Scrooge McDuck can answer.) As they enter and leave your sanctuary, make sure that they pass through the light for their highest good and the highest good of all concerned.

Information Retrieval System. What information would help you be more wealthy? If it's for your highest good to know it at this time, you'll find it here. Or, you may be instructed where else to look for it.

Video Screen. Sit comfortably in front of your video screen. The light around it is off. See yourself on the screen in a situation in which you are unhealthy, unhappy, not abundant, unprosperous, not rich, unloving, uncaring, not sharing, unwilling to learn, not knowing what you want, lacking opportunity, not enjoying or out of balance. Then imagine a paintbrush is in your hand, heavy with black paint. Make a large **X** across that unwealthy image. The screen clears. The paint fades. The white light around the screen glows. Now see yourself in the corresponding wealthy situation. If you were unhealthy, see yourself glowing with vibrant health, doing healthy things, feeling healthy. If you saw yourself as unhappy, see yourself joyously happy, surrounded by happiness. Do this for all the attributes of wealth.

Ability Suits and Ability Suit Practice Area. Go to your ability suit closet. Look at the section labeled *WEALTH*. There you'll find thirteen suits. Can you guess their names? Yes, there's an ability suit for health, happiness, abundance, prosperity, riches, loving, caring, sharing, learning, knowing what you want, opportunity, enjoying and balance. Put one on. Now move over to the ability suit practice area and see, feel, hear, smell and even taste yourself living that ability to the full. When finished with that suit, take it off (it hangs itself up, you'll recall) and try another.

Ability suits are also good to put on before entering a real-life situation. If you're going into a situation that

To see a world in a grain of sand
And heaven in a wild flower,
To hold Infinity
in the palm of your hand,
And Eternity in an hour.

WILLIAM BLAKE

might challenge your balance, for example, put on the ability suit for balance before entering the situation (or even once you're already in it—it only takes a split second) and keep it on while the real-life situation continues. Feel free to wear more than one ability suit at a time. The suits for loving, caring and sharing, for example, are "color coordinated and accent each other magnificently," according to the latest *Ability Suit Quarterly*.

Health Center. What needs to be healed in you—on any level: physical, emotional, mental or spiritual—so you can experience more health, happiness, abundance, prosperity, riches, loving, caring, sharing, learning, knowing what you want, opportunity, enjoying and balance? Whatever it may be, it can be healed in your health center. If you don't know or aren't sure what needs to be healed, your health center has some of the best diagnosticians in the known Universe. (They tend to diagnose and heal in the same motion, however, so maybe you'll never know—you'll just be healed.) Also, feel free to invite friends and loved ones into your sanctuary through the people mover and ask them if they'd like a treatment or two in your health center. The health of those we love is part of our wealth, too.

Playroom. Have *fun* with your health, happiness, abundance, prosperity, riches, loving, caring, sharing, learning, knowing what you want, opportunity, enjoying and balance. Play with your wealth. Enjoy yourself. Invite in people you'd enjoy playing with on the people mover.

Sacred Room. Spend time here meditating, contemplating, praying and doing spiritual exercises about life, wealth in general, or about each aspect of wealth in particular.

Master Teacher. One of the most powerful and practical tools in your sanctuary is your Master Teacher. (Do you think a Master Teacher minds being called a "tool"? Probably not. Master Teachers are used to being called *a lot* of things.) Sit with your Master Teacher—perhaps in your sacred room—and discuss your health, happiness, abundance, prosperity, riches, loving, caring, sharing,

The eye of the master
will do more work
than both his hands.

BENJAMIN FRANKLIN

learning, knowing what you want, opportunity, enjoying and balance with your Master Teacher. Ask questions. Listen to the answers.

In daily life, remember that your MT is always there. Listen for the Master Teacher's voice no matter where you are or what you're doing. It's a direct connection to your wealth.

Andy, you gits up at noon,
then you rushes to get dressed,
then you rushes to the restaurant
for breakfast. After you eat,
you rushes to the park
to take a nap,
after you take your nap
then you rushes back
to eat again;
then you rushes home,
rushes to get undressed
and then you rushes to bed.
I tell ya Andy,
there's just so much
a body can stand.

KINGFISH
"AMOS 'N' ANDY"

Go Slow

"My boat sleeps four comfortably," William F. Buckley, Jr., explained, "but five is three too many." And so it seems with life. If we can do four things happily, joyfully and productively within an hour, when we add a fifth, it's three too many. We become hurried, harried and unhappy.

"We live in a vastly complex society which has been able to provide us with a multitude of material things, and this is good," wrote Euell Gibbons, "but people are beginning to suspect that we have paid a high spiritual price for our plenty."

That was written about twenty years ago. People no longer *suspect* we're paying a high spiritual price, people *know* it. The solution? Slow down. Relax. At least once a day, take some time for meditation, contemplation, prayer, spiritual exercises or just plain taking it easy.

Make time in the noise and the chatter of life for some silence. "A man is known by the silence he keeps," observed Oliver Herford. "Silence is wonderful to listen to," said Thomas Hardy.

Silence is so, well, *golden* that entire philosophies have been based upon it. In fact, some people never seem to shut up about silence. "Carlyle finally compressed his Gospel of Silence," noted John Morley, "into thirty handsome octavos."

One thing we get from silence is the value of what we might *hear*. "Learn to listen," advised Frank Tyger. "Opportunity could be knocking at your door very softly."

Meditation, contemplation, prayer and spiritual exercises help us answer that burning question, "Who am I?" "Prayer gives a man the opportunity of getting to know a gentleman he hardly ever meets," said William Inge. "I do not mean his maker, but himself." Tom Masson pointed out, "The best way to study human nature is when nobody else is present."

O ye Gods,
grant us what is good
whether we pray for it or not,
but keep evil from us
even though we pray for it.

PLATO

Whenever you meditate, contemplate, pray, do spiritual exercises or "just sits," it's good to ask the white light to surround, fill and protect you, knowing only that which is for your highest good and the highest good of all concerned will take place during your quiet time.

Before starting, prepare your physical environment. Arrange not to be disturbed. Unplug the phone. Put a note on the door. Wear ear plugs if noises might distract you. (We like the soft foam-rubber kind sold under such trade names as E.A.R., HUSHER and DECIDAMP.) Take care of your bodily needs. Have some water nearby if you get thirsty, and maybe some tissues, too.

Contemplation is thinking *about* something, often something of an uplifting nature. You could contemplate any of the hundreds of quotes or ideas in this book. Often, when we hear a new and potentially useful idea, we say, "I'll have to think about that." Contemplation is a good time to "think about that," to consider the truth of it, to imagine the changes and improvements it might make in your life.

Or, you could contemplate a nonverbal object, such as a flower, or a concept, such as God. The idea of contemplation is to set aside a certain amount of quiet time to think about just *that,* whatever you decide "that" will be.

Meditation. There are so many techniques of meditation, taught by so many organizations, that it's hard to define the word properly. We'll give a capsule summary of some techniques from John-Roger's book, *Inner Worlds of Meditation.* (For more complete descriptions, you can get the book for $7 postpaid, from Mandeville Press, Box 3935, Los Angeles, CA 90051.)

You might want to try various meditations to see what they're like. With meditation, please keep in mind that *you'll never know until you do it.* We may somehow like to think we know what the effects of a given meditation will be just by reading the description, and that, in fact, is exactly what happens. We *think* we know; we don't *really* know. We suggest you try it, gain the experience, and decide from that more stable base of knowledge what is

*I'm going to take the moment
to contemplate
most of the Western religions.
I'm looking for something
soft on morality,
generous with holidays,
and with a very short
initiation period.*

DAVID ADDISON
"MOONLIGHTING"

best for you at this time. And please remember to "call in the light" before beginning. We suggest you do not do these meditations while driving a car, operating dangerous machinery or where you need to be alert.

Breathing Meditation. Sit comfortably, close your eyes, and simply be aware of your breath. Follow it in and out. Don't "try" to breathe; don't consciously alter your rhythm of breathing; just follow the breath as it naturally flows in and out. If you get lost in thoughts, return to your breath. This can be a very refreshing meditation—twenty minutes can feel like a night's sleep. It's also especially effective when you're feeling emotionally upset.

Tones. Some people like to add a word or sound to help the mind focus as the breath goes in and out. Some people use *one* or *God* or *AUM (OHM)* or *love*. These—or any others—are fine. As you breathe in, say to yourself, mentally, "love." As you breathe out, "love." A few other tones you might want to try:

- **HU.** HU is an ancient sound for the higher power. One of the first names humans ever gave to a supreme being was HU. Some good words begin with HU: *humor, human, hub* (the center), *hug, huge, hue, humus* ("The Good Earth"), *humble,* and, of course, *hula.* HU is pronounced "Hugh." You can say it silently as you breathe in, and again as you breathe out. Or, you can pronounce the letter H on the inhale and the letter U on the exhale. You might also try saying HU out loud as you exhale, but don't do it out loud more than fifteen times in one sitting; the energies it produces can be powerful.

- **ANI-HU.** This tone brings with it compassion, empathy and unity. You can chant it silently (ANI on the inhale, HU on the exhale) or out loud (ANI-HU on the exhale). It makes a lovely group chant and tends to harmonize the group—in more ways than one.

- **HOO.** This can be used like the HU. Some people prefer it. It's one syllable, pronounced like the word *who.*

I do most of my work
sitting down;
that's where I shine.

ROBERT BENCHLEY

- **RA.** RA is a tone for bringing great amounts of physical energy into the body. You can do it standing or sitting. Standing tends to bring in more energy. Take a deep breath and, as you exhale, chant, out loud, "ERRRRRRRRAAAAAAAAA" until your air runs out. Take another deep breath and repeat it; then again. After three RAs, breathe normally for a few seconds. Then do another set of three, pause, then another set of three. We suggest you don't do more than three sets of three at any one time.

- **SO-HAWNG.** The SO-HAWNG meditation is a good one to use when your mind wants to do one thing and your emotions another. SO-HAWNG tends to unify the two, getting them on the same track. This tone is done silently. You breathe in on SO and out on HAWNG. Try it with your eyes closed for about five minutes and see how you feel. You may feel ready to accomplish some task you've been putting off for a long time.

- **THO.** THO is a tone of healing. The correct pronunciation of it is important. Take a deep breath, and as you breathe out say, "THooooo." The TH is accented; it's a sharp, percussive sound (and it may tickle your upper lip). It's followed by "ooooooo" as an extended version of the word *oh*. To do the THO meditation, sit comfortably, close your eyes, inhale and exhale twice, take a third deep breath, and on the third exhale, say, "THoooooo." Repeat three times this series of three breaths with THO aloud on the third breath. That's enough. It's powerful. Feel the healing energies move through your body. You can also chant THO inwardly as a formal meditation or any time during the day, even while doing something else. (But, again, as with all meditations, not while driving a car or operating potentially dangerous equipment.)

Flame Meditation. This uses the power of fire to dissolve negativity. Put a candle on a table and sit so you

*I am just going
to pray for you at St. Paul's,
but with no very lively
hope of success.*

SYDNEY SMITH

1771–1845

can look directly into the flame, not down on it. Allow your energy to flow *up* and *out* into the candle. You may feel negativity or have negative thoughts. Don't pay any attention to their content; just release them into the flame. If you feel your energy dropping back down inside of you as though you were going into a trance, blow out the candle and stop the meditation. The idea is to keep the energy flowing up and out and into the flame. Do it for no more than five minutes to start. See how you feel for a day or so afterward. You may have more vivid dreams. If you feel fine otherwise, you might try it for longer periods. Twenty minutes a day would be a lot.

Water Meditation. Take some water in a clear glass, hold it between your hands (without your hands touching each other), and simply look down into the glass. Observe whatever you observe. You may see colors. You may see energy emanating from your hands. You may just see yourself holding a glass of water. Observe the water for five minutes, gradually working up to fifteen. Drink the water at the end of the meditation. Your energies have made it a "tonic," giving you whatever you may need at that time. As an experiment, you can take two glasses, each half-filled with tap water. Set one aside, and do the water meditation with the other. Then taste each. Don't be surprised if the one you "charged" tastes different.

E. The E sound is chanted out loud after meditation to "ground" you and bring your focus back to the physical. It's a steady "Eeeeeeeeeeeee" as though you were pronouncing the letter E. It begins at the lower register of your voice, travels to the upper range, then back down again in one breath. You begin as a bass, go through tenor, alto, onto soprano, and back to bass again. As you do this, imagine that the sound is in your feet when you're in the lower register, gradually going higher in your body as your voice goes higher, finally reaching the top of your head at the highest note of the eeee, and then back down your body as the voice lowers. If you try it, you'll see that it's far easier to do than it is to explain. Do two or three E sounds after each meditation session.

I meditated for hours on end.
Chanted.
I was finding God
all over the place.
He kept ditching me.
You gotta understand,
I thought I was on my way
to Nirvana.
All I ended up with
was recurrent flashbacks
of the original Mouseketeers.

REVEREND JIM IGNATOWSKI

"TAXI"

☆

These tones and meditations have worked for many people. We don't ask you to *believe* they work. We simply ask you, if you like, to try them and see what happens. If they do work, you don't need belief; you've got knowledge. Your results will dictate whether you'll use them often, sometimes, seldom or never.

Some may work better for you than others; that's only natural. Use the ones that work best for you now and, every so often, return to the others to see if they will offer more.

Some people think meditation takes time *away* from physical accomplishment. Taken to extremes, of course, that's true. Most people, however, find that meditation *creates* more time than it *takes*.

Meditation is for rest, healing, balance and information. All these are helpful in the attainment of a goal. Here's an additional technique you might want to add to your meditation. It's designed to make both the meditation and the time outside of meditation more effective.

One of the primary complaints people have about meditating is, "My thoughts won't leave me alone." Perhaps the mind is trying to communicate something valuable. If the thought is something to do, write it down (or record it on a tape recorder). Then return to the meditation. This allows the mind to move onto something else—such as meditation, for example.

As the "to do" list fills, the mind empties. If the thought, "Call the bank," reappears, you need only tell the mind, "It's on the list. You can let that one go." And it will. (It is important, however, to *do* the things on the list—or at least to consider them from a nonmeditative state. If you don't, the mind will not pay any more attention to your writing it down than you do, and it will continue to bring it up, over and over.)

I do benefits for all religions—
I'd hate to blow the hereafter
on a technicality.

BOB HOPE

When finished meditating, not only will you have had a better meditation; you will also have a "to do" list that is very useful. One insight gleaned during meditation might save *hours*, perhaps *days* of unnecessary work. That's what we mean when we say—from a purely practical point of view—meditation can make more time than it takes.

Nothing can be attained
without suffering
but at the same time
one must begin
by sacrificing suffering.

GURUDJIEFF

Go Fast

Fast can mean to speed up ("Faster! Faster!") or to grasp tightly ("Hold fast!"). It can also mean to let go, to abstain from ("I'm on a fast"). We're going to discuss *fast* in the latter sense.

Fasting usually refers to abstaining from food, but we'd like to expand the definition to also include abstaining from negativity. For some people, the toughest sacrifice of all is to sacrifice suffering.

Most people think anger, depression, fear, hurt feelings, guilt and all the so-called negative emotions are the "natural" responses to certain situations.

What if they're not? What if we were programmed to respond that way, and, if we worked hard at it, we could program ourselves to respond in another way?

It's OK to feel good when things go bad.

"But," some say, "people who feel good when things go bad aren't *normal!*" Perhaps, but as R. D. Laing pointed out, "Normal men have killed perhaps 100,000,000 of their fellow normal men in the last fifty years."

To feel good when things go bad is not just abnormal; it's beyond revolutionary; it's downright *radical*.

Fortunately, feeling is an inner process. Most people won't know how abnormal you are. *They* can all be feeling miserable at the news of fresh disaster in the papers or on television or from gossip, and *you* can be feeling perfectly wonderful. They probably won't notice. This is good, because martyrdom is so hard on the body.

Yes, it's a risk to enjoy yourself all the time, but, more than risk, it's a lot of *work*. "Thinking is hard work," observed Thomas Edison. Fasting from negativity and sacrificing suffering requires not just thinking, but *re*thinking every negative response you currently hold to be "automatic."

*I think it's very important
to be positive
about everything in your life
that's negative.
You can turn a twist on it.*

BARBRA STREISAND

Turn a Twist on It

What if things were neither good nor evil, but simply *were?* What would life be like if we recaptured the state of original innocence, before the original sin, the first mistake? "We are stardust, we are golden," observed Joni Mitchell, "and we've got to get ourselves back to the garden."

In the garden, we could see that nothing was good or evil *in itself,* but that everything had both positive and negative *uses.* It is not what something *is,* but how something is *used* that determines its relative good or evil.

A knife, for example, is neutral in itself. It can be used to kill or to cure, to harm or to help. What if this were true for *everything* in our lives? What if each of the "bad" things we wish we could get rid of had a positive side? What if we could, as Barbra Streisand put it, "turn a twist on it"?

Let's start with **childhood.** What if all those experiences we didn't like about our childhood are the same ones that made us strong, resilient, determined, funny or any of the other aspects of our character we admire?

Barbra Streisand again: "I can either complain about my mother not believing in me, or I can tell you it served me in some way to become who I am."

Without everything—*everything*—that happened in your childhood, you wouldn't be the remarkable person you are today. Oh, sure, if things had been different, a "problem area" might not be there, but the qualities developed to compensate for that "problem" might not be there, either.

And what about **problems?** What if problems were, as Duke Ellington called them, "a chance for you to do your best"? What if even the problems themselves had both a good and bad use, and if we saw them differently, we could use problems for our learning, upliftment and growth?

An adventure is only
an inconvenience,
rightly considered.

G. K. CHESTERTON

We can view problems—and all of life itself, for that matter—in a new light by changing two things: our attitude and our altitude. When one lifts, the other lifts, and we see the opportunity hidden behind the problem.

With the right attitude, we move *through* the problem. We get on the other side and, lo, there's the benefit. With altitude, we lift above the problem and see the blessing just beyond it. Then we can see the problem as merely a way of delivering the blessing to us—a protective covering, if you will. We don't curse the gift wrapping. We remove it with enthusiasm to get to the gift.

Sometimes the gift is simply that we're stronger. Sometimes the gift is a lesson. Usually it's both. In this way, problems are a form of exercise and a form of study.

"Never regard study as a duty," wrote Albert Einstein, "but as the enviable opportunity to learn to know the liberating influence of beauty in the realm of the spirit for your own personal joy and to the profit of the community to which your later work belongs."

How seldom do we look at problems in *that* light? It's the advantage of seeing a problem with an elevated attitude and altitude. Here's an example from Ernie Wise and Eric Morecambe on seeing life from the attitude of "no problem."

ERNIE: Is this my bill?

ERIC: Yes, sir.

ERNIE: I'm terribly sorry—it looks as if I've got just enough money to pay for the dinner, but I've got nothing to tip you with.

ERIC: Let me add that bill up again, sir.

"Consider that people are like tea bags," wrote Dan McKinnon. "They don't know their own strength until they get into hot water."

Aunt Maggie was every bit
as worried as Mother
but they'd take turns
cheering each other up.
Both of them were confirmed
pessimists but never
at the same time.
Whichever one picked up
the pessimism first
evidently had a claim on it.
The other would automatically
assume the role of optimist,
although always with
a certain lack of conviction.

STEVE ALLEN

Let's take a look at some specific "problems" and see how we might be able to turn a twist on them.

Fear. This is an easy one: fear is the energy to do your best in a new situation. The feeling of fear (anxiety, nervousness, shyness, or any of its other aliases) is really *preparation energy.* It's getting you ready to excel, to succeed, to do your best and to learn the most.

Does this mean we'll do whatever we fear perfectly? Hardly. We'll probably fail any number of times, but that's how we learn—one way, at least. "There is the greatest practical benefit in making a few failures early in life," said T. H. Huxley, and Robert Louis Stevenson agreed: "Give me the young man who has brains enough to make a fool of himself."

Anger. Anger is the energy to make change. We use it to make a change in the outer world. "I suppose I overdo it," said Theodore Roosevelt, "but when I'm mad at a man I want to climb right up his chest." Of someone like that, Thomas Ybarra wrote, "He owned and operated a ferocious temper." The explosive quality of anger may be taking it a bit too far—except in certain fight-or-flight situations that really *are* matters of life and death.

Well-modulated anger, however—carefully released over time and in the right situations—can be the stimulus to great change. Some of the most important social, political and cultural changes have been made because people were simply *angry* with the injustices, unfairnesses and absurdities they saw around them.

Alas, even with anger, the world still does not always give us what we want, when we want it, in the way we want it. What do we do? Usually we just sit and seethe. "His huff arrived," reported Alexander Woollcott, "and he departed in it."

When we do this, we aren't using the full capacity of anger's energy for change. We can, at that point, use it to change *ourselves.* We can change the shoulds, musts, have-tos and other judgments making us angry in the first place. It's not what *happens* to us, but how we *re-*

His renown has been purchased,
not by deeds of violence and blood,
but by the diligent dispensation
of pleasure.

WASHINGTON IRVING

1820

Of what question is
the following the answer:
"Washington Irving"?
The question:
"Who was the first President
of the United States, Max?"

ANONYMOUS

(AND WITH GOOD REASON)

spond to what happens to us that matters. When the outer world does not live up to our expectations, we can use the anger to change the response of resentment within ourselves.

If we *do* want to change what we find unfair in the world, we do not have to maintain our anger to do so. Usually, that just burns people out. They become embittered by the struggle and give up. Anger is best used as a *spark* for the will—"I *will* make a change." We can then use the residual anger to change the "should" within ourselves. We can still make the change "out there"—and often more effectively.

Besides, there's another reason for not getting angry. As reported in the *Reader's Digest:* "Keep your temper. Do not quarrel with an angry person, but give him a soft answer. It is commanded by the Holy Writ and, furthermore, it makes him madder than anything else you could say."

Guilt. Guilt is getting angry at ourselves—we didn't live up to our own expectations; therefore we feel guilty. Again, we can use the energy to change the outer action (if we *say* we're not going to eat the cake, then we can use the energy to *not* eat the cake), or (since we're probably going to eat the cake anyway) we can use guilt to change the belief that we should, must and have-to behave in a certain way.

"Regret is an appalling waste of energy," wrote Katherine Mansfield; "you can't build on it; it's only good for wallowing in." Don't waste. Don't wallow. Change. Rather than feel like a bad person, tell yourself that you're a good person, and that good people sometimes eat cake even when they know they shouldn't. The energy for change is there: use it.

Hurt Feelings. We hurt because we care about something, and it is taken from us or is not behaving the way we want something we love to behave. Under the hurt is the caring. Caring is healing. Move to the caring. Let that caring energy heal the hurt.

*You've got to watch your mind
all the time or you'll awaken
and find a strange picture
on your press.*

LORD BUCKLEY

*One of the hardest things
for any man to do
is to fall down on the ice
when it is wet and
then get up and
praise the Lord.*

JOSH BILLINGS

The only thing keeping our caring from healing our hurting is the mistaken belief that someone or something outside ourselves is necessary for our emotional well-being. The caring we feel for another we can just as easily feel for ourselves—more easily, in fact: it only has to go from one part of our heart to another; not a long journey at all.

Unworthiness. Good news about unworthiness? Sure: unworthiness keeps us on track. Once we choose what we *really* want in life—what we want more than anything else—unworthiness will gladly let us know that we're not worthy of everything else.

The trick, of course, is to program ourselves to feel worthy of our Big Goal, then let unworthiness have its say on all the other goals in the world—the goals we're not pursuing anyway because we want our Big One. In this way, unworthiness will keep us on track, on target and on time. (We'll be discussing the "knowing what you want" aspect of wealth shortly.)

Stubbornness. Stubbornness is really determination. Stubbornness is taking our will power and turning it into won't power. The twist? All we have to do is turn it back again. Be determined you *will* have what you want, not stubbornly battling what you *won't*.

"Like all weak men," observed Somerset Maugham, "he laid an exaggerated stress on not changing one's mind." Or, consider this from Bertrand Russell: "*I* am firm; *you* are obstinate; *he* is a pig-headed fool." When we don't know what we *want*, but only know what we *don't* want, will power can easily become won't power.

All we need to do is will *toward* our goal, our Big Dream, what we want most. Then stubbornness becomes determination. One additional thought on will: will is to be used *within* us to move us to greater growth, not *without* to control others.

Getting the hang of this? If we turn a twist on it, see a problem from another altitude or with a different attitude,

*Remember that you
ought to behave in life
as you would at a banquet.
As something is being passed
around it comes to you;
stretch out your hand,
take a portion of it politely.
It passes on; do not detain it.
Or it has not come to you yet;
do not project your desire to meet it,
but wait until it comes
in front of you.
So act toward children,
so toward a wife,
so toward office,
so toward wealth.*

EPICTETUS

50–120 A.D.

we can find a positive use for *anything* that happens to us. Let's try one more.

Overweight. What an abundant culture we live in to have overweight as a major problem. Let's look at weight for what it is. Weight is fat; fat is stored energy; therefore weight is an excess of stored energy.

Think, then, about *using* the weight, not *losing* the weight. Think of all the things you want to do. Your weight is the energy necessary to do a good many of them—perhaps all.

There's no more reason to resent excess weight than there is to resent an excessively heavy diamond. "This ring weighs too much; I can hardly lift my hand," is a complaint you've probably never heard. So, to say, "I weigh too much," is another way of saying, "I have too much energy." There is no such thing as too much energy—with enough altitude and the right attitude. Use it *to* lose it.

She got even
in a way that
was almost cruel.
She forgave them.

RALPH McGILL
ON ELEANOR ROOSEVELT

WEALTH 101
Getting What You Want –
Enjoying What You've Got

WEALTH 101
Getting What You Want –
Enjoying What You've Got

WEALTH 101
Getting What You Want –
Enjoying What You've Got

HOORAY!

YOU DID IT!

Wow!

If you can count your money you don't have a billion dollars.
J. PAUL GETTY

If you can count your money you don't have a billion dollars.
J. PAUL GETTY

If you can count your money you don't have a billion dollars.
J. PAUL GETTY

There are several ways to apportion the family income, all of them unsatisfactory.
ROBERT BENCHLEY

There are several ways to apportion the family income, all of them unsatisfactory.
ROBERT BENCHLEY

There are several ways to apportion the family income, all of them unsatisfactory.
ROBERT BENCHLEY

Seek wealth, it's good.
IVAN BOESKY

Seek wealth, it's good.
IVAN BOESKY

Seek wealth, it's good.
IVAN BOESKY

THE **LIFE 101** SERIES

THE **LIFE 101** SERIES

THE **LIFE 101** SERIES

BUSINESS REPLY MAIL
FIRST CLASS   PERMIT NO. 68914   LOS ANGELES, CA

POSTAGE WILL BE PAID BY ADDRESSEE

PRELUDE PRESS
8159 Santa Monica Boulevard
Los Angeles, California 90046

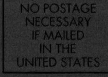

NO POSTAGE
NECESSARY
IF MAILED
IN THE
UNITED STATES

The books in the *LIFE 101* Series (all by John-Roger and Peter McWilliams) are:

LIFE 101
Everything We Wish We Had Learned About Life in School—But Didn't

YOU CAN'T AFFORD THE LUXURY OF A NEGATIVE THOUGHT
A Book for People with Any Life-Threatening Illness—Including Life

DO IT!
Let's Get Off Our Buts

WEALTH 101:
Getting What You Want—Enjoying What You've Got

Available at your local bookseller, or by calling 1-800-LIFE-101

Thank You.

The books in the *LIFE 101* Series (all by John-Roger and Peter McWilliams) are:

LIFE 101
Everything We Wish We Had Learned About Life in School—But Didn't

YOU CAN'T AFFORD THE LUXURY OF A NEGATIVE THOUGHT
A Book for People with Any Life-Threatening Illness—Including Life

DO IT!
Let's Get Off Our Buts

WEALTH 101:
Getting What You Want—Enjoying What You've Got

Available at your local bookseller, or by calling 1-800-LIFE-101

Thank You.

The books in the *LIFE 101* Series (all by John-Roger and Peter McWilliams) are:

LIFE 101
Everything We Wish We Had Learned About Life in School—But Didn't

YOU CAN'T AFFORD THE LUXURY OF A NEGATIVE THOUGHT
A Book for People with Any Life-Threatening Illness—Including Life

DO IT!
Let's Get Off Our Buts

WEALTH 101:
Getting What You Want—Enjoying What You've Got

Available at your local bookseller, or by calling 1-800-LIFE-101

Thank You.

WE WANT TO TELL YOU ABOUT OUR OTHER BOOKS!

Please send us your name and address so we can tell you about other Prelude Press books and audio tapes.

 Please place me on your mailing list.

 Please send free catalog.

 Please send free audio sampler tape.

NAME_____

ADDRESS_____

CITY_____STATE_____ZIP_____

Forgiveness

The word *forgive* is made up of two very nice words: *for*, to be in favor of; and *give*, to contribute, to supply, to endow. Each time we forgive, we affirm that we are in favor of giving.

Whom do we give to? The person we forgive? Sometimes. Ourselves? Always. The Aramaic word for forgive is *shaw*. It means, simply, to untie. This was the word Jesus—the master of forgiveness—used to describe the process. When we forgive, we untie ourselves from the past. We are free, then, to move, unburdened, into the present.

There are two aspects of forgiveness—two things to forgive.

The first is what happened—the situation or action that "wronged" us. We'll call this the *transgression*.

The second is the decision *we* made to feel wronged by the transgression—the conclusion we came to that "this is wrong and shouldn't be happening." We'll call this the *judgment*.

If there weren't a judgment, there would be no transgression. How often have we been upset by something that had no desire to upset us? Ever been rejected by an elevator? Conversely, if someone *tries* to transgress upon us, and we don't see it that way, there's nothing to forgive—the intended slight didn't "get" us.

Naturally, over time, the goal is not to get "got"—to be so complete in our own loving and satisfaction that our reaction to a potential transgression is "So what?" not "That so-and-so!" Until we reach that state of tranquility, however, we will, at times, react with judgment and feel transgressed upon. It's then we need to forgive.

Forgiveness begins when we realize that *we* are doing it—that is, it's not being done *to* us. With practice, the period of time it takes to make this realization gets shorter and shorter. What might have taken us a week to

That old law about
"an eye for an eye"
leaves everybody blind.

MARTIN LUTHER KING, JR.

realize now takes a day. What took a day now takes an hour. What took an hour now takes five minutes. With many former "slights," we move into almost instantaneous recognition and forgiveness.

The process of forgiveness is simple, almost mechanical, in fact. It's a good idea to call in the light before starting. First we forgive the transgression (let it go), then we forgive the judgment (let that go, too).

To do this, we simply say, "I forgive _____ (the transgressor) for _____ (the transgression)."

Then we say, "I forgive myself for judging _____ (the transgressor) and for judging _____ (the transgression)."

That's it. The next thing to do is *forget it*. Turn from it and move on with your life. "A retentive memory may be a good thing," wrote Elbert Hubbard, "but the ability to forget is the true token of greatness." For those who like their lessons in rhyme, here's Suzanne Douglass:

> To err is human
> To forgive takes restraint;
> To forget you forgave
> Is the mark of a saint.

Some people feel revenge is necessary before forgiveness can take place. "One should forgive one's enemies," said Heinrich Heine, "but not before they are hanged." Unfortunately, the hatred we would carry around until all our enemies die would kill us first—certainly inside, and, perhaps, literally.

"Revenge is often like biting a dog because the dog bit you," explained Austin O'Malley. Let it go. Forgive it. Forget it.

Of course, just because we're choosing the wealthy way of forgiving and forgetting, doesn't mean we're absolved of personal responsibility to make amends when *we* have done the transgressing.

"If I owe Smith ten dollars, and God forgives me," observed Robert Ingersoll, "that doesn't pay Smith."

*Only time can heal
your broken heart,
just as only time can heal
his broken arms and legs.*

MISS PIGGY

Pay Smith.

Forgive yourself for not paying Smith on time, or for not paying Smith as much as Smith *thinks* Smith is entitled to, but work on paying Smith what *you* think Smith is entitled to as soon as you can.

Sometimes Smith will settle for less—then the debt is paid. Sometimes we must go through legal proceedings, such as bankruptcy or divorce. Then the debt—while not paid—is settled. Forgive it, forget it, move on with your life.

"So, if Smith owes me, and doesn't pay, I'm supposed to forgive and forget, but if I owe Smith, I should pay him off. What kind of system is that?"

A wealthy system—wealthy, if you define wealth as health, happiness, abundance, prosperity, riches, loving, caring, sharing, learning, knowing what you want, opportunity, enjoying and balance.

If we can make amends, we do. If not, we don't. Sometimes a heartfelt apology is all we can do. The other person may or may not accept this. It's not our job to make him or her accept it; it was only our job to apologize sincerely and to do what we could to make amends. And then move on.

But we forgive ourselves *before* making amends. We do not need to make amends *in order* to be forgiven. We make amends because it lets us feel better about ourselves. The forgiveness is a given we have already given to ourselves.

Which brings us to the subject of agreements.

*That's not a lie,
it's a terminological inexactitude.*

ALEXANDER HAIG

Agreements

If you want to be wealthy—in the ways we've defined wealth in this book—keep all of your agreements, and don't expect other people to keep any of theirs.

Whenever we put our wealth in the hands of others and expect them to deliver, we're asking for trouble. Other people are, for the most part, beyond our control. "I am a believer in punctuality," wrote Edward Lucas, "though it makes me very lonely."

Where do we place our wealth? In our own hands. Can we always control ourselves? Of course not. But at least we have the right to *try*. At least we know whom we have to work on in order to avoid disappointment next time. At least we know that person will be around to be worked on.

When we keep our agreements, we become increasingly trustworthy, loyal, reliable, credible, dependable, solid, steady, sure, believable, authoritative, accurate and true. Why do we do this? To impress others? No. To impress ourselves? Absolutely.

When we give our word and we keep it, we trust ourselves more, we feel greater confidence, we feel better about ourselves. We know that, when we say we're going to do a thing, we're going to do it. Period.

Self-trust is not an ideal; it's a foundation. It's not a belief; it's a ground of being. It is not a "good idea" that one decides to incorporate; it is a day-by-day, kept-agreement-by-kept-agreement process.

Another way of looking at it is this: keeping agreements is an affirmation. No matter how many times we say to ourselves, "I am trustworthy, I trust myself," if we continually prove our lack of trustworthiness by not keeping our word, the affirmation will not stand.

"But I put in all this work and built this great building. What happened?" You built it on sand.

*The liar's punishment
is not in the least
that he is not believed,
but that he cannot
believe anyone else.*

GEORGE BERNARD SHAW

The guidelines for keeping agreements are easy to give—and yet so hard to take. They are

1. Don't make agreements you don't plan to keep.

2. Keep the agreements you make.

3. If you *must* change an agreement, renegotiate it.

That's it. A good way to separate "good ideas" from firm commitments is to write all commitments down. So often we think, "I really should" see a play, exercise, read a book, whatever. When we don't, we have (yet another) broken agreement with ourselves. Write the "real" ones down.

"Let's have lunch next week," "Talk to you tomorrow," "I'll love you forever," and all those things we say to others we know are probably not true, all add up. Make an agreement specific. Write it down. Or don't say it in the first place.

If we go to ridiculous lengths to keep all our agreements, it will show us how many silly agreements we actually make. It also demonstrates (to us) that our word is worth something. We will have the dual blessing of (A) not making so many agreements in the future, and (B) feeling better about ourselves—more trustworthy.

When we know we keep our agreements, we can then set a goal *and mean it.* "What I have said, that I will bring about," quotes Isaiah 46:11; "what I have planned, that I will do." We know we can commit, and that our commitment *counts.* A part of us listens and activates the goal-fulfillment mechanism within us.

When there are too many goals—too many unkept agreements—then nothing happens. The goal-fulfillment mechanism doesn't listen. "Oh, another commitment. Great. Put it on the pile over there. I'm going back to sleep."

The solution? Find a goal, the Big Goal, your Heart's Desire. Commit to *that* one. Declare all the others—and everything not directly on the path to that goal—complete, finished, over, no longer a goal, done.

*The boy gathers
materials for a temple,
and then when he is thirty
concludes to build
a woodshed.*

THOREAU

What Are You *Doing* with Your Life?

Too often, we look around and wonder "what's it all about?" The "it" we are pondering may be the nature of life in general or the purpose of the Universe, but more often than not the "it" is simply our *lives*. "What's my life about?"

We sometimes find ourselves echoing Henry Martin: "The egg timer is pinging. The toaster is popping. The coffeepot is perking. Is this it, Alice? Is this the great American dream?" Or, as Mama mused on "Mama's Family": "There's got to be more to life than sittin' here watchin' 'Days of Our Lives' and foldin' your Fruit of the Looms."

This unfulfilled feeling can lead to despair, desolation and conversations with friends that sound like Mort Gerberg's cartoon of one performing seal saying to the other, "Of course, what I *really* want to do is direct."

We may be doing all that we were programmed to do—by parents, teachers, culture, and Madison Avenue—believing it will make us happy. All too often, it does not. The solution is a simple but very difficult one: Choose what *you* want to do, and (even more difficult) *do it*. (There couldn't be a better place to plug our book *DO IT! Let's Get Off Our Buts.)*

"Take care to get what you like," said George Bernard Shaw, "or you will end by liking what you get." Unfortunately, too many of us neither take care to get what we like, *nor* do we like what we get.

What we choose to do with our lives is really not important. In 500 or 1,000 or 10,000 years our choice won't make any difference anyway. One thing is as important as another in the overall scheme of things. Being a good president is no more significant than being a good parent. The question is, what do *you* want to do?

"We must select the illusion which appeals to our temperament and embrace it with passion," wrote Cyril Connolly, "if we want to be happy."

Be not simply good;
be good for something.

THOREAU

Where are these dreams, these heart's desires? Inside us. If we weren't born with them, they certainly found their way into us early on. "If children grew up according to early indications," quoth Goethe, "we should have nothing but geniuses."

The evil specter of "be normal," "get along" and "fit in" takes us from what we truly want to do—the things we have a natural curiosity about and enthusiasm for—and sets us on the road to mediocrity, conformity and unhappiness.

To the degree that we find and fulfill our heart's desires, to that degree we live satisfied—and wealthy—lives. "It is said that a man's life can be measured by the dreams he fulfills," said Mr. Roarke of "Fantasy Island." If Mr. Roarke is too sophisticated or perhaps too esoteric, here's Shirley Feeney from "Laverne and Shirley": "Dreams are the soul's pantry. Keep it well stocked and your soul will never hunger."

Rather than following our dreams with enthusiasm and passion—as children do—and finding all of life fascinating, we divide our day into "work hours" and "play hours."

During the work hours, we do something we don't like in exchange for money. During the play hours—since we've used most of our energy "slaving away" at work— we become passive and want to be entertained. We watch television, listen to music and go to the movies. We want to "escape from life." What most people look for when they want "someone to love" is, really, an escape, a diversion— someone to entertain them.

On the other hand, the work we do in pursuit of our dreams is exhilarating. "Work is the true elixir of life," said Sir Theodore Martin at ninety-two. "The busiest man is the happiest man. Excellence in any art or profession is attained only by hard and persistent work. Never believe that you are perfect. When a man imagines, even after years of striving, that he has attained perfection, his decline begins."

*The superstition
that all our hours of work
are a minus quantity
in the happiness of life,
and all the hours of idleness
are plus ones,
is a most ludicrous
and pernicious doctrine,
and its greatest support
comes from our not taking
sufficient trouble,
not making a real effort,
to make work
as near pleasure as it can be.*

LORD BALFOUR

Which brings us neatly to another illusion created to pacify large groups of people who are not pursuing their dreams: that some day we will have *it,* and *then* we can take it easy. People think that when they "make it big," "strike it rich," or—more conservatively—when they retire, they can relax and enjoy life.

That's not true. Once you make it, you've got to maintain it. And, if you wait until retirement to enjoy life, the habit of non-enjoyment will be so firmly ingrained that enjoyment will be difficult.

The solution? Find your dream and pursue it with a passion. No, that won't make your life perfect—but it will make your life *yours.*

Great minds have purposes,
others have wishes.

WASHINGTON IRVING

What Is Your Purpose?

We've talked a lot about the aspect of wealth we call "knowing what you want"—the Big Dream, your Heart's Desire, the Grand Goal. Now let's do something about it— let's discover it.

First, it's a good idea to discover what's even bigger than the Big Dream, even grander than the Grand Goal. That is our purpose.

Goals and dreams change over a lifetime. We achieve them; we live them; we get new ones. Our purpose remains constant our whole life.

If we asked, "What would you like for dinner?" tonight it might be chicken, tomorrow meat loaf, the next day an omelette. These are goals.

If we asked, "What have you had for dinner every night of your life, and what will you have for dinner every night from now on?" you would probably reply, "Food." Food is the purpose of dinner. Chicken, meat loaf and omelettes are goals within that purpose.

Another way of viewing purpose is this: purpose is direction; goals are the stops along the way. Let's say the direction (purpose) is "east." No matter how far east we travel, there's still an infinite amount of east to go. (That's what comes from living on a round planet.) The goals, however, on an eastward journey might include New York, Chicago, Los Angeles, Honolulu and so on.

A purpose is a guiding light, a divining rod. Any goal is fine, as long as it's "on purpose." On *our* purpose.

A purpose is very personal. It fits us like a glove. And yet, a purpose is general enough to fill a whole lifetime with goals and experiences.

Let's hear what some great minds have said about purpose.

If you look good
and dress well,
you don't need
a purpose in life.

ROBERT PANTE

JAMES THURBER: All men should strive to learn before they die / What they are running from, and to, and why.

CARL JUNG: As far as we can discern, the sole purpose of human existence is to kindle a light in the darkness of mere being.

LEO ROSTEN: I cannot believe that the purpose of life is to be "happy." I think the purpose of life is to be useful, to be responsible, to be honorable, to be compassionate. It is, above all, to matter: to count, to stand for something, to have made some difference that you lived at all.

EXODUS 9:16: But I have raised you up for this very purpose, that I might show you my power and that my name might be proclaimed in all the earth.

1 CORINTHIANS 3:8: The man who plants and the man who waters have one purpose.

FRANKLIN D. ROOSEVELT: Happiness lies not in the mere possession of money; it lies in the joy of achievement, in the thrill of creative effort.

JOHN F. KENNEDY: Do you realize the responsibility I carry? I'm the only person standing between Richard Nixon and the White House.

HUGH BLACK: It is the paradox of life that the way to miss pleasure is to seek it first. The very first condition of lasting happiness is that a life should be full of purpose, aiming at something outside self.

LOGAN PEARSALL SMITH: Yes there is a meaning; at least for me, there is one thing that matters—to set a chime of words tinkling in the minds of a few fastidious people.

*I go on working
for the same reason that
a hen goes on laying eggs.*

H. L. MENCKEN

PETER JAY: My purpose—I have a mission to explain.

THE DALAI LAMA: We live very close together. So, our prime purpose in this life is to *help* others. And if you can't help them at least don't hurt them.

Like affirmations, purposes often begin "I am" and are followed by an adjective or two, and then a noun. "I am a (adjective, adjective noun)." "I am a gifted, joyful performer." "I am a loving, giving friend." "I am a caring, compassionate teacher."

Unlike affirmations, however, a purpose is not *created*, it is *discovered*.

To discover your purpose, start making a list of all the positive qualities about yourself (the adjectives), and another list of all the things you like to be (the nouns). Take your time with the list. Look for overall patterns in your life and in your desires. You can ask good friends to contribute.

When the list seems fairly complete, start playing with the words. Does one of the things (nouns) seem to describe you most? Which of the qualities (adjectives) seem to best describe your attitude? Eliminate words that are not *quite* you, or words that are contained within other, more general words. "Caring" may combine "loving," "compassionate" and "giving," for example. Or, "giving" may combine "caring," "loving" and "compassionate." We're not looking for dictionary definitions here. It's what the words mean to *you* that matters.

At a certain point, a few words will "click," and that will be your purpose. There may not be a bolt from the sky, but you will look at it and say, "Yes. This is what I've always done, and this is what I'll always be doing."

That is your purpose.

We suggest you keep your purpose to yourself; your little secret. Plant it like a seed, and let it grow. Don't pull it up to show others or to see how well it's doing. You'll know. You'll feel its roots go deep.

There are a million things
in this universe
you can have,
and there are a million things
you can't have.
It's no fun facing that,
but that's the way things are.

CAPTAIN KIRK

"STAR TREK"

You Can Have Anything You Want, But You Can't Have Everything You Want

We said it before and we *said* we'd say it again—so we're saying it: you can have *anything* you want, but you can't have *everything* you want. We say it so many times because what seems to be (to us, anyway) a fairly obvious observation of life has nonetheless gotten us into a great deal of trouble.

On one hand, the keepers of the traditional cultural beliefs are not very happy with the idea that "you can have anything you want." They counsel us to "fit in," "make do with what you've got" and "don't make waves." When we say to these people, "Yes, you can have anything you want—no matter how remarkable and wonderful," it reminds them of all the dreams they abandoned in order to "get along." Naturally, they don't like being reminded of this, so they blame us, as authors of self-help books, for saying crazy things and upsetting them.

On the other hand, the idea "you can't have everything you want" has made us relatively unpopular with those who espouse the idea "You can have it *all!*" The truth, of course, is that we *can't* have it all—there's just too much "all" and not enough time. Even if we *could* get it all, when would we find time to *use* it? "Everything happens to everybody sooner or later," said George Bernard Shaw, "if there is time enough." The last bit in that is the kicker—"if there's time enough." We only have so many years in this lifetime. There's not time enough for everything to happen to us.

Taking the rather—we like to think—*balanced* view that you can have anything you want but you can't have everything you want, has two distinct advantages.

First, it allows us to select the thing that we want the *most,* and then pursue that with all the vigor, passion, and resources we can muster. It keeps us from being scat-

The Argentinians believed
in Mrs. Perón. So much so,
that when she died,
they petitioned the pope
to make her a saint.
His Holiness declined.
But if he'd consented,
what a triumph for style
that would have been.
A double fox stole,
ankle-strapped shoes,
and eternal life.
Nobody's ever had that.

QUENTIN CRISP

tered between dozens of goals, and living our lives as described by Stephen Leacock: "He flung himself upon his horse and rode madly off in all directions."

Second, taking the balanced view allows us to let go of all the things that—although they would be nice to have—are not as important as our primary dream. Fran Lebowitz relates one of those "wouldn't it be loverly" dreams: "The phone rings. I am not amused. This is not my favorite way to wake up. My favorite way to wake up is to have a certain French movie star whisper to me softly at two thirty in the afternoon that if I want to get to Sweden in time to pick up my Nobel Prize for Literature I had better ring for breakfast. This occurs rather less often than one might wish." Indeed it does.

Letting go of wanting things we know we're not going to have time to get is an important element of wealth. When we don't let go of all the things we're not going to get, we are ripe for misery, ingratitude and poverty. "Grasp all, lose all," said the fourteenth-century proverb.

Wanting it all also opens us to *complaining*. Does this mock grievance from Alan Bennett sound familiar? "I don't think the state does enough for artists and writers generally in the way of subsidy and tax relief and so on. I mean, as an artist and a writer, I have to be surrounded by beautiful things and beautiful people. And beautiful people cost money."

Sometimes we must stoically face the world like Raymond Chandler's detective Philip Marlowe: "I got up on my feet and went over to the bowl in the corner and threw cold water on my face. After a while I felt a little better, but very little. I needed a drink, I needed a lot of life insurance, I needed a vacation, I needed a home in the country. What I had was a coat, a hat and a gun. I put them on and went out of the room."

Knowing what we want the most, and then letting everything else go—both important elements of wealth—begin with the simple, but often painful, realization: you can have anything you want, but you can't have everything you want.

*What the world needs
is more geniuses
with humility.
There are so few of us left.*

OSCAR LEVANT

What Have You Accomplished?

Before choosing what we want to do, it might be a good idea to take a look at what we've achieved.

For reasons we've explained before, we tend to not be aware of the goals we've achieved, the projects that we've accomplished, the lessons we've learned and the growth we've experienced.

We forget them.

Even if they're still with us, we take them for granted. It's as though they never happened.

We tend to look back on our lives and remember what we *didn't* get, what we *failed* to achieve, what we *refused* to learn and the growth that *didn't* take place.

Therefore, we don't think highly of ourselves or of our ability to get what we want. We don't think we're worthy of more. We suffer from low self-esteem. We have doubt, uncertainty and lack of confidence when contemplating future achievements.

Fortunately, there's a rather simple technique for building our self-esteem and confidence, for reaffirming our ability to get things done. (As with all our techniques, it may be simple, but it's not necessarily easy.)

The technique is this:

Get a pad of paper, a notebook or a pile of 3x5 index cards.

Start listing all the things that you've accomplished in the past five years. (If you're using 3x5 cards, write one achievement per card. Writing them on index cards will come in handy for a future exercise we'll be doing.)

Take some time with this.

Free associate. One accomplishment may remind you of a dozen others.

*Do not put off till tomorrow
what can be enjoyed today.*

JOSH BILLINGS

*Writing is turning
one's worst moments
into money.*

J. P. DONLEAVY

Consider the areas of work and career, relationships and family, social and political goals, religious and spiritual accomplishments.

What have you done for your health, happiness and well-being?

What have you done for other people?

What degrees, awards, citations or lotteries have you won?

What significant books have you read, movies have you seen, television have you watched?

Have you moved? Gotten a new car? A new job? Started your own company? Gotten married? Traveled? Learned a new language? Obtained a new skill?

What habits have you broken? What new, life-enhancing behaviors have you replaced them with?

What losses have you survived? Before each was a loss, was it a gain? If so, write down both the survival and the gain.

How much money have you made in the past five years?

What new people have you met?

Have you learned a new sport, a new game, or how to program your VCR?

Feel free to consult diaries, date books, scrapbooks, memento files, the memories of friends, or anything else that will help you remember all that you've achieved and accomplished in the past five years.

Please don't just *remember* these things—write them down.

Put this book aside now and take some time with your list. (By the time it's done, you can add to the end of it "compiled this list!")

When your list is fairly complete, please turn the page and continue reading.

I came to the conclusion
that one of the reasons
why I'm so blessed,
I think, is because
I reach so many people,
and you never know whose life
you are touching or affecting.
And so, because your blessings
come back to you
based upon how you give them out...
that's why I'm so...
You know what I'm saying?
You get it? OK, good.

OPRAH WINFREY

Now take some time to review your list. Isn't it amazing how much you did in the last five years? Over time, you'll probably remember other achievements that didn't make the list. That's fine. That's how the memory works. Take a moment to add them to your list.

If you add to your list all the things that might be considered "daily maintenance"—the meals you've eaten, the baths you've taken, the teeth you've brushed, the sleep you've slept—you start to get a sense of the enormous amount of *energy* we have to accomplish things.

Imagine this huge amount of energy directed toward *one* primary goal. It should be obvious that this one goal could be fairly large—gargantuan, perhaps.

And what if this goal were your heart's desire—your big dream? Then what? It's fairly clear that obtaining that big dream would be almost guaranteed.

With the same amount of energy from the last five years at your disposal for the next five years, it's easy to see that you *can* have anything you want—you just can't have...well, you know the rest.

All in all I'd rather
have been a judge than a miner.
And what is more,
being a miner, as soon as
you are too old and tired
and sick and stupid
to do the job properly,
you have to go.
Well, the very opposite
applies with judges.

PETER COOK

Obtaining Is Easy; *Maintaining* Is Hard

Hidden in all success is a little surprise. After pursuing and achieving a goal, people frequently ask, "Why didn't someone warn me about *this?*"

The "this" is *maintenance.*

If you live in an apartment and then achieve your goal of moving into your own house, for example, the first time something goes wrong, you habitually may want to "call the landlord."

You are then forced to make a discovery similar to that of Pope John XXIII: "It often happens that I wake at night and begin to think about a serious problem and decide I must tell the Pope about it. Then I wake up completely and remember that I *am* the Pope."

When you own your own house, you *am* the landlord.

With a new car comes insurance, worries ("If I park it here, and this car opens its door, it might dent my car, but if I park it over there, somebody might break in") and that delightful accessory that seems to come with all new cars—the payment book. ("To get back on your feet," as someone said, "miss two car payments.")

Some acquisitions are low maintenance—a rock collection, for example. Other acquisitions are high maintenance—a career goal in a highly competitive field, children, and almost any kind of relationship. "Friendship is like money," wrote Samuel Butler, "easier made than kept."

Developing a taste is one thing; *feeding* the taste is another. (Why do people work so hard to "develop a taste" for expensive things like caviar or oysters?) "My problem lies," observed Errol Flynn, "in reconciling my gross habits with my net income."

That *maintaining* is often more difficult than *obtaining* is not a new idea. In the book of Daniel (11:20), writ-

*People who live
in glass houses
have to answer the bell.*

BRUCE PATTERSON

ten about 600 B.C., it explains what one needs to do when one inherits a kingdom: "His successor will send out a tax collector to maintain the royal splendor."

Once we have something, maintaining it becomes a habit. We may have stopped getting satisfaction from something long ago, but we maintain it because, well, that's what we've always done. "Luxury comes as a guest," observed Joni Mitchell, "to take a slave." For many people, getting rid of high-maintenance, low-satisfaction possessions, habits, career choices and even people can be a major step toward wealth.

This notion, of course, goes contrary to the cultural belief that "in order to be wealthier, I have to get *more*." For many, greater wealth is achieved by having *less*.

In addition, we are about to ask you to choose what you *really* want. Part of choosing what you really want—with your eyes fully open—is to honestly look at what it will cost to *maintain* what you want when you finally get it.

Having a child may be nice, but it requires a 24-hour-a-day, 7-day-a-week commitment for at least 18 years. Being at the top of a given profession may be nice, but in that profession 18-hour work days may be the norm.

So make your choice with open eyes. People are better at what they do—and enjoy it more—when they choose it after looking at it from all angles. One important angle is, "What will it cost to maintain?"

*No wind favors him
who has no destined port.*

MICHEL DE MONTAIGNE

What Do You Want?

A major cause of tension in our lives is setting goals we can't reach, that we wouldn't want even if we got them. It's not that we *can't* reach any one of them, you understand; it's just that, with all the other goals we are already seeking, many of the goals we think we want we'll never have.

It's a sad but true fact—if we aren't actively pursuing what we want, we don't really want it. We may *think* we want to write a book, but if we haven't sat down and written a word in, say, a year, we probably don't *really* want to write the book.

We may *say* we're going to start an exercise program and look like Arnold Schwarzenegger or Jane Fonda, but if we're not actually exercising at least three times a week, we probably don't *truly* want that goal either.

Yes, we may want it, but we are not willing to place it in front of all the other things we really want more. As Samuel Johnson phrased it: "Worth seeing? Yes, but not worth going to see."

A good way to see what you *really* want is to take a look at what you are currently doing. After doing the exercise in this chapter, you may find you already *are* living your dream; that you have nothing left to do but be grateful for the wealth you already have. Or, you may find that "there'll be some changes made," and you'll get busy making them. In that case, there really *is* something you want that you currently don't have.

Please don't use this chapter to make yet another list of goals, not acted upon, that become even more shoulds, musts, and have-tos. If, once you realize there's a heart's desire you have not been following, and you do not immediately begin following it—doing something physical about it each day—then you probably don't *really* want it, or are not willing to go through what it takes to get it. In either case, it would be better to let it go.

Blessed is that man
who has found his work.

ELBERT HUBBARD

If, on the other hand, you see a goal and immediately become involved in the process of fulfilling it—no matter how uncomfortable or difficult—then you probably have latched on to your heart's desire and will ride it to fulfillment.

When we talk about dreams and goals, keep in mind that your dreams may be *simpler* than even the ones you are currently pursuing. In school, for example, they try to convince us that learning all sorts of things we have no desire to learn will be "good for us." Many of us have been programmed to follow the same advice in life.

We may work at a job that pays more money, just because it pays more money. It's as though the amount of money we make is the only criterion for employment. "A business that makes nothing but money," said Henry Ford, "is a poor kind of business." The same is true of individual work. If you make nothing at work but money, it's a poor sort of work.

Not that work is supposed to be one fulfilling joy after another. Work is, after all, *work*. "The true profession of a man," wrote Hermann Hesse, "is to find his way to himself." *That's work*. Along the way, however, we can make some money. "The law of work does seem utterly unfair—but there it is, and nothing can change it," said Mark Twain; "the higher the pay in enjoyment the worker gets out of it, the higher shall be his pay in money also."

Not that life becomes a bed of roses, you understand. "I'm not happy when I'm writing," said Fannie Hurst, "but I'm more unhappy when I'm not." Some days, we pursue our dream not because it feels better, but because not pursuing it hurts more.

If we all followed our hearts' desires, the world would continue on its course. People don't need to be *forced* into various categories of employment. If there's a need, there's someone who *wants* to fulfill that need. "So far I've found that most high-level executives prefer the boardroom to the Bahamas," wrote William Theobald. "They don't really enjoy leisure time; they feel their work is their leisure."

In life, as in football,
you won't go far
unless you know
where the goalposts are.

ARNOLD GLASOW

These people are *happy* to work 18-hour days. They wouldn't have it any other way.

On the other hand, many people have rather simple desires. "What is my loftiest ambition?" Oliver Herford asked himself. He answered: "I've always wanted to throw an egg into an electric fan."

When we ask, "What do you want?" there is no right or wrong answer. There is only *your* answer—the one that's right for you. The answer we think we *should* have—but that we don't really want—is not the right answer. It's not exactly the *wrong* answer. It'll lead to lots of busy-ness—as much busy-ness as it would take to fulfill a dream—but, alas, with far less satisfaction.

So, as we go along, look to your inner barometer—your personal indicator of truth. If you ask, your Master Teacher will help you, too. "To thine own self be true."

The exercise in this chapter is best done with 3x5 cards. We suggest getting at least 500 of them. You *can* do the exercise by making lists on sheets of paper, but 3x5 cards are much easier when the selecting and sorting begin.

If you have—from the earlier exercise in "What Have You Accomplished?"—the cards (or lists) of the things you've already done, go through them and separate the things that are current in your life—what you still have. Everything you still have will probably need at least *some* maintaining. Maintenance is time, and time is dreams.

After you've sorted the cards, start adding all the other things you want to keep in your life. Write one item per card: "Apartment," "Car," "Relationship with_____," "Haagen Dazs bars," etc.

When this pile of cards is fairly complete (you don't need to list each article of clothing on separate cards—one card saying "Wardrobe" is sufficient), then start answering the question, "What do you want?" Write one want per card. Free associate. Some may seem silly, some trivial, others impossibly difficult. Write them all down anyway—one per card.

There are few moments
during her recital
when one can relax
and feel confident
that she will make her goal,
which is the end of the song.

PAUL HUME

Take some time with this process. You may want to write for a while, take a walk, and come back to it. You may want to spend several days jotting down your wants on cards. Don't worry if you repeat a want or two—we'll sort those out later. Pause here in reading the book until your list seems complete.

☆

Now, go through and read each card with your purpose in mind. Would obtaining this goal be counter to your purpose? If the goal goes against your purpose, remove it. Say good-bye to that goal, and discard the card. Go through all the cards in this way. Now you know that all the goals that are left are "on purpose."

That done, sort each of the cards into one of five categories:

> Career/Professional
> Marriage/Family
> Social/Political
> Religious/Spiritual
> Fun/Recreation/Relationships

Put each want into the category that best describes it. Some wants may straddle a category or two. Choose the category that *best* describes your motivation in desiring that goal. You will end up with five piles of cards. That done, read through each of the five piles (Career/Professional, Marriage/Family, Social/Political, Religious/Spiritual, Fun/Recreation/Relationships).

Which category has the most appeal *overall?* While you're considering that, let's take a moment for a little explanation.

When we choose an area of goals under the general categories of Career/Professional, Marriage/Family, Social/Political, Religious/Spiritual and Fun/Recreation/Relationships, we can often achieve many individual goals *within* each category for about the same effort as having

The high prize of life,
the crowning fortune of a man,
is to be born with a bias
to some pursuit
which finds him
in employment and happiness.

EMERSON

any one of them. If you live in Kansas, for example, the goals of "live in Los Angeles" and "become a successful actor" fit together nicely. In fact, moving to Los Angeles (or New York) seems to be an almost necessary step in becoming a successful actor. If you *want* to move to Los Angeles (or New York), so much the better. The move becomes, as they say, a "freebie."

When you choose a category and make that category the primary focus of your life—the category to which you will sacrifice all the other categories, if necessary—you can get a lot of freebies along with it.

Or, you can pick a series of smaller goals from two or more of the categories, and still achieve each of them. This is what people often mean when they say a "well-balanced life." You'll find you'll have enough time each day to successfully pursue each of the smaller goals.

Or, as a third alternative, you could choose one specific goal you want more than anything else and give up everything—short of fulfilling basic bodily functions—until that goal is achieved. That goal in hand, you can then select the next specific goal, and put all your available energy toward it.

It's a matter of preference, a matter of style, and sometimes it's a matter of the goal. To become an Olympic medalist in certain sports, for example, one must achieve it before a certain age. This may mean putting off a great many other goals until after Olympic glory.

The trick here is not to mix and match the choices. Choose *one* path:

1. A primary category
2. A series of smaller goals from different categories
3. One big specific goal

Then *follow that*. Mixing and matching paths leads to the illusion that we can have more than we have time to achieve. As we've explained before, this only leads to misery.

Explanation over; back to the cards.

*To love what you do
and feel that it matters
—how could anything
be more fun?*

KATHERINE GRAHAM

Does one of the five piles—Career/Professional, Marriage/Family, Social/Political, Religious/Spiritual, Fun/Recreation/Relationships—seem far more intriguing than any of the other piles? Or, are there small goals within various piles that have an appeal? Or, is there one, burning, specific goal that is more important than any other goal or any other category?

(Be careful you don't kid yourself with the second option. Choosing a *major* Career/Professional goal *and* a *major* Marriage/Family goal *and* a *major* Religious/Spiritual goal *and* a *major* Social/Political goal *and* a *major* Recreation/Fun/Relationships goal is not the, well, wealthy approach. Even writing that sentence was exhausting. It's easy to see how exhausting—and impractical—trying to live it would be. It is, in fact, the life many people are *trying* to live—or at least *think* they want to (or should) live—hence, a great deal of misery. In option number two, we're talking about choosing some simple, not-too-taxing, easily do-able goals.)

When you've selected which path to take, *if you chose by category,* sort your cards as follows: look through each of the cards in your selected category, and pick the one goal that is *most* important within that category. Set it aside. Of the remaining cards, pick the goal that is now *most* important. Set that one aside. Continue sorting in this way until all the cards are in order. Look through the cards again. Set the sorted category aside, and say goodbye to all the other cards in all the other categories.

If you are selecting smaller goals from several categories: go through all the cards and choose the goal you want *most.* Set that aside. Now go through all the piles again and, of the remaining cards, choose the goal you want most. Set that card aside. Continue choosing until you get a *maximum* of ten goals. (The fewer the goals, the more quickly you will be able to achieve them. The more goals, the more time it will take to achieve them.) Put these ten goals aside, and say good-bye to all the other goals on all the other cards.

*When a fantasy turns you on,
you're obligated to God
and nature to start doing it
—right away.*

STEWART BRAND

If you are choosing one goal: go through all the cards and pick the goal that is *the* most important to you. Knowing that goal, go through the cards and pick any cards that *automatically* go with that one goal. ("Run a marathon," for example, would automatically include "Get in shape," "Eat a healthier diet," and "Go jogging every morning." It would *not* automatically include "Find dream lover," "Get a new car," or "Get a raise.") Set your major goal aside, and all the goals that automatically go with it, and say good-bye to all the other goals.

Saying good-bye to all the other goals is not easy. We may struggle with it. We may tell ourselves, "Oh, I have time for *this* one." Ten or fifteen "this ones" later, and we wind up where we started—over goaled, over tired, out of time, and under satisfied. As the saying goes, "Why put off till tomorrow what you'll never do anyway?"

Focus, instead, on the goals you've *chosen*. Take a look at your Big Dream. You *can* have this dream. It's the one you've selected. Focus not on the dreams you can't have; focus on the one you can—the one you want the most.

Be grateful for that.

Now, all it takes is, well, *doing it*. But first, let's take a look at a few tips on the best way to phrase goals.

*We don't know
how to celebrate
because we don't know
what to celebrate.*

PETER BROOK

How to Phrase a Goal

In order for something to be a *goal,* and not just a *direction,* it must be written in clearly defined, quantifiable terms.

So many people know what they want, yet fail to achieve it because they think they have a goal when they merely have a direction. "I want to be a successful actor" is a direction. The first time we successfully act in *anything,* that "goal" is fulfilled—we *are* a successful actor. The goal-fulfilling mechanism within us shuts down.

Conversely, no matter how many movies we do or how much money we make or how many Oscars we win, the "goal" of "I want to be a successful actor" is never fully realized—there's always potentially more successful acting ahead. Therefore, we never know when to celebrate the achievement of a goal.

A *quantifiable* goal is one in which the end results can be counted and measured. If your goal is, "I want to be a successful actor," ask yourself, "What is successful?" Then phrase the goal according to the quantifiable criterion of success: "I am making $100,000 per year as an actor," "Siskel and Ebert give my performance in a major feature film two thumbs up," "I star in my own series on a major television network." It's easy to tell when each of these goals has or has not been achieved. It is impossible to tell—with absolute certainty—when "I'm a successful actor" is attained.

Another important aspect of setting a goal is to state it in the present—like an affirmation. "I want a new car," is not a goal. It is a statement of want. "I have a new car," is a goal. (Be careful that the word "new" is defined as "newly manufactured," not "new to me.")

Even better, include a description of yourself in the goal: "I am satisfied and productive in my new job earning $50,000 or more per year." "I am happy and fulfilled in my relationship with a kind, loving person." (Come to think of it, we'd better make that one "I'm happy and fulfilled in

Ricky Ricardo: *There you go again, wanting something that you haven't got.*

Lucy Ricardo: *I do not. I just want to see what I haven't got that I don't want.*

"I LOVE LUCY"

my relationship with another loving and caring person." The first goal could well apply to our relationship with ourselves.)

Rewrite each of your goals so that an objective, outside observer would be able to tell whether you had or had not achieved them.

If you *really* want to turn up the heat, add *timelines* to your goals. Simply add the date by which each goal is to be achieved. This puts off the tendency to say, "I'll get my goal—later." Timelines make the goals real within a measurable segment of reality. (Don't say, for example, "within six months." Six months is always six months away. Set a specific date. Or, each month, shorten the time by one month—"six months" becomes "five months," and so on.)

One final thought about goals: For the most part, keep your goals to yourself. After you've achieved a goal, tell anyone you want. Shout it from the rooftops. Send out a press release. Go on "Oprah" and talk about it. Prior to that, keep it to yourself. We don't need to be talked out of our goals.

As Sally Kempton said, "It's hard to fight an enemy who has outposts in your head." We have challenge enough fighting the "enemies" who already have outposts in our head. We don't need the doubt, concern, caution, "good advice," and reservations of the people around us—especially those who "only want to help."

In a few rare instances—for example, a support group specifically meeting to encourage each others' goals—sharing your goals *might* be in order. When in doubt, err on the side of silence.

If needed, take the time now to rewrite your goals.

*All through the five acts
he played the King
as though under
momentary apprehension
that someone else
was about to play the Ace.*

EUGENE FIELD

Commit to and Affirm Your Goal

Now it's time to commit to your goal. This can be scary. Most of us have been trained to take the lukewarm approach to achieving our goals: "I'll try it a little bit and see what happens." The trouble is, lukewarm commitment generally produces lukewarm results. Based on the lukewarm results, people often say, "Well *that* didn't work out. It's a good thing I didn't commit myself!"

It was, in fact, the lack of commitment that produced the lackluster results. Nowhere have we seen the power of commitment more eloquently and clearly stated than in this from W. H. Murray:

> **Until one is committed, there is hesitancy, the chance to draw back, always ineffectiveness. Concerning all acts of initiative (and creation) there is one elementary truth, the ignorance of which kills countless ideas and splendid plans: that the moment one definitely commits oneself, then Providence moves too. All sorts of things occur to help one that would never otherwise have occurred. A whole stream of events issues from the decision, raising in one's favor all manner of unforeseen incidents and meetings and material assistance, which no man could have dreamed would have come his way. I have learned a deep respect for one of Goethe's couplets:**
>> *Whatever you can do,*
>> *or dream you can, begin it.*
>> *Boldness has genius, power*
>> *and magic in it.*

A great way to commit is to treat your goal as an affirmation. Get out your toothpicks, and say it (or each of them, if you have more than one) at least 1,000 times. In addition, you might try these affirmations:

"I am committed to my goal."

"I am living my dream."

"I am grateful for my goal."

"I am enjoying my heart's desire."

*My dear, I don't care
what they do, so long as
they don't do it in the street
and frighten the horses.*

MRS. PATRICK CAMPBELL

And Let the Rest of the World Go By

Once we know our goal, our own personal dream, the most wonderful thing happens: we can relax about *absolutely everything else*.

If something isn't connected to our goal—or directly preventing us from achieving it—we don't have to worry about it. In fact, we don't have to even *think* about it. We can let those who have that as their major goal think about it, and we can move ahead with our own.

This, of course, can make us happy and, as Clarence Darrow pointed out, "If a man is happy in America it is considered he is doing something wrong."

Yes, people will do everything they can to involve you in *their* goals, dreams, and desires. It is important to keep in mind that *those are theirs*.

Naturally, we will feel guilty. We say "naturally" not because guilt is a natural reaction, but because that's what we've been programmed to feel when we don't do what other people expect us to do. Stay on your path. Remain aligned to your dream. Use the energy of guilt (the energy for change) to make the changes that will get you closer to *your* goal. Use the anxiety ("If I don't do what they want, they won't like me anymore,") as free energy, and use it toward your goal.

It's not that other people's dreams, goals, and desires are not worthwhile—frequently they are. It's not that we don't care about what people want us to become involved in—often we do. It's just that we don't care about them *as much* as we care about our own dream.

The world is simply too full of worthwhile projects, injustices in need of justice, and unfairness in general for each of us to conquer them all. Now that we've decided what *is* important in our lives, it's a good idea to keep focused on that, and not to scatter our energies—either emotional, mental or physical—in directions not directly on our path.

*One way to get
high blood-pressure
is to go mountain climbing
over molehills.*

EARL WILSON

As Cynthia Heimel explained, "The person who says, believes, and acts on the phrase 'I ain't taking any shit from anybody' is a very busy person indeed. This person must be ever vigilant against news vendors who shortchange him, cab drivers who take him the wrong way around, waiters who serve the other guy first, florists who are charging ten cents more per tulip than the one down the block, pharmacists who make you wait too long and cars that cut you off at the light: they are a veritable miasma of righteous indignation and never have a minute to relax and have a good time."

Would you rather be right or be righteous? Would you rather have what you *really* want, or be justifying your life by whining, "I did all that I could"? Would you rather have your dream, or live in someone else's nightmare?

As the old saying goes, "If it ain't broke, don't fix it." Let us paraphrase that to read, "If it's not your heart's desire, don't bother with it."

One thing, certainly, not to bother with is gossip. "Of course I wouldn't say anything about her unless I could say something good," said Bill King. "And, oh boy, is this good..." "The public have an insatiable curiosity to know everything," wrote Oscar Wilde, "except what is worth knowing."

What other people are doing with their lives is their business. You have no time for it if you want to achieve your goal. "The things most people want to know about," observed George Bernard Shaw, "are usually none of their business." Your business is achieving your goal.

Of course, following this suggestion doesn't guarantee that you won't be involved in gossip—you will: as the subject of it.

You aren't responsible for anyone else's goals but your own. You aren't responsible for anyone else's happiness but your own. Taking to heart the first of these sentences quite often helps with the second.

Why is this thus?
What is the reason
of this thusness?

ARTEMUS WARD

1834–1867

The Remainder of This Section

We'll continue with suggestions on fulfilling dreams and achieving goals in the next section of the book, "Getting More of What You Want." For now, we're returning to the central theme of this section—enjoyment. To get us in the mood—guess what? Yes! Quotes on enjoyment...

ELBERT HUBBARD: It is easy to get everything you want, provided you first learn to do without the things you can not get.

FONTENELLE: A great obstacle to happiness is to anticipate too great a happiness.

BERTRAND RUSSELL: To be without some of the things you want is an indispensable part of happiness.

RANDY NEWMAN: People become who they are. Even Beethoven became Beethoven.

MARY WILSON LITTLE: There is no pleasure in having nothing to do; the fun is in having lots to do and not doing it.

KAHLIL GIBRAN: Work is love made visible.

HENRY FORD: Work is our sanity, our self respect, our salvation. So far from being a curse, work is the greatest blessing.

THOMAS JEFFERSON: It is wonderful how much may be done if we are always doing.

JAMES BARRIE: We are all of us failures—at least, the best of us are.

ANDREW CARNEGIE: Surplus wealth is a sacred trust which its possessor is bound to administer in his lifetime for the good of the community.

AMENEMOPE: Do not strain to seek increases, What you have, let it suffice you.

WILLIAM WYCHERLEY: Go to your business, pleasure, whilst I go to my pleasure, business.

JOHN CHURTON COLLINS: To profit from good advice requires more wisdom than to give it.

The remainder of this section is a series of ideas, techniques, suggestions and "good advice," designed to enhance our experience of enthusiasm, contentment, and joy.

If we live, we live;
if we die, we die;
if we suffer, we suffer;
if we are terrified, we are terrified.
There is no problem about it.

ALAN WATTS

Acceptance

Acceptance is simply acknowledging that what is, is.

The difficulty many people have with acceptance is that they confuse *acceptance* with *approval*. "I'm not going to accept *that*. It's no good." By accepting something, we're not saying it's good—nor are we saying it's desirable, preferred, the way we want it or that it fulfills our personal preferences in any other way.

Acceptance is simply acknowledging that what is, is.

The opposite of acceptance is denial. When we deny something that is, we create struggle. Struggle is not fun—especially when there's no way we can win the struggle.

If we drop something, we can deny gravity as much as we like. The object will hit the ground with the same force and results. The only difference is that, in addition to a broken object, we also experienced frustration. Accepting that gravity is, that the object will probably break, and there's not much we can do about it will not keep the object from breaking, but will eliminate our inner struggle that somehow there *shouldn't* be any gravity and that things dropped *shouldn't* break.

In addition, just because we accept something doesn't mean we can't work to change it. In fact, acceptance of what is seems to be a prerequisite to effective change. As we pointed out in the previous chapter, however, unless something is directly interfering with the realization of your dream, it's probably best not to try and change it, but to accept it as it is and move on toward your goal.

Acceptance allows us to abandon the futile struggle between what we think "should" be happening and what's actually going on. In other words, we pierce the illusion that the world should be the way we want it to be, and we wake up to reality.

One of the great tools for achieving acceptance is *observation*.

*I can detach myself
from the world.
If there is a better world
to detach oneself from
than the one functioning
at the moment
I have yet to hear of it.*

P. G. WODEHOUSE

Observation

Observation is a technique to explore our *reactions* to what goes on around (and within) us. As we observe the reactions, we can detach from them—become less "reactive." Ultimately, observation lets us get in touch with what's *really* going on. It begins as a meditation, practiced for short periods of time, and can eventually expand to become a way of viewing life.

One technique of observation is to sit comfortably with your eyes closed. Call in the light. Tell yourself you're not going to move any part of your body for a certain number of minutes. (Begin with five minutes and build up.) If something itches, don't scratch it. Observe the itch. Observe your desire to scratch it. Observe your emotional reaction to not scratching it. Observe the demands you make on yourself. If you want to shift positions, don't. Observe your desire to switch positions. If you want to wiggle your toes, don't. Observe your desire to wiggle your toes.

We can also practice observation when going about our daily life. Find within yourself a sense of inner calm, contentment, peace—your portable paradise. Use the light, affirmation, prayer, or whatever it takes for you to find your inner calm. Then go through life as you normally would, except the challenge is: "Never abandon your inner calm." If something happens you don't like, observe your dislike. Don't become upset about it. If something happens that's disappointing, observe the disappointment. Don't *get* disappointed about it.

If life is too "real" for you to do this successfully for any period of time, try practicing observation while watching television or movies. If you begin to lose your emotional balance, just remind yourself, "It's only a movie." With enough practice, you'll be able to say, "It's only life," with the same degree of conviction.

The technique of observation shows us not only where we are trapped—where our responses are causing us to sacrifice our enjoyment—but also the way out of the trap.

Well, Norton,
I guess there'll be
no more bus rides for me.
I've come to the end of the line.
I'm going to that
big bus depot in the sky.
It's a one-way trip
with no transfers.

RALPH KRAMDEN
"THE HONEYMOONERS"

The bus bringeth and
the bus taketh away.
You know, that's a lot like life.

FLOYD LAWSON
"THE ANDY GRIFFITH SHOW"

Accept Death

Bertrand Russell relates this story: "The late F. W. H. Myers used to tell how he asked a man at a dinner table what he thought would happen to him when he died. The man tried to ignore the question, but, on being pressed, replied: 'Oh well, I suppose I shall inherit eternal bliss, but I wish you wouldn't talk about such unpleasant subjects.'"

When we bring up the subject of death, that's how many people respond. Most people don't like thinking about what happens "after." "Eternity is a terrible thought," wrote Tom Stoppard. "I mean, where's it going to end?"

Most people live in denial of death. "I detest life insurance agents," said Stephen Leacock. "They always argue that I shall some day die, which is not so." "I don't fear death because I don't fear anything I don't understand," explained Hedy Lamarr. "When I start to think about it, I order a massage and it goes away."

That death, however, is inevitable is, well, inevitable. "One can survive everything nowadays," observed Oscar Wilde, "except death."

What, then, is the appropriate use for death? "We should so use the next world," wrote Samuel Butler, "that it should advance us in that which is before it."

When we take the time to explore death, the feelings most people have about death (fear, terror, dread) don't make sense. Culturally, we only have three beliefs about death—none of them bad. They are

When we die, we're dead. *Life is a biochemical electrical phenomenon, and when the body ceases to function, we cease to be*. If this is one's belief about death, there's nothing to fear, because there is nothing—no experience, no awareness, nothing. Just complete, total uninterrupted, utter unconsciousness.

*AIDS has come upon
us with cruel abandon.
It has forced us to confront
and deal with the frailty
of our being and the reality of death.
It has forced us into a realization
that we must cherish every moment
of the glorious experience
of this thing we call life.
We are learning to value our own lives
and the lives of our loved ones
as if any moment may be the last.*

ELIZABETH TAYLOR

*Capture the moment, whoever you are.
None of us is here forever.*

ADRIAN
1958–1991

It's heaven or hell through all eternity. *In the end, we are judged once and for all, and those who believe go to heaven, those who don't go to hell, and that's that.* There's not much to fear in that, because most believers believe that, when all is said and done, they are going to heaven. Hell, after all, is reserved for nonbelievers and *truly bad* believers.

We keep coming back until we get it right. *We, as a soul, keep picking up body after body, incarnation after incarnation, until we learn all we need to know, and then move on to our next level of expression.* If this is the way it is, then death is no more significant than moving from one house to another, or ending one semester in school and starting another.

Most of us allow our childhood beliefs about death—formed when we were young and unable to understand the concept of death—to subconsciously rule our emotions as adults. An important part of enjoying life here is to understand that we won't always be here—that each moment is precious.

We like to think of death as expressed by Truman Capote's last words. When asked by a friend, "Are you all right?" he answered "No, I'm not. But I soon will be."

If we work at it, we can arrange our lives so that—at the moment of our passing—we will be able to answer the same question, "Yes, I am. And I soon will be, too."

I can't tell a lie
—not even when I hear one.

JOHN KENDRICK BANGS

Trust

Whom can we trust? So often misery is explained by the words, "But I *trusted* them."

Ultimately, the only person we can trust is ourself.

What we can trust is the intuitive sense we have about how another person might or might not behave in a specific situation. How often have we trusted someone, received the short end of the stick, and then reacted, "I knew it!"

In fact, we *do* know it. Our intuition told us precisely what would happen—and it did. Why don't we listen to our intuition? Because there are so many other voices inside vying for our attention that it's hard to hear our intuition over the din.

Besides that, we are conditioned to consider all attempts to "tell the future" that are not mathematically, statistically or scientifically based to be nonsense. Even people who *do* believe in our ability to predict what might happen to us think it is the gift of a small group of psychics, sensitives and seers.

In fact, we know a lot more about what's going to happen than we are culturally conditioned to believe. This is especially true when it comes to our big dream and the fulfillment of it.

No, we may not know *everything* about the future—what a pathetically dull life *that* would be. But we do know how we feel about certain people and situations. Quite often, these feelings are accurate.

To develop our trust in ourselves requires simple observation. Next time "the voice" is telling us to do or not to do something, take note of it. Then see what happens. Was it right? Was it wrong? Perhaps it was fear speaking—or greed.

After listening to the many voices and investigating their effects, begin to differentiate the voice of intuition

Be careful,
and you will save many men
from the sin of robbing you.

ED HOWE

from the other (sometimes louder and more insistent) voices inside us.

The next time something happens, and you say to yourself "I knew it!" and congratulate yourself for following your inner guidance, think back to how that inner guidance communicated itself to you. What did it feel and sound like? Over time, we can learn to differentiate this voice (or, for some people, feeling) from all the others.

When we get to know our intuition well, we can trust it. It will tell us whether someone is being truthful with us or lying. It will also tell us when *we* are being honest, or just kidding ourselves.

It may take some time to develop a solid connection with our intuition, but it's worth it. It forms the basis of a true, lasting and reliable trust.

Why do they call them tellers?
They never tell you anything.
They just ask questions.
And why do they call it interest?
It's boring. And another thing
—how come the Trust Department
has all their pens
chained to the table?

COACH ERNIE PANTUSSO
"CHEERS"

What Would a Master Do?

When people aren't successful, they sometimes wonder, "Why not?" They get answers, then they wonder why those answers don't seem to meet their needs. They get the wrong answers, and they get upset about it. Perhaps they're really getting the right answers, but asking the wrong questions.

Too many people ask nothing but "Why" questions. They analyze and analyze a problem until what they have is a perfectly analyzed problem—but no solution. "You can analyze a glass of water and you're left with a lot of chemical components," said J. B. S. Haldane, "but nothing you can drink."

"Why?" questions can drive us crazy. "What?" questions drive us sane.

"Why?" questions ultimately leave us dangling at the end of our knowledge. We can quickly reach the frontiers of not only our own ignorance, but of the ignorance of all humanity. A child knows that with six "Why?" questions in a row, he or she can stump any adult. So often, we do this stumping to ourselves.

"What?" questions, on the other hand, lead us to practical solutions. They direct us toward information and action. "What happened?" "What can be done to fix it?" "What do I do now?"

By asking questions that begin with "What?" rather than "Why?" we may not understand as much, but we accomplish more.

One of the great "What?" questions to ask is "What would a master do?" You can call on your own Master Teacher and ask, "What would you do in this situation?" Or you can ask about specific types of masters. "What would a master problem-solver do?" "What would a master healer do?" "What would a master plumber do?"

What would a master writer do to end this chapter?

The world is a stage,
the stage is a world
of entertainment!

HOWARD DIETZ

That's Entertainment!

When we discuss acceptance and observation, some people say, "Do you expect me to detach myself from life and walk around like a zombie?"

No, not at all. As humans, we are here to do, learn and enjoy. Doing, learning and enjoying require *involvement.* Sometimes involvement is pleasant; sometimes involvement is not so pleasant. In fact, some of our most profound lessons are learned through unpleasant experiences.

"But I don't want to feel unpleasant things!" some people protest. The people who say this are quite often the ones who stagger out of a movie theater, their cheeks dripping with tears, saying "That's the best movie I've ever seen!"

When we go to the movies, theater, a concert, read a novel or watch television, we *expect* to have emotional reactions. In fact, the more emotions—and the more extreme each emotion—the more fulfilled we feel when the entertainment is over. If, within a single performance, we are moved to both laughter and tears, we pronounce the entertainment "good." If we are moved to laughter and tears several times—especially if the periods of laughter and tears are intense and prolonged—we declare the piece "spectacular!"

How many times have we watched Scarlett pining after Ashley and being pursued by Rhett—complete with Civil War, birthin' babies, and Yankee scalawags—only to have her wind up pining for Rhett at the end? It's known as melodrama. Things are always darkest just before they go completely black. Yet, we watch it over and over again—and love it. We *enjoy* being miserable.

Why, then, in life, don't we give ourselves the same break? As we've said before, it's not what happens to us but how we *respond* to what happens to us that creates the quality of our life. When we relax into our feelings— *all* of our feelings, the ones we label good and the ones we

NOTICE TO OUR GUESTS
If there is anything you need
and don't see,
please let us know,
and we will show you
how to do without it.

MARY TOARMINA McWILLIAMS FADDEN

label bad—we seem to have a good time. We give ourselves permission to do this when we go to an organized entertainment—play, movie, television, game, etc.

Why not give ourselves the same permission with the rest of life? Why not imagine that life is one immense entertainment? What if the world were one majestic holographic, SurroundSound, 70 millimeter, Technicolor extravaganza of virtual reality—entirely designed for our bemused amusement?

We don't use "amusement" in the sense of "light entertainment." We use it in the sense of "amusement park." We see ourselves thin and fat, have our reality distorted; things pop out that frighten us; we get lost; weird voices threaten to do us harm—and we call this the fun house.

We stand in line for an hour to ride the roller coaster, all the while saying "Why am I doing this? I'm scared." The ride takes five minutes and we regret every second of it. As soon as it's over, someone is bound to say, "Let's do it again!"

We compete in tossing, throwing and shooting games *we know* are rigged—struggling to win a prize that we wouldn't want even if we got it.

We visit the freak show, and are simultaneously appalled and fascinated by the extremes of nature. We exit feeling terribly normal—and grateful for it. (Meanwhile, the freaks make their living just sitting there being watched by boobs like us.)

We leave the amusement park—sunburned, slightly ill from the dreadful food, and exhausted—saying, "What a wonderful day!"

Or, consider a movie. It could be full of romance, action, adventure, betrayal, suspense, terror, absurdity, thrills, or chills—and we jump right in. We enjoy every moment of it.

So why don't we enjoy every moment of life? If life is one great entertainment, why don't we know it? In fact, it seems a major taboo to enjoy ourselves when things are going "bad." Why is this?

Life is like an overlong drama
through which we sit
being nagged by
the vague memories
of having read the reviews.

JOHN UPDIKE

The answer might be found in a story, which we first heard from Alan Watts. Imagine that the ultimate entertainment device had been invented—the Entertainertron. Film, television, laser discs, virtual reality and all the rest had reached such sophisticated proportions, that the illusion was complete. We could see, feel, hear, smell, taste and touch so fully that we would be convinced that it was *really* happening to us.

With this device, we could imagine ourselves going anywhere, doing anything, experiencing whatever we wanted. First, we would probably do all the fun stuff— have passionate romances with one perfect lover after another, eat sumptuous feasts, live in expensive mansions, drive exotic cars, win beauty contests, be adored by the entire world and so on.

The good stuff would be endless. After a little while, however, we might begin to feel a little bored. After a lot longer, we might feel a lot bored. To keep things interesting, we might begin to take an occasional "walk on the wild side."

Knowing that we could always imagine our way out again—in the same way we know we can always get up and leave the movie theater or push the stop button on the VCR—we could explore some rather intense experiences from the darker side of life.

After enough time, we would have explored all the dark, wicked, evil, depraved aspects of life, and these— being completely familiar—might become boring too. What to do?

Ah, enter the New Improved model—the Entertainertron Plus! The new element of the Entertainertron Plus was a button marked "Forget." It could be set for any period of time—and for that period of time we would forget that the adventure we were imagining was merely an entertainment. We would think it was *real*. No matter what we did or what we thought, it would still continue to appear real until the amount of time we had set on the Forget switch had expired.

Oh don't the days
seem lank and long
When all goes right
and nothing goes wrong,
And isn't your life extremely flat
With nothing whatever to grumble at!

W. S. GILBERT

Oh, isn't life
a terrible thing,
thank God?

DYLAN THOMAS

This, of course, added a whole new element of excitement, involvement and, well, *reality* to the journeys of our imagination. We'd probably begin by setting the timer for short periods—one minute, five minutes, an hour—but as time went on, we'd probably set the timer for longer and longer periods.

In this future time, perhaps medical science had increased the life span by hundreds of years. This means we could take our Entertainertron Plus on some long and exotic journeys. We could set the forgetfulness button to 30 years, 50 years, 70 years, 90 years. For the span of an entire lifetime (as we know lifetimes now) we could forget that we were lost in our own imagination.

After doing this for a number of years, however, we began growing bored with the lives that we made up. Even the Forget button wasn't as exciting as before. We wanted something more. Something new. Something different. Something exciting and completely unpredictable. We wanted, of course, the Entertainertron II!

In addition to the Forget button, the Entertainertron II had yet another button. This button was marked "Surprise." According to the Entertainertron II instruction manual, when we hit the Surprise button, something completely unexpected would happen, for an undetermined length of time, and while it was happening we would completely forget that we were really in the Entertainertron II.

After a quick bite to eat and a trip to the rest room (this adventure might take a while), we put on the Entertainertron II, held our breath, pushed the Surprise button...and we found ourselves where we are right now, thinking what we're thinking right now, feeling what we're feeling right now, with everything in our life precisely the way it is right now—reading this book.

Did you ever go to a horror film as a child and spend the entire time hiding under the seat? Or, perhaps you were more sophisticated, and simply closed your eyes during the juicier parts. Perhaps you then went home think-

*Everyone
is in
the best seat.*

JOHN CAGE

ing, "That wasn't so bad. In fact, that was fun. I wish I had kept my eyes open a little more."

Perhaps that's how we'll feel about this life when it's over. Perhaps we'll look back and wish that we had *experienced* more of it. Perhaps we'll wish we hadn't avoided, run away from and numbed ourselves to so many incidents of life. Perhaps we'll regret using a good portion of our energy trying to make life—which is essentially a roller coaster—into a smooth, flat, bump-free train ride.

So often we say, when complaining of a movie we don't like, "It went on and on, and nothing happened." How many of us spend a great deal of our energy trying to arrange life so that "nothing happens."

Nothing adventured, nothing attained.

And what part—what role—do we, individually, play in this entertainment of life? We are, of course, the star. Everyone else is merely our supporting cast. (The trouble is, the supporting cast is under the delusion that each of *them* is the star. It's one of the challenges that you, as the *genuine* star, must rise to. Consider it one of life's running jokes.)

To play our role well, we must explore all the potential for drama and comedy we have within us. We must explore our dark side and our light side; our Benito Mussolini and our Mother Theresa, our evil and our good.

Once we realize that all the roles are inside us, we can enjoy playing them all—the extremes and everything in between. We can play the lover and the liar, the prince and the pauper, the tragedian and the clown. Some days will be melodrama, other days will be farce, most days will be both.

And, with certain intimates, we will take off the make-up and swap stories about the ups, the downs, the highs, the lows, the agonies of defeat and the thrills of victory that are all part of an entertainer's life.

I'm only the Pope,
what can I do?

POPE JOHN XXIII

Don't Get Serious on Yourself

Did you ever sign a letter "Seriously yours"? Probably not. "Sincerely yours" is as formal as we usually get—even in a business environment. If we don't become any more formal than "Sincerely yours" in a business letter, why should we become more formal than that with ourselves?

The key to enjoying the show—the entertainment—of life, and to playing your character(s) in that entertainment, is to get fully involved—but not to take it all too seriously. Life is a sexually transmitted terminal illness. You can consider that either terribly terrible or terribly funny. However you see it is not going to *change* it, but it will change the way you *feel* about it.

Just as we can see a rose as a beautiful flower with a thorny stem or a dangerously thorned stick with a flower on one end, so too can we see life as either a comedy with occasional tragic moments or a tragedy with occasional comic relief. The way we see it is our choice—there's plenty of evidence to support either interpretation.

How we view life begins with how we view ourselves. If we take ourselves too seriously, life will be a serious place, indeed. If we take ourselves lightly, life will become lighter.

One of the greatest gifts of life—and one we take for granted so often—is laughter. What a barren and unbearable place this would be without laughter. When we count our blessings and make lists of things to be grateful for, let's not forget laughter.

And let's not forget about laughter's biological twin—crying. Tears not only provide a release and comfort during times of pain; they also provide an eloquent voice for moments of deep joy and gratitude.

Both laughter and tears feel wonderful. They only don't feel good when we resist them.

*Don't take yourself
too seriously.
And don't be too serious about
not taking yourself
too seriously.*

HOWARD OGDEN

Did you ever notice the source of our funniest stories, the life anecdotes our friends want us to tell again and again? (At least they *ask* us to tell them again and again—that's what makes those dear people our friends.) Usually the basis for a funny story is an incident which—at the time it happened—made us miserable.

The more frustrating and arrogant the hotel clerk, the ruder the waiter, the worse the turbulence and the longer the airplane circled the field before landing, the more flagrantly unfaithful our lover, the more dismal the sex, the more incompetent the doctor, the more sadistic the dentist, the more boring the concert, the more dishonest the lawyer, the more deceitful the politician, the more intricate the red tape, the more painful the tax audit, the more inconveniencing the car theft, the drunker the cab driver, the more confusing the instruction book, the more catastrophic the dinner party, the greater the rejection and the longer the sentence, the funnier we'll make it.

Knowing this, the next time we're involved in a frustrating situation, all we have to do is take a deep breath and tell ourselves, "Relax. This is funny." If we're going to laugh at it later—and we will, we will—we might as well laugh at it now.

If it'll be funny then, it's funny now.

If the only difference between finding something funny and finding something frustrating is the *time* that passed, we can learn to shorten the time from anathema to anecdote. What would normally take six weeks to become a good story, we can make into a good story within three weeks; then two, one, a day, an hour, five minutes, while it's happening.

It's back to our old friends altitude and attitude.

Not that we should laugh at *everything* in life—but then, on the other hand, why not?

*My choice early in life
was either to be a piano player
in a whorehouse
or a politician.
And to tell the truth,
there's hardly any difference.*

HARRY S TRUMAN

So What?

Werner Erhard was listening one day to a woman recount—in great dramatic detail—the tragedies of her life. After a while, the woman paused, fully expecting Werner to become involved in her troubles—to brilliantly analyze her plight and to help in her struggle to solve her problems.

Instead, he looked at her and simply said, "So what?"

The question caught the woman off guard. She reviewed all that she had told him in this new light. "Yes," she finally said, "So what?" With this one question, both her attitude shifted and her altitude lifted.

"So what?" is a question that can help us enjoy life. We can use it to feel lighter, less attached to the burdens of life, to free ourselves from the wishes, wants, desires—and especially problems—other people want us to make our own.

Naturally, when other people are telling us their troubles—hoping to find a new recruit in their army of agony—we don't have to say "So what?" out loud. We can sit and say it quietly to ourselves—all the while maintaining a pained expression on our face and nodding sympathetically. (Oh, if Oscars were only given for life performances!)

The same applies to our own life and problems. Naturally, we will feel some guilt asking ourselves questions that make us feel better about our problems. Culturally, most of us are trained only to ask questions that make us feel *worse* about problems. ("You went to bed with her/him?" "How many times?" "Is she/he better than I am?" "Do you have any videos?" "Can I see them?")

One of the great let's-make-it-worse-if-we-possibly-can questions most of us have mastered is "What if?"

"What if the plane crashes?" "What if I don't have any flight insurance?" "What if I buy flight insurance and the plane doesn't crash?" "What if the plane crashes, and I

*A man does not
have to be an angel
in order to be a saint.*

ALBERT SCHWEITZER

don't die, but I am hurt, and while the ambulance is rushing me to the hospital it hits another car and then I'm killed, does my flight insurance cover that?" "What if they don't have my special meal on the plane?" "What if they have my special meal on the plane, and the plane crashes before I can eat it?" "What if they have my special meal on the plane and somebody else pretends to be me and eats it before I can get to it?" "What if my baggage doesn't get put on this flight?" "What if my baggage is put on another flight and that flight crashes?" "What if *both* planes crash?"

The list goes on and on.

Harold H. Bloomfield, M.D., prescribes a simple solution to the "What if?" problems of life: add the word *so* to each "what if?" "So what if..." "What if I run out of gas?" becomes "So what if I run out of gas?" "What if they don't like me?" becomes "So what if they don't like me?" "What if I make a mistake and look like a fool?" becomes "So what if I make a mistake and look like a fool?"

Yes, of course, there are situations of genuine concern that require action—sometimes immediate action, sometimes gradual and consistent action—but these situations are relatively few when compared to the number of situations we worry about.

Which situations to do something about and which ones to "So what?" about? Obviously, if the survival of our physical bodies is at stake, it would be reasonable to do something about it. *Soon.* If it's something connected to our big dream, that, too, is something to take action on. Combining those two is probably enough action to fill a day. Everything else becomes "So what?" as we let the rest of the world go by.

Forget goals.
Value the process.

JIM BOUTON

After a time,
you may find that
having is not
so pleasing a thing,
after all, as wanting.
It is not logical,
but it is often true.

SPOCK
"STAR TREK"

Enjoy the Climb

What are we going to do when we achieve our current big dream? Find another big dream, of course. What do mountain climbers do when they reach the top of a mountain? Find another mountain.

Although the top of the mountain is enjoyable, if that's the only time we enjoy ourselves, we're not going to spend much time enjoying. It's a good idea, then, to learn to enjoy the climb.

So often, people firmly established at the height of success will look back on the time of "struggle" as "the happiest years of my life." In other words, winning is fun—that's the purpose of the game—but enjoyment, for the most part, is to be found in the *playing*.

Enjoy, too, the climb mates. As you pursue your goal, you will no doubt find others traveling on parallel paths. For as long as your paths run parallel, enjoy them. When your paths no longer run parallel, know that—after you round the next bend—there will be other people making their climb on newly parallel paths.

Stay focused on the goal, and enjoy the journey.

*Lots of times
you have to pretend
to join a parade in which
you're not really interested
in order to get
where you're going.*

GEORGE MORLEY

Co-operation

In intelligence and military circles, the organization of personnel and resources is often called an *operation*. In the same way, the mobilization of our personal resources is also an operation. We might call it Operation Big Dream.

It's important to remember that all the people who might get in the way of our operation—by using resources we want to use, by directly opposing us, or by simply being in the way—are really *not* the enemy. They are simply people who are mounting their own operations—their own Operation Big Dream. (The biggest mobilization most people ever get involved in, however, is Operation Wait and See. They are a hindrance primarily because they are not moving toward any specific goal, but merely wandering around the playing field.)

Whatever other people's operations—be they Operation Big Dream or Operation Wait and See—when our Operation Big Dream comes close to theirs, we can move into a state of friction (also known as battle) or move into a state of co-operation.

We suggest co-operation.

Like oncoming cars passing each other on a narrow road, sometimes we pull over; sometimes they pull over; sometimes we back up; sometimes they back up. It's a state of cooperation. We do it in a friendly, cordial way— even if it means momentarily stopping or even backing up. Soon we're back on the road, heading toward our goal.

If the other car *demands* the right of way, yield to it. In a true state of cooperation, we'd hardly be aware of its demand: We would be looking for a way that we could clear the road so that both cars could pass. If we stubbornly stand our ground at each and every challenge to our forward motion, before long we will have consumed all of our resources, and the entire operation will grind to a halt.

Mr. Salter's side
of the conversation
was limited to expressions
of assent. When Lord Copper
was right he said,
"Definitely, Lord Copper";
when he was wrong,
"Up to a point."
"Let me see,
what's the name of the place
I mean? Capital of Japan?
Yokohama, isn't it?"
"Up to a point, Lord Copper."
"And Hong Kong belongs
to us, doesn't it?"
"Definitely, Lord Copper."

EVELYN WAUGH

Take a lesson from the river as it twists its way around boulders, hills and mountains, winding its way to the sea. The goal is the sea. The river does not "demand" to travel in a straight line "because a straight line is the shortest distance between two points." Old Man River cooperates with Old Mother Nature, and both benefit from each other's co-operations.

Or, think of a quarterback running to make a touchdown. The idea is to reach the end zone. He gets no extra points for obtaining his goal via the shortest possible route. He will go over, under, around and through the opposing team. He cooperates with them by skillfully avoiding them. He does not stop to do battle with each opposing team member. He continues toward his goal.

And so it is we can move toward our goal—our big dream. It won't be one relentless straight line as we plow unceasingly toward our goal. It'll be two steps forward, one step back, one step to the left, four steps to the right, two more steps forward.

As we begin pursuing a dream, we may be more like a stream—we must concern ourselves with every little rock and boulder on our path. As we continue on—gathering strength and resources—a boulder we would have had to go around before we can simply go over. We barely notice it. We cannot, however, as a stream, expect to have the power to overcome obstacles that a river has. Quite often, the highest form of cooperation is avoiding confrontation.

Never fear: that which we *must* confront will present itself to us, again and again, until we do confront it.

We are not saying to live the life of ostriches. We are saying that with Operation Big Dream—as with all major operations—resources are limited and should be conserved at every opportunity. One of the best forms of conservation is cooperation.

*Faith is the bird
that feels the light
and sings when
the dawn is still dark.*

RABINDRANATH TAGORE

Faithing

Many people use faith in the same way they use hope—believing that something will get better, then taking no action to improve it. Here we agree with St. Paul, "Faith without works is dead."

That's why we use the word *faithing*. The *ing* adds *action* to the concept of *faith*.

When we have faith in action, we don't even have to think about it. We have faith that when we put our foot on the brake, our car will stop. We don't have to say affirmations or statements of faith, "I have faith in the braking ability of my car." We act, and our faith is rewarded.

If, however, we haven't been properly maintaining our car, we need *lots* of what people commonly call faith—which is really another form of fear. We need *faith* that our car will start, move and stop every time we want it to start, move and stop. Another word for this is *worry*.

True faith is knowing—knowing to the point of forgetting we know—that our car will start, move and stop.

The process of faithing, then, might be called "preventive maintenance." Through our action—mental, emotional, and physical—we prepare. Our preparation is so complete that, when it comes time to use our resources in the direction of our dream, we don't even have to think about it—it simply takes place. Our knowing that it will work—within a reasonable latitude—is the fruit of our faithing.

Like a master of martial arts, when we are fully prepared we are seldom challenged. When we are challenged, we rise to the occasion with ease and grace. The result of faithing—of proper preparation—then, is *confidence*.

With confidence, we need not worry about every this and that. We can relax and enjoy the moment. We know that, when necessary, we will rise to the occasion.

Just as Noah didn't worry when it started raining, or the little pig who built his house of bricks didn't worry

Man: *Do you belong here?*

Fonzie: *I belong everywhere.*

"HAPPY DAYS"

when the wolf began huffing and puffing, so we too—with proper faithing—can relax and enjoy the rain on the roof and the wind at the door.

She had that
indefinable beauty
that comes from happiness,
enthusiasm, success
—a beauty that is nothing
more or less than
a harmony of temperament
and circumstances.

FLAUBERT

Enthusiasm

Enthusiasm is a wonderful word. It means, literally, "one with the energy of God (or the divine)." *En* (to be one with), and *theos* (God or the divine).

When we are pursuing our dream, our heart's desire, something we are passionate about, it's natural to feel enthusiastic about it. When we feel enthusiastic, work—no matter what the work may be—becomes a joy.

We are, however, culturally conditioned not to enjoy work. "My father taught me how to work," said Abraham Lincoln, "but not how to enjoy it." In order to overcome this unfortunate bit of cultural conditioning, we need to encourage enthusiasm.

Encourage is a beautiful word, too. It means "to be one with the energy of the heart." *En* (to be one with), and *cour* (French for *heart)*. The simplest way of saying this is: Love it.

As we said before, more than just a feeling, loving is a decision—a choice. We *choose* to bring the qualities of loving to the situation at hand. These qualities differ for each of us, as each of us has a different definition of love, but usually they encompass ideas such as devotion, affection, loyalty, fondness, adoration and delight.

When we approach the present moment with the attitude of loving, we encourage enthusiasm. The divine energy flows through us, and we no longer have to consciously *choose* to be devoted, affectionate, loyal, fond, adoring and delightful—we simply are.

*Man must choose
whether to be rich in things
or in the freedom to use them.*

IVAN ILLICH

Freedom Is Found in Discipline

Most people think freedom is doing whatever they want, whenever they want. This is not freedom. This is fanciful indulgence.

Indulgence because it is simply exercising a whim of iron, which seldom leads to satisfaction. Fanciful because—even if you had infinite amounts of money—the laws of time, space, and human existence simply don't permit us to have whatever we want whenever we want.

If you wanted to be in Morocco *right now,* no amount of money or anything else is going to get you there *right now.* Even with your own private Concorde parked at the side door, you're still several hours from Morocco. (Just in case you happen to be reading this book in Morocco, please substitute "Montana" for "Morocco" in that last example.) (What are you doing in Morocco, anyway?)

Freedom is found in *discipline.*

Discipline, unfortunately, is a word that's gotten a lot of bad press. It's been used too often by too many people (parents, teachers, bosses) who want *us* to toe the mark in order to get what *they* want.

The word *discipline* comes from the word *disciple*—a devoted student and follower. If we look at rules as tools—guidelines for achieving our goal—we can study and follow rules with such devotion (discipline) that we become free to live our dream.

Rules, then, become not just the road map we follow to get to a destination, but the road itself.

When we know the rules of the road—what highway to take, where to turn off, how to drive a car, keeping the car well maintained and supplied with gas—we are then free to enjoy the journey. We can chat with friends, watch the scenery, listen to tapes, play music, sing, and even make telephone calls. (Ah, isn't technology wonderful?)

To get to that state of enjoyment, however, took a great deal of work—of discipline. For most teenagers,

*Most people
put off till tomorrow
that which they should
have done yesterday.*

EDGAR WATSON HOWE

however, learning to drive a car is far from a tedious task—it's exciting, thrilling and something we'd fantasize about for years before it happened.

So, too, we can approach all we need to learn in order to move freely toward our big dream with the same degree of enthusiasm, joy, and excitement. We become the disciple of our life, our goal, our path.

In this, we find freedom.

*I have a memory
like an elephant.
In fact, elephants
often consult me.*

NOEL COWARD

Remember the Good

So many good things happen to us each day, each hour, each minute.

In the next minute, for example, your heart will keep beating, your lungs will keep breathing, your senses will keep functioning and you will read lots of words in this wonderful book. (False modesty was never high on our list of achievements. Besides, if you've gotten this far in the book, you must think it's at least *marginally* wonderful. Or, perhaps you're just reading to see how much worse it can get. Either way, we don't think you'll be disappointed. Is a minute up yet? Are you a fast reader? Well, it took us about a minute to write this, so we're going to move on.)

We'd like to suggest an even more wonderful book to you. It's one that you'd write yourself, day by day. It would be your own personal book of lists. The lists would be made up of all the good that happens to you and all the good you do.

We, of course, don't mean *all* the good that happens to you and *all* the good you do. If that were the case, you'd be doing nothing but writing. As we pointed out before, the blessings already are, and they never seem to stop.

The book we're suggesting you write, then, would be the highlights of the good that happens to you and the good you do—*The Best of the Good.*

Get a blank book of some kind, and start writing down the good. Spend some time each day—perhaps just before bed—remembering the good that happened to you and the good that you did during that day. Write it in your book. (Which you might choose to call your "good book.")

These need not be elaborate journal entries or descriptions. A few words will do. "Saw a beautiful sunrise." "Surpassed my sales quota." "Had dinner with _____." "Visited _____ in the hospital." "Saw a great movie." And so on.

*We may allow ourselves
a brief period of rejoicing.*

WINSTON CHURCHILL
ON THE DAY WORLD WAR II ENDED

Remembering the good each day and writing it down is only the first step in remembering the good. The second step is to review, on a regular basis, your entire good book.

As you read through it, you'll remember all the good that happened to you over the weeks, months and, eventually, years.

The amount of good in our lives is overwhelming. When we see it listed in front of us—in black and white—it begins to overwhelm even the programming determined to convince us "My life is no good," "Nothing good ever happens to me," or "I can't do anything right."

Remembering the good lets us feel good about ourselves. Another word for feeling good about ourselves is self-esteem. We begin to esteem ourselves—to place a high value on ourselves, to respect ourselves, to prize, honor, admire and appreciate ourselves.

All it takes is remembering the good, and the technique for that is writing it down.

Take the time to develop your self-esteem.

You're worth it.

*To feel themselves
in the presence
of true greatness
many men find it
necessary only to be alone.*

TOM MASSON

Love Yourself

One of the biggest—and silliest—taboos in our culture is the taboo against loving ourselves. The moment we express any degree of positive self-regard, we are labeled as vain, egocentric, self-centered (so whose self do they want us to be centered around?), stuck up, stuck on ourselves, and just plain stuck.

Jesus' admonition to love our neighbor as ourselves is good advice. The problem is, since we treat ourselves so poorly, even if we love our neighbor *better* than ourselves, it's still not very much. Hence, the prevailing condition of tension, competition, deception, and the "get what you can while the getting's good and get out" attitude in human relationships.

In case you need to see it in print, here it is: It's not just OK to love yourself, it's *great*. It's terrific if you are the most important person in your life. It's just fine if, when you hear the words "love, honor and cherish," you think first of yourself. "To love yourself," said Oscar Wilde, "is the beginning of a lifelong romance."

Our culture seems built on the myth that until you find a wonderful person to love—who happens to love you back—you are not a whole human being, your life is not complete, your "better half" is missing.

Such nonsense. You already *have* a wonderful person to love. You already eat with this person every meal, bathe with this person every bath, and sleep with this person every night.

This person, of course, is you.

When we say "love yourself" we don't just mean feel good about yourself—although that's certainly a part of it. Feeling good about yourself is self-esteem, and we discussed an important technique for enhancing that in the previous chapter. We're also talking about loving yourself in the sense of *choosing* to do the right thing for you in any given situation, no matter *how* you feel.

So Harry says,
"You don't like me any more. Why not?"
And he says, "Because you've got
so terribly pretentious."
And Harry says, "Pretentious? <u>Moi?</u>"

JOHN CLEESE AND CONNIE BOOTH

Cliff Claven: You ever heard
of the lone wolf, Carla?
The lone wolf, <u>c'est moi.</u>
A man by himself, needing no one.
I touch no one, no one touches me.
I am a rock. I am an island.

Carla Tortelli: You am a boob.

"CHEERS"

If we don't feel like exercising, and we know exercising is the best thing for us to do at that moment, we love ourselves enough to exercise anyway. If we want the extra piece of chocolate cake, but know the extra piece of chocolate cake would not be the best thing for us at that moment, we don't eat the chocolate cake, whether we feel like eating it or not. If there are 500 envelopes to stuff that might get us one step closer to our goal, and we don't *feel* like stuffing 500 envelopes, we love ourselves enough to stuff the envelopes anyway.

As we said before, loving is more than just a feeling, it's a decision—a choice.

But we don't just pull out loving as a whip to crack when there's something we don't want to do. Loving is also arranging time each day to do some things we genuinely enjoy—bicycling, reading, watching videos, time with friends. Even if it's only for a few minutes on very busy days, we take time to do something we genuinely enjoy.

Part of loving yourself is accepting the discomfort of moving through taboos. Feeling good is a taboo in our culture, and feeling good *about yourself* is an even greater taboo. It's taboo upon taboo. ("Taboo Upon Taboo"—it sounds like a 1940s song by Xavier Cugat, doesn't it?) Accepting the taboo and feeling good about ourselves, feeling better and better about ourselves each day—even though it may be uncomfortable—is an important part of loving ourselves.

Loving ourselves also includes breaking bad habits, habits such as focusing upon the negative in any given situation. When we learn the habit of focusing upon the positive, the natural result is happiness.

Isn't happiness a gift you'd like to give to someone you love? Focus on the good around you—right now—and happiness is a gift you'll give yourself. (For lots more information on breaking the habit of negative thinking, please see our book, *You Can't Afford the Luxury of a Negative Thought.*)

He is his own best friend,
and takes delight in privacy;
whereas the man
of no virtue or ability
is his own worst enemy
and is afraid of solitude.

ARISTOTLE

Like any love affair, our love of ourselves will have its ups and downs, its good times and bad, its fights and its reconciliations. That's to be expected. Enjoy the entire process. Sometimes it's a sitcom, sometimes it's a foreign film with subtitles and sometimes it's an action-adventure flick.

Remember forgiveness. That's just another way of saying remember love.

Pursue your goal. To live your heart's desire is one of the most loving things you can do.

Be grateful. You already are living a heart's desire you had at an earlier time.

Enjoy the moment. Give yourself the gift of the precious present.

You are a walking, talking, living, breathing miracle. Marvel in the miracle of yourself. Astonish yourself. Be awe-full with yourself. Wipe away the cobwebs of the cultural conditioning that tell you you're not good enough—that you're not worthy.

You are more than good enough. You are more than worthy. You are incredible.

And very, very precious.

Anticipate charity by
preventing poverty;
assist the reduced fellowman,
either by a considerable gift,
or a sum of money,
or by teaching him a trade,
or by putting him
in the way of business,
so that he may earn
an honest livelihood,
and not be forced
to the dreadful alternative
of holding out his hand
for charity. This is
the highest step and
the summit of
charity's golden ladder.

MAIMONIDES MOSES BEN MAIMON
1135–1204

Service

When we love ourselves, we notice the most remarkable occurrence—our love fulfills us very quickly. What was once an empty cup that we would take from person to person begging for a drop of kindness, compassion and caring soon becomes—through being kind, compassionate and caring to ourselves—filled to overflowing.

Our cup runneth over.

What to do with the overflow? Like being given 500 gallons of ice cream on a hot day with no freezer in sight—we give it away.

Taking such good care of ourselves that we have an abundance of love to give to others is called service.

Service is one of life's deepest joys.

Doing for others, alas, has gathered something of a bad name for two very good reasons. First, too often people have done good for others when they should have been doing good for themselves. Hence, service is sometimes confused with self-sacrifice, self-denial, and "giving until it hurts." We don't consider this service. We consider this silly.

Second, service has quite often fallen into the hands of the "do-gooders." These are people who don't want to give, they want to reform. "See how wonderful I am to fill your need," says the do-gooder, "that's because I believe this certain thing. If you believe this certain thing, too, you will be wonderful and happy and go around doing good things for other people just like wonderful, happy me." Service with strings is not service—it's manipulation.

Service is giving with absolutely no desire to get anything in return. The good feeling we get by being of service is more than enough payment.

Service is also an affirmation of our wealth. It is saying, "Thank you, I have more than I need." This is one of the most profound and powerful affirmations of wealth in existence. (We'll explore that concept further in the chap-

*Noble deeds and
hot baths are
the best cures
for depression.*

DODIE SMITH

*'Tis more blessed
to give than to receive;
for example,
wedding presents.*

H. L. MENCKEN

ter "Seeding and Tithing.") By demonstrating that we have more than we need through service, we not only affirm the wealth that we have, but we open wide the door to receive more.

Where do we serve? Whom do we serve? All we need is to be open to service, and the need will find us. It may be a phone call from a friend, an article in the paper, a person we meet in the course of business, a park full of litter, or a homeless person on the street.

There's an old saying, "When the student is ready, the teacher appears," and its corollary, "When the teacher is ready, the student appears." It is equally true that "When the server is ready, the service appears."

What do we give? We give of what we have. Sometimes it's money, sometimes it's information, sometimes it's a smile, sometimes it's an encouraging word, sometimes it's sending flowers, sometimes it's our talent, and sometimes it's the nitty gritty work of physically jumping in and getting the job done.

And let's be completely honest about this: We serve for purely selfish reasons—we serve because it *feels so good*. Knowing this, when you're in need, one of the greatest acts of service you can do is allow yourself to be served.

It's hard, then, during true acts of service, telling the server from the served, just as, in a love affair, it's hard telling the lover from the loved.

For anything worth having
one must pay the price;
and the price is always work,
patience, love, self-sacrifice.

JOHN BURROUGHS

PART FOUR

GETTING MORE OF WHAT YOU WANT

It might seem as though this would be a point of major transition: From this point on we stop *enjoying* and start *obtaining*. "Abandon all pleasure," you might expect us to say at this point; "there's no time for it!"

As you've been reading along in the book, however, you may have noticed that we are of the opinion that fulfilling your heart's desire—your big dream—is not an unenjoyable act.

Sure, it's a lot of hard work, and yes, of course, it means forgoing a lot of momentary pleasures, but pursuing one's goal and living one's dream have more built-in enjoyment and—especially—satisfaction than a life devoted merely to pleasure. In fact, a life devoted solely to pleasure, that does not include any portion of one's big dream, is a good working definition of hell.

In this section—yes, finally—we are going to discuss how to get more money. This section is full of techniques on how to get more of the spendable stuff. We'll look at the limiting beliefs we have about money in our culture, the expansive beliefs, how to eliminate the former and enhance the latter.

Let's start by seeing if money is what you *really* want.

My father worked
for the same firm
for twelve years.
They fired him.
They replaced him
with a tiny gadget this big.
It does everything
that my father does,
only it does it much better.
The depressing thing is
my mother ran out
and bought one.

WOODY ALLEN

Are You Sure It's *Money* You Really Want?

Because money is such a powerful symbol of energy, we often fall into the trap of thinking that if we want something, we need money in order to get it.

Quite often, when we *think* we want money, what we really want are either *resources* or *experiences*.

If we want a resource—let's say transportation—we might automatically think, "Oh, I need some money to buy a car." Yes, money would buy us a car. But by thinking money is the *only* way to get the transportation we need, we limit not only our thinking and creativity, but also the ways in which our desire for transportation can be fulfilled.

Someone might, for example, loan us a car. Or, perhaps we learn that public transportation will take us everywhere we need to go—and we get to catch up on our reading at the same time. Or, the eccentric next door neighbor puts her chauffeured limousine at our disposal. (Why not?)

The same is true of *experiences*. Let's say the experience we want is foreign travel. We might think, "I'd better save my money so that I can travel to foreign countries." Yes, money will pay for foreign travel. Yet there are other ways. You could get a job as a traveling companion, join the Peace Corps, fall in love with a diplomat, or—more to the point—have a diplomat fall in love with *you*.

When we expand the methods by which our desires can be fulfilled—including ways we haven't even thought of—we also expand the ways in which the Universe can fulfill those desires.

The Universe has so many, many ways to fulfill desires. Often people limit themselves by saying, "I need money! Money, money and *only* money will fulfill my needs." That's like saying "Caviar, caviar and *only* caviar will fill my hunger." Yes, caviar would probably do it, but

The love of money as a possession—
as distinguished from
the love of money
as a means to the enjoyments
and realities of life—
will be recognized for what it is,
a somewhat disgusting morbidity,
one of those semi-criminal,
semi-pathological propensities
which one hands over
with a shudder
to the specialists in mental disease.

JOHN MAYNARD KEYNES

so would several thousand other foods. Furthermore, caviar is somewhat scarcer than, say, hot dogs. From the standpoint of sheer availability, it's easier to satisfy hunger through hot dogs than caviar.

The same is true of money. Because so many people *think* that *only* money will fill their needs, money is relatively scarce. *Resources* and *experiences,* on the other hand, are abundant.

No, they're not always free—you'll probably have to work for them. But you'll probably have to do less work directly pursuing resources and experiences than it would take to get the money and buy them. As they say in those television ads for discount stores, "Eliminate the middle man!"

When we "eliminate the middle man" (money) and go directly after the resources and experiences we want, it's often easier—and less trouble—to get them.

Take a look at your big dream, your heart's desire. Some of it will probably require money, yes, but much of it—perhaps more than you originally thought—can be fulfilled by going directly after the resources and experiences to fulfill your dream.

Another way of saying this is that we'll have a lot more *opportunities* to fulfill our dream if we expand our thinking to include methods other than money. We begin to see opportunities where we never saw opportunities before.

Opportunity, of course, is one of the attributes of wealth. By looking for *opportunities*—and not just money—we begin to realize how much more wealth we already have, how much wealthier we already are. If we remember to appreciate and be grateful for that newly discovered wealth, we continue the cycle of expansion, which allows us to get even more.

That said, let's take some time looking at how to get more of that *specific* opportunity—money.

*The only point
in making money is,
you can tell some big shot
where to go.*

HUMPHREY BOGART

If You Want More Money...

There are so many cultural beliefs about money pulling on us at any one time, it's no wonder most people feel confused. The amount of money we currently have is a direct result of the limiting (negative) and the expansive (positive) beliefs we have bought about money.

That *we* "bought" them is important. Just because the culture has a belief about money, doesn't mean we have to buy it. When we do buy it, however, it's ours—until we decide to get rid of it.

If we want to have more money, there are two fundamental things we must do:

1. Reduce the number of limiting (negative) beliefs we have about money; and

2. Increase the number of expansive (positive) beliefs we have about money.

We implement these two methods in a variety of ways. Primarily, however, we *actively* challenge the validity of the limiting beliefs, and we affirm the wisdom of the expansive beliefs.

Let's start by looking at some of the limiting beliefs we have about money in our culture.

I find all this money
a considerable burden.

J. PAUL GETTY

Why It's Amazing
We Ever Have Any Money

Take a look at some of these limiting beliefs about money. See if you—even to a slight degree—"bought" any of them.

> It takes money to make money.
>
> Poor is pure.
>
> Money is dirty ("filthy rich").
>
> People resent rich people.
>
> Wealthy people are snobbish.
>
> It is easier for a camel to go through the eye of a needle than for a rich man to enter the kingdom of God.
>
> Money is the root of all evil.
>
> You need training and education to get money.
>
> Money can't buy you love.
>
> You can't take it with you.
>
> Money is too much responsibility.
>
> It takes hard work to make money.
>
> Money isn't everything.
>
> The best things in life are free.
>
> Money isn't spiritual or holy.

Whew! It's easy to see how believing even a few of those not only keeps money away from us, but might even make us want to get rid of the money we have.

Let's challenge those limiting beliefs.

*Money never made
a fool of anybody;
it only shows 'em up.*

ELBERT HUBBARD

Challenging the Limiting Beliefs about Money

Let's take a look at each of the limiting beliefs in the last chapter—which represent our culture's primary limiting beliefs about money—and ask ourselves one fundamental question about each of them: "Is this true?"

Something need not be true, of course, to control our lives. It is only necessary that we *believe* something is true for it to have an effect upon our lives. For centuries, humanity believed the world was flat and behaved as though that were true, limiting exploration and expansion. The world is not flat. The world never was flat. The belief, however, that the world *was* flat made people behave as though it were.

The same is true of our beliefs about money—if we *believe* a limiting statement is true, it will limit us. The first step is to find out whether it's true or not. The second step is to stop believing it's true, if it's not. Let's take the first step now.

In order to prove that something is not true for each person—and, consequently, not necessarily true about us—we only need to find *one* exception to every "rule." If someone else was number one, we can be number two.

It takes money to make money. It takes a dream, a commitment to that dream, and the relentless, passionate pursuit of that dream until it is realized to make *anything* in this world—including money. There is story after story of people who started with nothing and made great sums of money. There are also stories of people who started with large sums of money and wound up on skid row. If you expand your container of wealth—and money is the energy you need to make your dream come true—money will come to you.

Poor is pure. Money is dirty. Being poor is intrinsically no purer—neither in mind, body, emotions nor physical surroundings—than being rich. In fact, money can

Success didn't spoil me;
I've always been insufferable.

FRAN LEBOWITZ

help make things purer if that's what a person wants. Some of the grinding poverty we've seen has nothing to do with purity. Not that a poor person must be impure or that a rich person can't be impure (on whatever level you define impurity). It's just that one's purity has little to do with the amount of money one has.

People resent rich people. Sure, some people resent rich people. Some people resent that "The Star Spangled Banner" is difficult to sing. Some people resent it when it rains. Some people resent people who don't resent anything. Those who want to resent will do so, and they will also find—for them—the *perfect* reasons to do so. Because resentful people are often jealous people, being jealous of other people's money is a perfect excuse to resent them. It's not a logical excuse, or a *reasonable* excuse, you understand, but it is a *perfect* excuse.

On the other hand, some people *respect* rich people. They may have their perfect reasons that are no more reasonable or logical than the reasons of those who resent rich people, but, nevertheless, there are those who worship the rich. Not getting money because others may resent you for having it is a form of worshiping the god of other people's opinion. This is one of the strangest of the "strange gods" people sacrifice their heart's desires to. The fact is, some people are going to resent you no matter *what* you do—or don't do. You might as well follow your dream and be resented for following it rather than being resented for some other reason.

Wealthy people are snobbish. Some wealthy people are snobby, and some poor people are snobby. Some wealthy people are down to earth, and some poor people are down to earth. Being snobby has to do with complacency, prejudice and unchallenged bad habits—not money. Snobby people are punished by their own snobbery, just as those who resent snobs are punished by their own resentment. Snobbishness is certainly *not* a natural outcome of having lots of money.

*The urbane activity
with which a man receives money
is really marvelous, considering
that we so earnestly believe
money to be the root
of all earthly ills,
and that on no account
can a monied man enter heaven.
Ah! how cheerfully
we consign ourselves to perdition!*

HERMAN MELVILLE

It is easier for a camel to go through the eye of a needle than for a rich man to enter the kingdom of God. This is, of course, a biblical quotation. It is one of those thrice-witnessed events in the life of Jesus, written about by Matthew (19:24), Mark (10:25) and Luke (18:25). In our research, we discovered several explanations as to what Jesus may have meant by a camel going through the eye of a needle. It's clear in all of them, however, that he was not referring to a great big camel and a little teeny needle. Jesus taught in parables, and the following is our favorite interpretation of that parable.

One of the gates in the walled city of Jerusalem is called the Needle. Within each gate of the city was a smaller gate called "the eye." "The eye of the Needle," then, would refer to the small gate within the larger gate known as the Needle. On holy days, the main gates would be closed, but the eyes would be opened. (Hmmm. That's significant in and of itself.) Going through the eye of the Needle was possible—in fact it was done all the time—but it required doing three things.

First, one had to wait in line, as holy days had some of the heaviest traffic in and out of the city, and closing the main gates and opening only the eyes kept traffic nicely congested. Second, one had to unburden the camel of whatever it was carrying. (One got to keep it, but one had to carry it through by hand.) Third, the camel had to go through on its knees.

As we discussed before, Jesus was very clear about the location of the kingdom of God. "The kingdom of God is within you" (Luke 17:21). Jesus was talking about how difficult it was for someone attached to outer riches to discover the greater wealth within.

Knowing that his disciples knew about the eye of the Needle and camels passing through it, what might Jesus have been trying to tell them? What do you suppose he was trying to tell *us* about how to enter the kingdom of God?

*Lack of money
is the
root of all evil.*

GEORGE BERNARD SHAW

First, we must be patient. We must get in line, and take our turn. It also implies that we must be fair and know how to share.

Second, we cannot be attached to physical possessions. We can have them, use them when we need them, and learn to let them go when we're done. And sometimes—even though it's another's job to carry the burden—we have to carry it ourselves. This is another way of saying, "Do the work that needs to be done when it needs to be done."

Third, we must be humble—some might even call it reverent. Being on one's knees is a universal sign of this. It is not a sign of unworthiness or disgrace—camels, in fact, *enjoy* being on their knees. For humans, kneeling is a sign of honoring, and we must honor the greater—the more sacred—portion of ourselves to enter the kingdom of God within us.

It's easy to see, then, that although it's difficult for a rich *or* poor man to enter the kingdom of God, it can be done. Another often misinterpreted quotation from the Bible is...

Money is the root of all evil. This was not said by Jesus, but by St. Paul in a letter to Timothy. The full quotation is "For the love of money is a root of all kinds of evil" (1 Timothy 6:10). In the ancient Aramaic and Greek texts, the word *love* is more accurately interpreted in this context as *lust*. The sentence would then read "Lust of money is a root of all kinds of evil." In this sentence, "of money" could be replaced by any number of things. The basic idea is "Lust is evil."

As we mentioned before, *evil* is *live* spelled backwards. What makes lusting backwards living? When we lust, we say, "That out there is more important than what's in here, and I want that thing out there very, very badly." Sounds like a perfect affirmation for ingratitude, nonappreciation and not living in the moment, doesn't it? It is. Lusting—whether after money, fame, power, sex, having people do it "our way," or any other than here-and-now experience—destroys the moment. The moment destroyed

Money alone can't
bring you happiness,
but money alone
has not brought me unhappiness.
I won't say my previous husbands
thought only of my money,
but it had
a certain fascination for them.

BARBARA HUTTON

is not a wealthy one. We are doing things backwards, hence evil.

If money were in and of itself evil, the solution would be simple: Get rid of your money. But this is not what Paul counsels: "Command those who are rich in this present world not to be arrogant nor to put their hope in wealth, which is so uncertain, but to put their hope in God, who richly provides us with everything for our enjoyment. Command them to do good, to be rich in good deeds, and to be generous and willing to share. In this way they will lay up treasure for themselves as a firm foundation for the coming age, so that they may take hold of the life that is truly life" (1 Timothy 6:17–19).

In other words, don't just seek money—seek wealth. There is nothing wrong with having money.

You need training and education to get money. There are many stories of people who had little or no formal education—or who were notoriously bad in school—yet went on to great fame and fortune. There are also stories of people who earned so many degrees, they had more letters *after* their name than *in* it. These people sometimes ended up working for the people with little or no education.

Yes, we have to be "smart" about life (dare we plug our book *LIFE 101: Everything We Wish We Had Learned About Life In School—But Didn't?*), we need certain skills, information, education and knowledge about the area of our big dream, but a sheath of degrees does not guarantee money, and a complete lack of degrees (other than 98.6) is no automatic obstacle to money.

Money can't buy you love. As someone once said, "Whoever said money can't buy you love doesn't know where to shop." Loving others, expressed through money, can bring love in return.

You can't take it with you. You may not be able to take it with you—but wherever you can't take it, you won't need it anyway.

Money is too much responsibility. The more money you have, the more people you can hire to shoulder that

Money doesn't buy happiness,
but that's not the reason
so many people are poor.

LAURENCE J. PETERS

awful burden of responsibility for you. True, when we are given an ability, it becomes a responsibility. People with lots of money do have more responsibility for certain things in certain areas than people who have less money. Fortunately, you can hire people who will help you "spread it around" where it will do the most good.

It takes hard work to make money. It takes hard work to be poor, too. Life is full of hard work. The only thing worse than hard work is boredom—which is precisely what we get when we aren't working hard. To fulfill a dream—any dream—takes hard work—most of it internal. When the goal is achieved, however, the hard work is forgotten in the pleasure of success. After a brief pause, there follows another goal and more hard work. Such is life. You might as well work hard pursuing *your* dream than get paid mere money to help other people pursue theirs.

Money isn't everything. People who use this as the reason not to get money tend to be the same ones who, when cornered in an intellectual discussion, jump levels and say things like, "It's not that important, anyway." No, money isn't everything, but it is something—and sometimes it's the only something that will get us one step closer to our dream.

The best things in life are free. There are some very good things that are free, and some excellent things that come with a price tag. Having the money to buy the things in the latter category doesn't prevent us from enjoying the things in the former.

Money isn't spiritual or holy. Did you ever look closely at money? Try the back of the U.S. dollar bill, for example. It is full of more mystical symbols (radiant eyes in triangles over pyramids and such) than you'll find over the altar in most metaphysical churches. In addition, money can buy you the time, environment, training and paraphernalia for whatever religious or spiritual path you choose to pursue. As with most things, money is just one of many methods that can be used to fulfill a dream—including the dream of knowing God and Spirit better.

Study:
concentration of the mind
on whatever
will ultimately
put something in the pocket.

ELBERT HUBBARD

Now the real work of challenging the culturally ingrained limiting beliefs about money begins. The next time you feel shame, guilt, fear, unworthiness, hurt feelings, or anger regarding money, take the time to explore the belief causing the feeling.

Perhaps it's simple unworthiness: "I don't deserve it." Perhaps it's one of the limitations listed in this chapter. When you find the limiting belief within yourself, consciously challenge it. Explore it. Dissect it. Have a heart-to-heart talk with yourself. Convince yourself "It just ain't so."

Use your sanctuary, your Master Teacher, further study, meditation, paraphernalia (get a great big needle and a tiny stuffed camel and spend a few minutes putting the camel through the eye of the needle), or any other tools (we'll be using affirmations extensively in the next chapter) to eliminate the limiting belief from your consciousness.

As many of these limiting beliefs were ingrained in us very early and are reinforced constantly by the media and the general negativity around us, freeing ourselves from limiting beliefs about money is an uphill climb.

It's worth the climb.

The view from the top is wealthier, healthier and happier.

*

Money is the symbol of duty,
it is the sacrament
of having done for mankind
that which mankind wanted.

SAMUEL BUTLER

I've Been Poor and I've Been Rich and, Believe Me, Rich Is Better

In addition to the well-worn limiting beliefs about money, our culture is rich in expansive beliefs. Take each of those expansive beliefs you come upon, and make it an affirmation. If the culture doesn't seem to have a positive belief about money to fit your needs, create one.

In repeating affirmations a thousand times each, rather than using toothpicks, perhaps you'd like to use money. Get 110 bills of the highest denomination that you can muster. Use them in the same way we suggested using toothpicks on page 177.

Here are some affirmations to get you started.

"I like money."

"I love money."

"I use the energy of money to fulfill my dream."

"Money is honey. Money is sunny. Money is funny."

"I enjoy money."

"I appreciate money."

"I am grateful for money."

"Thank you. I have more money than I need."

"With money I do great good for myself and others."

There's always
room at the top—
after the investigation.

OLIVER HERFORD

A Metaphor for Money

Metaphors and analogies help us imagine things, accommodate concepts and create arenas in which to experience life. The most popular metaphor for the obtaining of money in our culture is that of a *struggle* or a *battle*. With those metaphors in mind, it's little wonder that people show a pronounced lack of enthusiasm when it comes time to go out and get some money.

Earlier, we presented the metaphor that life was an entertainment—a movie, television show, concert, book or maybe even an amusement park. We'd like to suggest a metaphor for pursuing your dream in general, and for pursuing money in particular. The metaphor we'd like to present is that of a *game*.

Games are activities we take part in not just because they are fun—although that's certainly one reason—but because they are intriguing, challenging, demanding, expanding, exciting, and require our utmost in skill, focus, concentration and creativity.

At the end of a game well played, we may be exhausted, but we are also satisfied. If the game is to engross us fully, it must have a degree of difficulty equal to our ability. If a game is too easy, it's no fun. If a game is too difficult, we feel defeated. It's when we know we *can* win, but have no guarantee that we *will* win, that games become truly exciting and worthy of our playing.

In order for a game to be truly interesting, we must become *involved* in it. We must become engrossed, captivated—lose ourselves in the playing. It must seem real, and part of the reality requires that we forget "it's only a game." We must play as though it *really mattered*.

While playing a game, we don't appreciate it when people interrupt our illusion. Even if we are losing and they're "only trying to help," we don't appreciate it. If, while we're playing Monopoly, for example, a bystander kept saying, "Those aren't real hotels; they're only pieces of plastic. That's not really Boardwalk; that's just a

The successful people
are the ones
who can think up things
for the rest of the world
to keep busy at.

DON MARQUIS

square on a game board. That's not real money; that's just play money." Before long, we'd throw the person out of the room.

For a game to be enthralling, there must be an element of risk—we'll have something to gain if we win, but something to lose if we don't. The loss has to be big enough to make things interesting (even if we only lose "our pride"), but not so great that we become incapacitated by fear. For this reason, we may do better walking a tightrope two feet above the ground than an identical tightrope twenty stories in the air.

Playing a game requires commitment. There's a big difference between "playing" and "playing around." Players are committed to the game and its outcome. Those just playing around aren't committed to much of anything, except perhaps annoying the other players.

If you choose to see obtaining more money as a game—an engrossing, challenging, dynamic game—rather than a struggle or a battle, then the pursuit of money can become exciting, satisfying and fun. Money, then, is just a way of keeping score.

*If you can
actually count your money
then you are not
really a rich man.*

J. PAUL GETTY

What Are You Worth?

In order to know whether you are winning or losing in the game of making more money, you must first have a starting point, a ground zero, a calibrated scale. This starting point is what you are worth right now. At a future point, you can calculate what you are worth and determine whether you are winning or losing.

There are two basic ways to measure financial worth. The first is *net worth*. All the money you have, and the monetary value of everything you own, less everything you owe, is your net worth.

The second way of measuring financial worth is *cash flow*. This is the amount of money that flows *through* you. If you make and spend $36,000 per year, you have a cash flow of $36,000 per year, or $3,000 per month.

Like making a flat map of the round earth, neither system is—nor can be—completely accurate. Calculating what you're worth works like a map. When trying to understand a portion of the world around us, even a distorted map is better than no map at all.

We can't recommend one system over another. Our highest recommendation must go to the one you would actually *use*.

Some people like the idea of using net worth, but we have met very few people who have actually taken the time to compile a complete net-worth inventory. Doing this seems to fall apart when it comes time to have things appraised. What's the value of that silver tea set Grandma left? $50, $500, $5,000? What about all those records from the 1960s? Most are probably worth 25 cents, yet a few may be worth $250—but which ones?

For many people, cash flow is the system that's easiest to figure. If most of your money goes directly into your checking account, all you need do to discover your cash flow is add up your deposits for the past year. With your monthly bank statements in front of you, this shouldn't

I started out with nothing.
I still have most of it.

MICHAEL DAVIS

take much time at all. If you work heavily on a cash or barter system, however, determining the cash flow may take additional remembering and calculating.

Whichever system you use, and however you choose to implement it, the most important thing is to be consistent. You're setting up a scoring system for the game of making money. As you establish your "baseline" score, you're also establishing the rules for calculating future scores.

If you're using the net worth system, and you estimated the value of all of your books at a certain price, the next time you establish your net worth, don't go through your library on a book-by-book basis. Continue to estimate all of them as a group. If you are on the cash flow system and decide not to include the value of birthday gifts in your determination, if you get a $20 toaster for your birthday one year, and $20 cash from the same person the following year, if you didn't count the toaster, don't count the cash.

People tend to get tired even *thinking* about discovering what they're worth—either net worth or cash flow. With all the confusing, conflicting and contradictory beliefs about money in our culture, many of us choose to simply go unconscious about money. "What I don't think about won't hurt me." To figure out what we are worth brings the idea of money more into our consciousness.

As with all endeavors, the only way out is through; therefore, the only way to greater consciousness about money is *through* the unconsciousness we already have. Go through the motions of calculating your monetary worth—even though you are barely conscious while doing so. When you arrive at a bottom-line figure, consciousness should return. An increased awareness of money—and your interaction with it—will be the long-term benefit.

Among other things, you'll see how conscious or unconscious you've been about money in regard to how much of it you have. What do you think you're worth? Write it down. After you calculate—in black and white—your

*I bless God
I do find that I am worth
more than ever I yet was,
which is £6,200, for which
the Holy Name of God be praised!*

SAMUEL PEPYS

1666

*Money is
God in action.*

FREDERICK J. EIKERENKOETTER II
"REVEREND IKE"

worth, ask yourself: "Am I worth more, less or about the same as what I thought?"

Whatever the answer, it will tell you something about how you view money—and, perhaps, yourself.

Figuring your financial worth on a regular basis—every six months, say—not only increases your consciousness of money, but lets you know whether you're winning or losing—and by how much—in the game of making more money.

*We are not interested
in the
possibilities of defeat.*

QUEEN VICTORIA

Winning and Losing vs.
Grinning and Choosing

Those who view getting money as a struggle or a battle often involve themselves not so much in *winning* but in—at all costs—*not losing*.

Loss they equate to defeat, devastation, death and annihilation. They spend so much time not losing, they forget almost entirely about what it is they want to win.

Not losing itself becomes a victory. When you ask these people, "What have you won?" they say—often with great pride—"I don't know, but at least I haven't lost!" People committed to not losing become rigid, firm, inflexible and dogmatic. They decide that by being "solid" they will get what they want. If what they want is not losing, they often get it. If what they want is winning, however, the essence of winning is found in flexibility, not rigidity.

Those committed to not losing spend a lot of time *deciding* rather than *choosing*. "You think too much, that is your trouble," Zorba told his young friend. "Clever people and grocers, they *weigh* everything."

Rather than choosing a method and seeing how it works, the non-losers of life mull it over and over in their minds until they eventually make a *decision*. Once the decision is made, that's it. "This is the way we'll go, this is how we'll get there, these are the rest stops along the way and what time we'll stop at each and if anyone or anything gets in the way—look out!" From that point on, all information of any kind is filtered out, and the non-loser plows ahead dogmatically—ignoring, perhaps, signs saying "Road Out," "Detour Ahead" and "Caution."

The term "the bitter end" was coined for non-losers. In the end, they are bitter. When they lose, it is a death in life. They kill all the wealth within them and around them. They pretend they didn't lose by destroying the game. "I didn't want it anyway," they mope.

Bitter people make sour grapes.

I'm not picking you up,
I'm picking you out.

LOS ANGELES PICK-UP LINE

CIRCA 1991

A key can be found in the word *decide*. The *cide* portion of the word comes from the Latin *cida,* for killer; *cidium,* for killing and *caedere,* for kill. We see *cide* in such words as homicide, genocide, herbicide, germicide, pesticide, insecticide, patricide and, of course, suicide.

Decisions are what were made by Mammy Yokum, "I has spoken!" and by the pharaoh from *The Ten Commandments,* "So let it be written. So let it be done!"

When we become attached to a *method*—that is, the *way* we get to our goal as opposed to the goal itself—we are in the land of cide. "I don't understand it," the deciders say, "It worked last week."

That's like a quarterback memorizing the path he took across the field to the triumphant touchdown the Saturday before. All week he rehearsed exactly what he did, where he stepped, and how he moved. He feels confident and ready. He takes three steps along his well-rehearsed path, however, and is slaughtered. "I don't understand it," he groans.

To get to our goal, we need to focus on the goal, be aware of what methods *in that moment* might get us to that goal and choose one method after another until one works.

The difference between choosing and deciding is that with choosing, if a choice doesn't work, we let it go and immediately make another choice.

A rat making its way through a maze to get to the cheese is a perfect example of choosing. It runs down this tunnel, around that bend, over this barrier and "What? No cheese? Oh well. I'm after cheese. I can smell it in here somewhere." And the rat heads off down other tunnels, around other bends, over other obstacles, until the cheese is found. None of the choices was wrong; each was simply a lesson in where the cheese was not. Once the rat knew where the cheese was not, it moved away from there—sometimes backtracking—in order to reach the cheese. The rat never rested, nor did it stop choosing, until the cheese was found.

Wilbur Post: *I'm counting on you to win tomorrow, but if you don't, be a good sport— lose with a smile.*

Mr. Ed: *I'd rather win with a sneer!*

"MR. ED"

In laboratory research, there is the phenomenon known as "the smart rat." On the first day in the maze, the smart rat will find the cheese with great speed. On the second day, however, the smart rat will go directly to the point where the cheese was the day before. Finding no cheese there, it looks around, obviously wondering, "The cheese *should* be here. Where is it?" The rat looks up, down, over and around wondering, "What's wrong with this maze today, anyway?" The rat then sits down and waits for the cheese to be delivered—it's obviously late—and will wait there until it starves to death. Meanwhile, in the next tunnel over sits the cheese. A few choices—and one fewer decision—later, and the rat would get what it wants.

So often we become smart rats. Through trial and error, we find a way that gets us noticeably closer to our goal. Then we *decide,* "This is the way." "We pointed you the way to go, and scratched your name in the sand," lamented Bob Dylan, "but you thought it was nothing more than a place for you to stand." When "the way" no longer works—that is, when it no longer gets us closer to our goal—we continue with it. Why? "Because it worked before!"

If something's not working, have the wit to let it go, no matter how well it worked in the past. We must choose again. Flow with the *ooooo* in choosing. If that doesn't work, we can grin and say, "Oh well," and move on to another choice—another method.

Those who are involved in winning rather than not losing—and winning is defined as getting to the *goal,* not in getting to the goal in the way we *think* we should get there—don't equate *losing* with *loss.* Losing is just another lesson.

In the heightened emotional state that follows loss, we are conditioned to use that energy to find reasons why the loss *shouldn't* have taken place—whom or what to blame. For the most part, to blame is to be-lame. Whether we blame others, external events, or ourselves, we are using our heightened awareness in the wrong direction.

When you have to
make a choice and
don't make it,
that is in itself
a choice.

WILLIAM JAMES

Rather, we could use our heightened awareness (which people often mislabel anger, hurt and fear) to find and learn the lesson presented by the loss.

Within each loss is a lesson. Sometimes, however, it takes a bit of ferreting out. That's why we're given the extra emotional and mental energy—to discover what we need to know to do better next time.

Sometimes the lesson is, "Be gentler." Other times the lesson is, "Be more forceful." Over time, we learn to find the balance between these two seemingly contradictory lessons—and in which situations to apply each.

Sometimes the lesson is simply, "Well, that won't work" and we move on to something else that may.

In *Singin' in the Rain,* Gene Kelly plays a dancer who comes to New York to find fame and fortune. He knocks on an agent's door, the agent opens the door, Kelly does his three-second audition dance, and waits for a response. If the response is not immediately favorable, he shrugs and moves on to the next door. His energy is boundless. He knows his goal, and if this particular agent isn't a method to that goal, oh well, perhaps the next one will be.

It's important for us to pursue our dreams with that same degree of unbounded enthusiasm. When we don't get what we want, we need only shrug it off and move on to the next method that may work. If it doesn't, we grin and choose again. And again. And again.

When will we have chosen enough? When we have our goal. Until then, keep grinning and choosing.

Grasshopper,
look beyond the game,
as you look beneath
the surface of the pool
to see its depths.

MASTER PO
"KUNG FU"

After a certain point
money is meaningless.
It ceases to be the goal.
The game is what counts.

ARISTOTLE ONASSIS

Creation or Competition?

There is a myth in our culture that says there's only so much "stuff" available, that other people already own it, and in order to get what we want, we have to take it from somebody else.

For those who believe this myth, fulfilling a dream—and especially getting the money necessary to fulfill that dream—must, almost by definition, be a battle and a struggle.

Who wants to let go of what they already have? No one. Obviously, we'll have to wrench it by force from their clutching hands. If that doesn't work, we'll have to trick them out of it. "By hook or by crook," as the saying goes.

This is known as *competition*. If this is how people believe wealth is won, no wonder so many people don't want to play. Who wants to enter *that* arena? It's not that that arena doesn't exist—it does. There, experienced gladiators stand atop mole hills playing King of the Mountain while less experienced gladiators battle them unto the death. In the stands, the crowds cheer, and the Emperor decides thumbs up or thumbs down—usually thumbs down.

There is, however, another system, another arena, another metaphor for pursuing our goal, living our dreams and getting what we want—including money.

That method is *creation*.

Creation is making something out of *seemingly* nothing. We say *seemingly* nothing because although our thoughts and creative energy are certainly *something,* they don't *seem* to be something until they have a physical manifestation.

If we spend a day at the beach and want our own sand castle, we don't have to take the one someone else built. There's lots of sand on the beach. All it takes is vision, commitment, a certain amount of physical energy and we, too, can have a sand castle.

Hello, good evening
and welcome to "Blackmail."
And to start tonight's program,
we go north
to Preston in Lancashire
and Mrs. Betty Teal.
Hello Mrs. Teal!
Now Mrs. Teal,
this is for fifteen pounds and
it's to stop us revealing
the name of your lover in Bolton.
So, Mrs. Teal,
send us fifteen pounds
by return of post please and
your husband Trevor and
your lovely children, Diane,
Janice and Juliet,
need never know the name
of your lover in Bolton.

"MONTY PYTHON"

While building our sand castle, we can be so involved in the process—and having so much fun—that people may come along and want to join us. This is known as *seduction*. We don't *force* others into helping us, we jump in and enjoy the process so much that our enjoyment becomes contagious. Most people don't have a dream of their own. They are more than happy to help push another's dream wagon, to march in another's parade.

One act of creation can be the spark to a world of other creative acts, springing *seemingly* out of nothing, but quite real indeed.

Where was the recording industry before Edison invented the phonograph? Where was the telecommunications industry before Alexander Graham Bell invented the telephone? For those who thought our sand castle analogy was too fanciful to be true, take a look at the computer industry: it's based entirely upon the silicon chip—and silicon is nothing but sand.

We only need look at our goal and ask, "How can I create this for myself?" rather than, "Who can I take it from?" If you want a career, you don't need to take someone else's—create your own. If you want a marriage, you don't have to take someone else's spouse—find your own.

The perfect attitude of creation and not competition came from film producer Samuel Goldwyn. When asked if he minded that a movie from a competing studio was doing so well, he replied: "Of course not. When people go to see that movie, they'll see the trailer for my next picture."

If your goal has competition built into it—in which you'll be struggling with others over a scarce position or commodity—you may want to restructure your goal slightly. You may want to reword it in a way that allows everyone to win.

Rather than "I am president of *that* corporation," try "I am president of *a* corporation that..." and give the attributes you admire about the corporation you would like to lead. This leaves room for any number of corporations

The wise and moral man
Shines like a fire on a hilltop,
Making money like the bee,
Who does not hurt the flower.

THE PALI CANON
500–250 B.C.

with attributes you admire to grow, thrive and prosper. If you were president of any one of them, your goal would be met.

Yes, sometimes on the playing field we will have to "play" with other people who are staunchly set in the combative mode. They will want precisely what we want and feel the need to attack us in order to get it.

Whenever possible, avoid those who want to compete with you over a specific method of achieving your goal. If some bullies come along and want your sand castle, let them have it. You can always build a better one.

If, on the other hand, someone comes along and wants your *beach house*—well, that's another matter. It's a question of weighing the time and energy it takes *not to lose* a certain patch of beachfront versus what could be created by applying the same time, energy and commitment in a positive direction.

As Sting wrote about Quentin Crisp—who was frequently taunted for his effeminate appearance—"Confront your enemies, avoid them when you can. A gentleman will walk but never run."

Or, as the Quaker said after being slapped on one cheek, turning the other cheek, and being slapped again, "Now that the scriptures have been fulfilled, I shall proceed to beat the hell out of thee."

Back to our old friend balance? Absolutely. Fights can usually be avoided—provided we are sure *we're* not the ones looking for the fight.

I can say,
"I am terribly frightened
and fear is terrible
and awful and
it makes me uncomfortable,
so I won't do that
because it's uncomfortable."
Or I could say
"Get used to being uncomfortable.
It is uncomfortable
doing something that's risky."
But so what?
Do you want to stagnate
and just be comfortable?

BARBRA STREISAND

The Comfort Zone

As we pursue our goal—trying on various new behaviors, methods and levels of income—we're going to feel uncomfortable. Count on it. That's part of the process.

The comfort zone is the area of activities that we've done often enough to feel comfortable doing. Anything new, different or untried lies outside the comfort zone—in the land of the uncomfortable.

As we approach the edges of our comfort zone, we feel one or more of five emotions: fear, guilt, unworthiness, hurt feelings and anger. These are generally the feelings people have when they say, "I'm uncomfortable."

For many people, the explanation, "I'm uncomfortable," is sufficient reason not to do anything new. It's little wonder, then, that these people seldom reach their dreams. They chose comfort over their goal.

To reach our goal—to live our dream—we must choose, moment by moment, to take steps in the direction of our dream no matter how uncomfortable we may feel. Reaching one's goal is not comfortable. It is, however, satisfying.

The subtle ways in which the comfort zone keeps us from our dreams are remarkable. The comfort zone reacts with its "Don't do it!" messages long before we take a physical action. When we even *think* about doing something new and different, the comfort zone reacts. We have been programmed to do whatever it takes to avoid fear, guilt, unworthiness, hurt feelings and/or anger. So, we think about something else—something more comfortable.

At the very foundation of manifestation, at the level of thought, the comfort zone attacks. We—often unconsciously—follow our programming and focus on what's familiar, what's comfortable.

In reality, the comfort zone is an important part of our inbuilt success mechanism. As we explored in the earlier chapter, "Turn a Twist on It," all the feelings that make up the comfort zone can be used *for* us—can be used to

If I repent of anything,
it is very likely
to be my good behavior.

THOREAU

help us achieve our dream. We've simply been misprogrammed as to their proper use.

This programming took place in childhood. For our parents to let us out of their sight, they had to train us, essentially, "Don't do anything new." The limited knowledge of a child can not tell the difference between drinking milk and drinking poison, between playing on the street and playing in a playground, between one neighbor's nice puppy and another neighbor's nasty pit bull. For their own safety, children are taught, "If it's new, don't do it."

When we are old enough to know the difference between that which is merely new and exciting and that which is genuinely physically harmful, no one draws us aside and says, "Oh, by the way, all those feelings of discomfort that you've been taught to avoid—you can start using those as additional tools to get what you want."

It takes a while to do this reprogramming. Fortunately, on the way to our dreams, we'll have lots of opportunities. Each time fear, guilt, unworthiness, hurt feelings and anger surface—and they will, they will—we can either choose to run from them, or use them as the energy to take yet another step toward our dream.

Fear becomes excitement—the energy to do our best in a new situation.

Guilt becomes the energy for making personal change—to change our behavior (sometimes) or to change our mistaken beliefs about what our behavior *should* be (most of the time).

Unworthiness keeps us on track. We tell ourselves that we *are* worthy of our dream, and then let the feelings of unworthiness we have about pursuing all the other dreams in the world guide us to success.

Hurt feelings remind us how much we care. If we didn't care, we wouldn't hurt. Hurt feelings can remind us to return to the caring. We use the energy to care for ourselves, thus healing whatever damage the hurting did. Then we direct the caring toward our goal, our big dream.

*The best way out
is always through.*

ROBERT FROST

Anger is the energy for change. In a persistent, consistent and determined way, we move toward our goal. It's only when we keep anger bottled up and not directed toward something we really want that it becomes explosive.

Successfully reprogramming the comfort zone is like learning how to swim. We can study theory and practice as much as we like, but the place of true learning is in the water. We'll sink, swallow water, panic and do all the things we wanted to avoid by learning to swim. It may seem, for a while, counterproductive. If, however, we stick to it, we learn to use the water as a way of getting what we want (fun, exercise, recreation) rather than as an enemy, waiting to do us in.

In order to use the comfort zone to get what we want, we must feel what we *currently* call uncomfortable. In a few years, we may automatically call fear excitement. For now, however, it's fear, and it's uncomfortable. Be willing to feel uncomfortable. Feel the fear and do it anyway. Take the next step toward your goal. Along the way, begin seeing the various emotions of the comfort zone as the friends they are.

One of the "freebie" benefits of pursuing our dream is learning to use the comfort zone as the support system it truly is. The primary benefit is our dream. The secondary benefit—which, perhaps, over time, becomes the primary benefit—is learning that nothing is truly good or bad within ourselves; that everything can be used for good if we so choose. We learn that the world is not "out to get us." That was just a childhood fantasy—a nightmare from our youth from which we can finally awake.

I used to think I was poor.
Then they told me
I wasn't poor, I was needy.
Then they told me
it was self-defeating
to think of myself as needy.
I was deprived.
Then they told me that
underprivileged was overused.
I was disadvantaged.
I still don't have a dime.
But I have a great vocabulary.

JULES FEIFFER

We Don't Receive Because We Don't Ask

When we are perfectly attuned to our highest good and the highest good of all concerned, we don't need to ask. Everything is given to us. Our needs are met before they become needs. Our wants are more than fulfilled. We feel whole and complete.

When we are not quite that in tune (and—let's face it—that seems to be most of the time), we *want*. When we want—and it lies on the path to our dream—it's best to fulfill the want. So often, however, even when it *is* on the path to our big dream, we don't receive what we want.

Often, we don't receive because we don't ask. We may ask one person who we carefully and thoughtfully considered would be the proper person to help us fulfill a want. If that person says no, we give up. This gives us a sense of deprivation, a feeling that asking only makes it worse. Not only don't we get what we want; we have rejection on top of it.

> PETER: I only hitchhiked once in my life. I stood on a street corner with my thumb out for about two minutes. Five cars passed me by. I took each as a personal rejection. I couldn't take it any more, so I walked.

Rather than asking less—which we've been programmed to do when we're told "No,"—we should, instead, ask *more*.

Interestingly, when we ask and receive, we begin to realize that the Universe is an abundant place. People who walk into a store and think, "I have enough money to buy anything in here I want," quite often don't buy a thing. Knowing they can have whatever they want, they realize they don't want anything.

On the other hand, people who feel so poor that they can't afford anything often want everything. Their con-

Or what man is there of you,
whom if his son ask bread,
will he give him a stone?
Or if he ask a fish,
will he give him a serpent?
If ye then, being evil,
know how to give good gifts
unto your children,
how much more shall your
Father which is in heaven
give good things
to them that ask him?

MATTHEW 7:9–11

sciousness of poverty creates a greater sense of poverty within them.

It seems paradoxical, but it is nonetheless true: the more we know we can have, the less we want.

One way to realize it's an abundant Universe is to ask and ask and ask until we get what we want. Even if we don't get the specific thing we're asking for, with each questing we expand our comfort zone and learn one more lesson about how to get what we're asking for.

Perhaps we learn that asking one person for $10 is less effective than asking ten people for $1 each. Or, perhaps we learn just the opposite: that the more we ask for, the more sincerely our request is considered.

When we get back in tune, realize the blessings already are and know that we are well taken care of by whoever or whatever it is that has always made sure an abundant supply of oxygen has surrounded us no matter where we've gone or what we've done during our entire lives, we can relax and enjoy the moment, feeling wealthy and content.

To want, however, is not a bad thing. Wanting just means it's time to learn a few more lessons—that school, once again, is in session.

So, ask.

Only the hand
that erases
can write
the true thing.

MEISTER ECKHART

Make Room for the New

Just as we needed to create a container to receive the inner manifestations of wealth, so too we need to make room in our outer environment for the material possessions we plan to receive. We do this by letting go of all the material possessions we are not currently using.

Letting go of what we are not using has several benefits:

1. *It allows energy to flow from us.* All of our material possessions are a form of stored energy. If we're not using that energy—that is, if we are not regularly using that physical object—the energy is stagnated, wasted. By freeing that object for another's use, we take back the energy we have invested in it and can apply that energy to our goal. It's amazing how much money, for example, we have tied up in things we no longer use. If we sell all the things we're not using, we can use it to pursue our big dream.

2. *It starts the energy flowing into us.* Life is energy. It flows in, it flows out. "In" is not good, "out" is not bad. Both, working together, are essential to life. When we inhale, we receive oxygen. When we exhale, we eliminate carbon dioxide. Both are vital. By breathing out, we make room for the next breath. Letting go of the material possessions we are not currently using is like an exhale: it allows us to take a full, deep breath. Letting go of things we're not using is a "kick start" for the increased flow of giving and receiving we desire.

3. *It creates a vacuum.* Nature abhors a vacuum and seeks to fill it. Now that we know *what* we want—the paraphernalia necessary for the obtaining and maintaining of our dream—eliminating what's not part of reaching our dream creates a vacuum. The vacuum is then filled with what we want. (Although we must be careful to say "No, thank you"

*First, have a definite,
clear, practical ideal—
a goal, an objective.
Second, have the necessary
means to achieve your ends—
wisdom, money,
materials and methods.
Third, adjust all your means
to that end.*

ARISTOTLE

to all the non-dream things that will seek to fill the vacuum. Some of them may be quite tempting, too.)

We call this *making room for the new*. It's a simple process—go through all of your material possessions, and of each ask yourself: "Have I used this in the past year?"

If the answer is no, place the object in the "recycle" pile. If the answer is yes, ask yourself another question: "Will this object be directly helpful in obtaining my goal?" If the answer is yes, you get to keep it. If the answer is no, put it in the recycle pile.

Letting go of possessions can be difficult. We are, by cultural conditioning, pack rats. We were trained that if we get something, we get to keep it. We forget that material possessions are simply here for our *use*.

When we're no longer using them, continuing to hold onto them is as silly—and unproductive—as holding your breath. "I'm not going to let go of any of *my* oxygen." Or, as unproductive as people who overeat and become dangerously overweight because "I can't stand to throw food away." It's better to let the food go to waste than to waist.

If you haven't used something within a year, you really don't want it anyway. If you *really did,* you would have used it at least *once* in the past 365 days.

Somebody, somewhere may have a use for this object, just as—at one point in the past—you had a use for it. Even if no one has a use for it, *you* have a use for the space that it's occupying. Donate, give away, recycle or discard what you can't trade or sell. Get rid of it.

The Universe is conservative with its resources. It tends not to give freely to hoarders. Energy was not meant to be hoarded, it was meant to be shared. The Universe loves flow. You take something in, use it, appreciate it, feel grateful for it, and let it go. We hand off that object to the next person in line for it, and turn to greet our next experience.

*Genius is
an infinite capacity
for taking pains.*

JANICE ELICE HOPKINS

*I'm very organized.
I have this
very elaborate schedule.
Sure sign
of mental health, huh?*

ELAINE NARDO

"TAXI"

Plan It

Plans are funny things: without them, we seldom get to our goal. When we've gotten to our goal, however, we look back and realize we haven't gotten there according to our plan. We must be willing, then, to make a plan, follow it, and when better options arise, let the plan go.

Keep moving toward the goal by the best methods available, using the best tools available. As you get closer to your goal, the methods and tools will probably change. Nonetheless, it's important to make a plan *now* with the methods and tools you currently envision.

Planning may be uncomfortable—making choices and putting them down in black and white often is—but the process is a simple one. Pick a date by which you want your goal achieved, write that down, and schedule all the things that need to happen between then and now.

Keep scheduling until you know what you have to do *next*. Always have a next action step towards your goal ready to take. If you say about your next action step, "I can't take that until next week," there's almost certainly a smaller action step that can be taken *now*. It might be as simple as a phone call, reading a book or gathering information. It might be planning your next day, writing down the good, or saying an affirmation. Arrange it so that there is always *something* you can do towards your goal at any given moment.

Also schedule the "maintenance" activities for what you already have. Maintaining what you have is called "living your dream." Planning for and methodically attaining what you don't already have is called "pursuing your dream."

Between living your dream and pursuing your dream, there's not much time left for anything else. But so what? Besides living and pursuing your dream, what else is there? It makes for a full day—and a full life. Plan it that way.

Seek not proud riches,
but such as
thou mayest get justly,
use soberly,
distribute cheerfully,
and leave contentedly.

SIR FRANCIS BACON

1625

How Much Money Do You Want?

As with all goals, the more specific and quantifiable your money goals are, the better.

The question is this: How much money do you *need* (not *greed)* to fulfill your goal? If you want to be an actor, for example, you don't need a Rolls Royce. A Honda will do. (Writers, however, *do* need Lexuses.) (Especially *these* writers.)

The question is: How much money do you need to get, by when, to achieve your goal, while maintaining (not indulging, but maintaining) your body along the way? Go through your plan. Begin calculating how much each of the things in your plan will cost.

Start with fixed expenses—those things necessary to keep body and soul in close proximity: rent, car payments, food, clothing, drinking water (don't forget to bring your own container), health care, seeding, tithing, the next book in THE *LIFE 101* SERIES—you know, the basics.

Then start adding the expenses necessary for pursuing your dream: tools, travel, research, phone calls and all the rest. Add it up and see what your yearly cash flow must be in order to fulfill your dream. Add ten percent to this figure because, well, things happen. We call this the *mishigas* margin.

This gives you a specific money goal to affirm. Make it an affirmation: "My cash flow is $_____ per year." Or "I am using my cash flow of $_____ per year to fulfill my dream," or perhaps "I'm grateful for my cash flow of $_____ per year." Say one—or all three—at least a thousand times using money, rather than toothpicks, to keep count. This charges your money goal and begins attracting cash to you.

Our friends and colleagues, Drs. Ron and Mary Hulnick, are masters of money management. Their book *Fiscal Fitness* is a classic in the field. It's the best book we know on the nuts and bolts of tracking, understanding and increasing cash flow. It's available for $40 from University of Santa Monica Press, 2107 Wilshire Blvd., Santa Monica, CA 90403 or by calling 310-829-7402.

*Most men believe
that it would benefit them
if they could get a little
from those who <u>have</u> more.
How much more
would it benefit them
if they would learn a little
from those who <u>know</u> more.*

WM. J. H. BOETCKER

Make a Treasure Map

So, enough already with repeating affirmations over and over. Let's try another method of affirming our wealth. We might call this a visual affirmation. It's known as a Treasure Map.

With your goal in mind, flip through magazines, newspapers, trendy catalogs and so on, finding visual images that illustrate some portion of your dream. Cut them out. You might also see words and phrases in headlines that describe your goal. Cut them out, too.

When you have a lot of images, go to an art store and buy a large piece of white cardboard or foam core board. While there, pick up some glue. (We don't know what kind of glue to recommend. Just say to the person in the art store, "I'm making a Treasure Map. What kind of glue should I use?")

Arrange the images and words on the cardboard. If you like, get photographs of your face, cut them out, and glue them over the faces of the people enjoying their dreams. When your arrangement looks exciting and appealing, glue everything down.

Have fun making this collage of your dreams. When completed, it is your Treasure Map. Hang it in a place where you'll see it often, but where you don't have to explain it. If anyone asks, and you don't wish to discuss it, just casually say, "Oh, that's a collage I made once."

Making a Treasure Map gets our whole body involved in the process of affirming our dream. It also involves that child inside you who loves to cut, paste and create. Feel free to add to it at any time—or make another. Each time you look at it, remember the fun you had making it.

You can pursue your dream with the same childlike fun and enthusiasm.

I've always been after
the trappings of great luxury
you see, I really, really have.
But all I've got hold of are
the trappings of great poverty.
I've got hold of the wrong load
of trappings, and a rotten load
of trappings they are too,
ones I could have very well
done without.

PETER COOK

Watch out for emergencies.
They are your big chance!

FRITZ REINER

Don't Study Poverty

One of the favorite reasons people have for not pursuing their dream is "the economy." If the economy is on the rise, they get Inflation Elation Fixation. If the economy is slowing down, they get Recession Depression Obsession. If the economy is stable, they will shake their heads slowly and mutter something about "the stagnant economy."

No matter where the economy is—or is headed—those who study poverty (and there are some real experts out there) have the perfect reason for not pursuing their dream.

The same people study crime statistics, and can prove—unequivocally—that you can not walk three blocks in New York City without being mugged, or breathe for three minutes in Los Angeles without being smogged.

Always remember: you're not a statistic, you're a human being. (Didn't the Elephant Man say that first?) Remember, too: during the most depressionary and inflationary times in history, people have fulfilled their dreams.

Remember Mae West, who, at the age of forty, got off the train in Hollywood, in the midst of the Great Depression, telling the press, "I'm not a little girl from a little town planning to make it in the big town. I'm a big girl from a big town, and I have every intention of making it in this small town." A year later, she was the biggest star in Hollywood. The only person in the United States who made more money than Mae was William Randolph Hearst.

Even if times are *so tough* that only one percent of the population is fulfilling their dreams, with the U.S. population at 250 million, that means 2,500,000 people will be fulfilling their dreams. *Certainly* you can be one of 2,500,000.

Study, instead, success stories—people who succeeded no matter *what* the odds. Those people are your peers now.

If thou wouldst keep money,
save money;
If thou wouldst reap money,
sow money.

THOMAS FULLER

Seeding and Tithing

We saved the best news about money—seeding and tithing—for last. These two elements alone—practiced faithfully—can bring incredible wealth.

Seeding is planting the crop.

Tithing is saying "thank you" when the harvest is in.

You might say seeding and tithing involve "giving money away." In fact, with seeding and tithing, we are investing in success. When we seed and tithe, we contribute to the organization that represents—to us—the highest good on the planet. Usually that's our church, spiritual group or the source of our religious or spiritual teachings. (We'll discuss in detail what or whom we seed and tithe to in the next chapter.)

To seed, we give from one to one hundred percent of what we want to receive (harvest). Seeding is a form of commitment. When we commit to something through words alone, a part of us says, "Oh, that's nice." When we commit to something and put *money* on the line, that same part says, "Oh, this is real!" and gets busy making it happen. Seeding helps us separate what we *really want* from what we just think we want.

Seeding also directly connects our goals to whatever we consider to be the highest source of energy on the planet. God, Spirit, Mother Nature, the Source—or whatever we choose to call the representative of the highest energy—becomes our partner in that project.

No, we're not buying God off. No matter how much we seed, if it is not for our highest good and the highest good of all concerned, what we seed for will not come to pass.

Sometimes, we seed for something and it does not take place, but all our desire for it disappears. Our seeding has come to fruition. What we thought we wanted was not for our highest good, but we were given the next best thing—and some would consider it an even better thing—the

*It is only the farmer
who faithfully plants seeds
in the Spring,
who reaps a harvest
in the Autumn.*

B. C. FORBES

elimination of the desire for it. If you no longer want something, you certainly won't miss not having it.

When what we seed for comes to pass, it is time for the harvest—a time for thanksgiving. We take ten percent of the harvest—of our material increase—and donate it to the same organization that represents the highest good.

This is known as tithing.

It's hard to express gratitude in a more concrete way than *money*. This is gratitude that goes beyond personal greed, fear of future wants and the "It's mine, I earned it, and I'm going to keep it *all*" petty attitudes of so many people. Gratitude proves us a worthy steward, and more is given to us.

Further, giving ten percent away—even if we were to throw it out the window—is a powerful affirmation. It is saying—demonstrating, actually—"Thank you. I have more than I need." There are few statements of wealth as powerful as that. By tithing, we aren't just *saying* that, we're *living that*.

As a successful gardener, we set a portion of the crop aside for future seeding, and the process begins again.

In the next three chapters, we'll look at seeding and tithing more carefully.

For too many
giving is occasional,
spasmodic, ill-proportioned.
It depends on what is left over
when other things
have had their full share.
Sometimes what it means
is that only the small change
lying in their pockets
goes to the support
of good and worthy causes.

ROBERT J. McCRACKEN, D.D.

To Whom or What Do We Seed and Tithe?

In one sense, it doesn't really matter where our seeding and tithing money goes. As an instruction to ourselves, "I really mean this," seeding works just as well if we throw the money out the window. As an affirmation of abundance, "I have more than I need," tithing works even if we throw the money out the door. (If we use this approach, it means the seeding and tithing of our neighbors is working, too.)

In another sense—connecting to the energy of the highest good, making the energy of creation a partner in our process of manifestation—to whom or what we seed and tithe is very important.

Give to that which represents to you the highest good.

If you believe in God, the highest good would, of course, be God—who is represented by the source of your religious or spiritual teaching. This is usually your church or spiritual group.

If you don't believe in God, or if you believe in God and don't have an organized group that goes along with your belief, then give to that organization which represents to you the highest good being done on the planet. This may be a charitable group, a nonprofit organization, an educational institution, a social cause, or even an individual whose work represents to you the highest good.

If no one organization or individual is "it" for you, you can seed and tithe the money to a fund and give the money away to various causes which represent to you individual expressions of the highest good.

The important thing is not to find *the* organization which represents the highest good, but which organization does the work that represents to *you* the highest good. You are connecting yourself with the source of energy. It is important that *you* feel this is the highest energy available.

Gardens are not made
by singing
"Oh, how beautiful,"
and sitting in the shade.

RUDYARD KIPLING

Whom or what you seed and tithe to is not a once-and-for-all commitment. Over time, you may find another organization that represents to you the highest good. At that point, begin seeding and tithing to that organization. Eventually, you may find another. As we evolve and grow, so does our perception of what is the highest good and who or what is performing that highest good to an outstanding degree.

If you have any doubts, spend some time in your sanctuary with your Master Teacher discussing it. To what or whom you seed and tithe is less important than *that* you seed and tithe. Make a choice. Begin the process.

Money
is the seed
of money.

JEAN JACQUES ROUSSEAU

1754

Seeding Step-by-Step

Seeding is precisely what the word says—planting a seed. As with planting most seeds, we, as gardeners, follow a few simple guidelines. Nature takes it from there.

1. Choose specifically what you are seeding for. This is the equivalent of going to the gardening store and selecting which packet of seeds to plant. If you have ever been to a gardening store, you know how overwhelming the selection of seed packets can be.

You cannot just say, "I think I'll plant some vegetables over here and some flowers over here." The gardening store person will want to know what *kind* of vegetables. "Uh, well, carrots I think." "What kind of carrots?" "You mean there's more than one kind of carrot?" Indeed, there is. And with flowers, it's not only what kind of flower, but which color. So it is with life. We have lots of choices. But when it comes right down to it, the seed we plant is the plant we'll get.

You already know your big dream, and you may want to seed for that. If you're not familiar with the seeding process, however, we suggest starting with a smaller, more immediate goal. It might be what you perceive to be one of the first steps toward reaching your goal. By choosing a smaller goal, you'll see not only *how* the seeding process works, but *that* it works.

This way, you'll have confidence in the process of seeding based on your own experience. You will not echo the novice gardener gesturing to a plot of freshly planted soil with a worried expression, "I have $128 worth of seeds in that ground. I hope something comes up."

You might want to start with a goal that can be realized within a week or two. Then your process of seeding can build from success to success, and you'll see that—like gardening and the flowering and fruiting of plants—the whole process is fundamentally in the hands of nature. It is, in fact, something of a miracle.

If a little does not go,
much cash will not come.

CHINESE PROVERB

As with all goals, make sure your seeding goal is *quantifiable*. Please reread the chapter "How to Phrase a Goal" if you need to review the process of quantifying goals. There should be no doubt whatsoever when the goal is attained. "I have carrots" is not as good as "I have 100 or more carrots at least six inches long."

2. Write the goal down. This not only helps you remember and review the goal; it also begins the action to fulfill the goal in a physical way.

Further, seeing a goal in black and white helps reveal any discrepancies or conflicts. W. C. Fields, an atheist his entire life, was asked on his deathbed why he was reading the Bible. "Looking for loopholes," Fields replied. When you see your goal in writing, it sometimes helps point out the loopholes.

For example, seeing our goal of 100 carrots above pointed out a loophole to us. What if we get our carrots, but the gophers get to them first and we get half-eaten carrots? After seeing our goal in writing, we would now probably rewrite it: "I have at least 100 whole, healthy carrots at least six inches long."

3. Determine what your goal is worth to you. What—in real, spendable money—is your goal worth? In some cases, this will be easy—your goal is a material object with a fair market value. In other cases, determining worth may be more difficult. If your goal is "I weigh a healthy 150 pounds" and you currently weigh 155 pounds, you will have to determine what weighing five pounds less is worth to you.* Here's where your Master Teacher can come in handy.

Keep in mind what *you* can afford to pay. Don't automatically say, "That would be worth a million dollars to me!" Do you *have* a million dollars? If someone came to

---

*Note, please, that we stated the goal of weight loss in positive terms. We did not say "I want to lose five pounds." We gave, instead, the ideal weight—or at least one of the weigh stations (no pun intended) along the way (they're all over the place!) to our ideal weight. If you can't find a way to state what you want without also stating what you don't want, say it in the most positive way possible. For example, rather than "Stop smoking," try, perhaps, "I am free from smoking."

Be not penny-wise:
riches have wings,
and sometimes
they fly away of themselves;
sometimes
they must be set flying
to bring in more.

SIR FRANCIS BACON

1625

your door and offered your goal to you right now for a million dollars, would you be able to buy it? If not, it's not worth that to *you*.

It's not that you can't have your goal, you understand. It's just that the value you place on it has to be proportionate to your net worth and cash flow. If you're worth $500,000,000 and your cash flow is $50,000,000 per year, then perhaps some things might be worth a million dollars to you. If your net worth is $100,000 and your cash flow is $30,000 per year, then *nothing* is worth a million dollars to you. No matter *what* it was, you probably wouldn't be able to gather a million dollars anyway.

If, however, the same person appeared at your door and offered you the same goal for $1,000, would you take it? Would you actually, literally, give this person $1,000 for that goal? If yes, then that's what it's worth to you.

Please keep in mind that establishing the price is not what the item would be worth on the "free market." Just as 150 pounds might be your ideal weight, it may be too light for some and too heavy for others. So, too, weighing 150 pounds may be worth $100 to you, $1,000 to the next person, $10,000 to another, and $100,000 to a multi-millionaire.

Carrots grow equally well for the rich as for the poor. Don't put off weighing 150 pounds if that's what you really want until you "have enough money to pay for it." If what you can afford to pay is $1 for it, pay that.

4. Plant the seed. You plant the seed by donating from one to one hundred percent of the value of your goal. When should it be one percent? When should it be three percent? When should it be fifty percent? When should it be one hundred percent? That's between you and your higher power (or, if you don't believe in a higher power, between you and your conscience). Some seeds are larger than others. Some seeds cost more than others.

In general, the sooner you want your goal, the greater should be the seed. If you're ill and say, "My health is worth $1,000" and you want your health back *fast,* seed

*In this world
it is not what we take up,
but what we give up,
that makes us rich.*

HENRY WARD BEECHER

*Practical prayer
is harder on
the soles of your shoes
than on
the knees of your trousers.*

AUSTIN O'MALLEY

one hundred percent. If you want a house, but are in no hurry to get a house, seed less.

The most important part of seeding is *intention,* not *amount.* One percent with clear intention works better than one-hundred percent with weak intention.

A great deal of seeding has to do with what you believe you need to give in order to receive. If you genuinely believe that by giving $1 you can receive $100, then your seed need only be one percent. If you believe you need to give $10 to get back $100, then your seeding would be ten percent. And so on.

Belief and intention are more than just emotional feelings. They are based upon pragmatic results. Did your seeding work at ten percent? If yes, then ten percent works. Does it work at one percent? If no, then try it at five percent. If it works at five percent, then you can seed at five percent. Watch carefully as your garden grows, and you can adjust your seeding accordingly.

If yours is a money goal, you might want to seed for a portion of it first. When that portion comes in, seed for the next portion of it. For example, if your money goal is $10,000, you might want to seed for $1,000 first. When the $1,000 comes in, then seed for $2,000. When the $2,000 comes in, seed for $4,000. Continue in this way until you have reached your money goal.

The same gradual process can be used for any goal. If your ideal weight is 150 and you currently weigh 175 pounds, plant the seed for weighing 170. When you reach that goal, plant the seed for weighing 165, etc.

5. Keep your seeding a secret. What you have seeded for—and all the details of your seeding—is entirely between you and your higher power. Telling another about it is like digging up a seed. The plant will die. Keep your seeding secret. Keep your seeding sacred. Let the roots grow deep.

When you have the fruits of your seeding—that is, when your goal has been clearly achieved—you can invite your friends over for a home-grown, home-cooked meal to

*I am a great believer in luck,
and I find the harder I work
the more I have of it.*

STEPHEN LEACOCK

*Don't stay in bed...
unless you make money in bed.*

GEORGE BURNS

celebrate. Then you can give all of your friends copies of this book and say "it's all described on page 465, but read all the stuff that goes before it first."

6. Tend your garden. Leave the seeds alone. Let them grow. Water them with affirmation and action, but don't check their progress every three minutes. A watched pot never boils; a watched plant never grows. Every so often—weekly, say—review the progress you've made on each goal. This generally takes very little time.

Occasionally, doubt may come in. Time for a little gardening. State the goal as an affirmation and say it to yourself a few hundred times. Or, perhaps, a treasure map of that particular goal is in order. Maybe it's time to go to your sanctuary and put on the ability suit connected with that goal, or do some work on your video screen. Or, perhaps, a brief chat with your Master Teacher will take care of any doubts.

7. Do the work necessary. Just as the soil needs tilling, so, too, your seedlings as they grow may require—in fact, probably will require—some physical work on your part. Whatever that work is, as it appears, do it.

8. Keep a record of your progress. As a goal is fulfilled, check it off your list, but continue to write new seedings on the same list. As time goes by, you will have page after page of seeds, successfully nurtured to completion. Please remember that seeding can work in one of two ways. First, we can get the thing we seed for—or something better. Second, the desire for what we seed for may go away completely. If, as we go down our list of planted seeds, we realize one day, "I don't want that anymore," we can check it off. The seeding has been fulfilled.

At each harvest comes the time of thanksgiving. That's where tithing comes in.

*"Bring the whole tithe
into the storehouse,
that there may be food
in my house.
Test me in this,"
says the Lord Almighty,
"and see if I will not
throw open the floodgates
of heaven and pour out
so much blessing
that you will not
have room enough for it."*

MALACHI 3:10

Tithing

The concept of tithing is an ancient one. By the time of Moses, 1490 B.C., it was already well established. *Tithe* means "a tenth." "A tithe of everything from the land, whether grain from the soil or fruit from the trees belongs to the Lord; it is holy to the Lord" (Leviticus 27:30).

In tithing, we give a tenth of our increase. If we make $100, we give $10. If someone gives us a gift worth $100, we give $10.

You can tithe with money, goods or services. Money is the cleanest. When it's time to tithe, some people kid themselves by going through the garage and donating everything that they no longer need—which the organization they tithe to may not need either.

If something is worth $50 and the organization does not need it, sell the item for $50 and donate the money. If your time is worth $10 an hour and the organization needs your services, let them know you're not volunteering—you're working at the rate of $10 an hour to pay your tithe. If the organization says, "We don't pay anyone to work for us, we're an all-volunteer organization," then go out and work for someone else for $10 an hour and donate that money to the organization.

You tithe only on the increase. This means after taxes but before anything else. ("Render unto Caesar" and all that.) If you work for someone else, and your taxes are automatically taken from your payroll check, you tithe on the amount of your check.

If you work for yourself, and your business and personal expenses are intermingled, go though each expenditure and ask, "Is this a business or personal expense?" If it's personal, tithe ten percent of that amount. If it's business, there is no need to tithe on that amount—that's your business increase. Tithe on *your* increase. (When you sell the business, however, tithe the full amount, after taxes, you receive.)

You may say to yourself,
"My power and the strength
of my hands have produced
this wealth for me."

DEUTERONOMY 8:17

But remember
the Lord your God,
for it is he
who gives you the ability
to produce wealth,
and so confirms his covenant
which he swore
to your forefathers,
as it is today.

DEUTERONOMY 8:18

Some expenses—such as telephone, may be both business and personal. Determine the percentage, say, twenty percent personal and eighty percent business—and tithe on the portion that is personal.

The attitude behind the tithe is all-important. The tithe made as a sacrifice will return its blessings to us—although they will come to us in a sacrificial way. People will begrudgingly give us what is ours because they feel that they have to. We'll get it, but the energy that comes with it will be, "I don't want to, but I have to."

If we give from the joy of thanksgiving, with a heart full of gratitude, then we will receive back in joy, thanksgiving and gratitude. People will not just give you what is yours; they will thank you for being in their lives. Tithing is a physical affirmation of both abundance and gratitude. The more abundant and grateful you feel as you give your tithe, the wealthier you will be.

When should you tithe? As the saying goes, "Pay God first." If you pay your bills every two weeks, let the first check be your tithing check. At least once a month, however, review your increase and tithe accordingly.

Don't let tithing replace whatever *donations* you regularly give to the organization of your choice. If you donated $500 to that organization last year, donate at least $500 this year *and* tithe in addition to that. A tithe is a way of saying, "Thank you for what I have newly received." A donation is a gift from you to materially support the work the organization does. You tithe for yourself; you donate for the organization.

If you have any further questions about tithing, go to your sanctuary and invite in on the people mover the Prince of Tithes. He'll be able to answer all your questions.

Tithing is a way of showing gratitude for whoever or whatever you feel is responsible for the gift of life. It's paying your rent to live in this world. It's your share of the air you breathe, the color of the trees, the sun in the morning and the moon at night. It's also a most tangible way of saying, "Thank you. I have more than I need."

Turning and turning
in the widening gyre
The falcon cannot hear the falconer;
Things fall apart;
the centre cannot hold;
Mere anarchy is loosed
upon the world,
The blood-dimmed tide is loosed,
and everywhere
The ceremony of innocence
is drowned;
The best lack all conviction,
while the worst
Are full of passionate intensity.

WILLIAM BUTLER YEATS

Money Magnet

In addition to seeding and tithing, some people like to keep a money magnet. A money magnet follows the same rules as tithing, except that you tithe to yourself. Take ten percent of your increase and keep it in cash, gold, precious stones, land or whatever represents solid material value to you.

The money magnet is for the child within. This is the inner voice that asks, as we pay our monthly bills, "What's in it for me?" So, you pay God first with your tithe, yourself second with your money magnet, then everyone else.

As the money magnet grows, the child within feels more and more confident and abundant. That little voice inside sometimes gives us negative affirmations about material wealth—those limiting worries and complaints that slow the flow of money out, therefore, slowing the flow of money in. With a money magnet, these become less and less frequent as this inner child worries less and less about money.

"If it's ten percent for seeding, ten percent for tithing, and ten percent for the money magnet, that's thirty percent," some people figure. "That only leaves seventy percent left for everything else. I can't live on seventy percent of what I make."

Well, first of all, you probably *could* live on seventy percent of what you make—perhaps not in the style to which you have become accustomed—but you could live.

That, of course, is not the main point. The main point is that seeding, tithing and the money magnet *increase* one's material abundance—quite significantly. Seventy percent of $100,000 is more expendable income than one hundred percent of $50,000.

Some people ask, "Can't I keep my money magnet in the bank where it will collect interest?" If you put your money in the bank, then the bank has your money mag-

*A lot of people
will also urge you
to put some money in a bank,
and in fact—within reason—
this is very good advice.
But don't go overboard.
Remember, what you are doing
is giving your money
to somebody else to hold on to,
and I think that it is worth
keeping in mind that
the businessmen who
run banks are so worried about
holding on to things that they put
little chains
on all their pens.*

MISS PIGGY*

---

*Miss Piggy, bless her porcine heart, satirized one of our previous books by calling
it *DO IT FOR ME! Let's Get Them Off Their Butts* by John and Peter McWillful.
God bless you, Miss Piggy! And God bless *humor.*

480

net. What are banks if nothing more than giant money magnets? They prove the principle of mutual attraction, "Like gathers like."

The banks that have the most money get more. If there were two banks next to each other, and one had $50 billion in assets and the other one had $238 in assets, which would you put more money into? The child within doesn't understand numbers in a bank book. He or she understands cash, gold, jewels, land. It is *this* child's interest you want to collect.

It's not a good idea to put your money magnet into anything that tends to depreciate in value—such as automobiles or machinery. It's better to invest in things that tend to appreciate. The child within appreciates that more.

When you have enough money in your money magnet, however, you can invest up to ninety percent of it in what might be called the "tools of the trade." If you're a writer, this may mean a word processor. If you're raising a family, it may mean a down payment on a house. If you're an actor, it may mean cosmetic surgery or a new set of teeth. Whatever might help you pursue your big dream in a big way would qualify.

Before making any such investment, however, be sure to get the permission of the child within. Your child may say, "It's about time we got a computer—I'm tired of retyping all the time." Or, your child may say, "That means we'll be poor again!" If you get the second type of answer, the time is not yet right for investing the money magnet.

As with homemade yogurt or sourdough bread, when investing the money magnet, always keep at least ten percent of it as a "starter."

For some people, the inner child is so confident in the worth of their spiritual or religious organization that, each year, the child is happy to donate ninety percent of the money magnet to that organization. Again, this is a choice to be made by the child within. Please respect his or her decision.

You should realize
that I have made no addition to my collection
of French Impressionists since I bought the
Washington Post.

EUGENE MAYER

The Pluto-American
Anti-Defamation League said
it will bring pressure to bear
on media to up-grade the image
of incredibly rich people.
The newly-formed group,
which hopes to combat
negative portrayals
of incredibly rich people
on television and in print,
cited the crucial role
that incredibly rich people
have played in American history,
and hopes to restore incredible richness
as a "positive aspect of American life."

OFF THE WALL STREET JOURNAL

As children love to play, so too your inner child loves to play with his or her money magnet. Count it. Spread it around the floor, throw it in the air, have fun with it.

It's a good idea to count your money magnet before writing the monthly checks. As the balance in the checking account goes down, the money magnet will remind the child within, "We're not poor." It alleviates a lot of worry.

(It's also a good idea, with each check you write, to remember the *good* that came because of that check—the food, electricity, medical care, enjoyment or whatever. Too often we look at *amounts,* not at the *experiences* that came from those amounts. Check writing can be an exercise in appreciation and gratitude.)

The money magnet gives the child within confidence, reassurance and joy. It creates a consciousness of wealth that acts as a magnet, pulling more and more material abundance to it. It also makes us feel wealthier.

If it isn't the sheriff,
it's the finance company;
I've got more attachments
on me than a vacuum cleaner.

JOHN BARRYMORE

Money Magnet Questionnaire

Please answer the following questions about your money magnet. Then tear out this page and mail it to us at the address in the front of the book.

1. How much is in your money magnet?

2. In what form do you keep your money magnet:
   ❑ cash   ❑ gold   ❑ jewels   ❑ other_____.

3. Where do you keep your money magnet?
   (Be specific—draw a diagram if necessary.)

4. Do you have a burglar alarm or any sort of security system?

5. If the answer to number 4 is yes, what is your security code, and how does one disarm your burglar alarm?

6. Do you have any vicious dogs, cats, goldfish, etc.?

7. Would a raw T-bone steak distract them for at least ten minutes?

8. At what hours of any day or night is no one home at your house or apartment?

9. What are the dates of your vacation this year?

If there are any significant changes in the above information, please send the updated information to us at your earliest opportunity.

Thank you.

*I cannot easily
buy a blankbook
to write thoughts in;
they are commonly ruled
for dollars and cents.*

THOREAU

Ten Essential Minutes a Day

Thus far in this book, we have given you a great many techniques for increasing wealth. If we were to choose one technique to be practiced on a daily basis above all others, it would be the one we're about to present.

It only takes ten minutes to do; that's why we call it "Ten Essential Minutes a Day." Seeding and tithing we consider essential, too, but they are not necessarily a daily practice.

To practice the ten essential minutes, get a notebook that's divided into at least six sections. A loose-leaf binder in which you can add and remove pages might be ideal. Get one that's attractive, though—one that doesn't cause flashbacks of high school.

Label the sections: ATTUNEMENT, AFFIRMATION, LONG-TERM GOALS, SHORT-TERM GOALS, APPRECIATION/GRATITUDE and LISTENING.

During the ten essential minutes, each section will receive from one to two minutes of attention. What to place in each section will become clear as we review, minute by minute, the ten essential minutes of the day:

> ONE MINUTE: ATTUNEMENT—Ask for the light, pray, meditate, contemplate. Attune yourself to your highest good. On this page in your notebook, you may want to remind yourself of the definition of wealth. We'll give you our definition again, and you're certainly welcome to adapt it to your own personal definition. "Wealth is health, happiness, abundance, prosperity, riches, loving, caring, sharing, learning, knowing what I want, opportunity, enjoying and balance."

> TWO MINUTES: ABUNDANCE AFFIRMATIONS—Use this time to review whatever affirmations you've used to enhance your abundance. "I am wealthy," "I am worthy of my

*Our greatest happiness
does not depend
on the condition of life
in which chance
has placed us,
but is always the result
of a good conscience,
good health, occupation, and
freedom in all just pursuits.*

THOMAS JEFFERSON

wealth," "I appreciate my wealth," "I am grateful for my wealth," and all the others—both new and old—that you find uplifting and important. Add to this list as you go along.

ONE MINUTE: LONG-TERM GOALS—Review and visualize the success of your big dream—your long-term goal. These are usually goals projected ahead three to five years. Some, however, may be as close as one year away. Use this minute each day to see, heal, hear, smell and taste the joy of living that dream.

TWO MINUTES: SHORT-TERM GOALS—Review the goals you have set to achieve within the next days, weeks, and months. When a goal is achieved, cross it off your list, but cross it off in a way that you can go back and review all that you've accomplished. Feel free, of course, to add new goals at any time.

TWO MINUTES: APPRECIATION AND GRATITUDE—Feel appreciation and gratitude for what you already have. This section could become the "good book" we discussed earlier in which you keep track of all the good things that you do and all the good things that happen to you. Keep adding to this list, but don't remove any pages. This section will become quite thick in time. The full two minutes may be taken just turning pages. Be grateful for the fact that you have so much to be grateful for, it can't even be reviewed in two minutes.

TWO MINUTES: LISTENING—Take the time, with your eyes closed, to listen to whatever inner guidance, ideas, suggestions or lessons you may hear. Keep the notebook on your lap, pen in hand. As each idea comes through, jot it down. These may be things that need to be done—steps in fulfilling your dream. You can

I keep the telephone
of my mind
open to peace, harmony, health,
love and abundance.
Then, whenever doubt,
anxiety or fear try to call me,
they keep getting a busy signal—
and soon they'll forget my number.

EDITH ARMSTRONG

get a rather complete "To Do" list for the day. The formal part of the process is over in two minutes. You may find, however, that the information you're getting is so valuable—and so practical—that you'll keep listening and writing.

This ten minutes each day is best spent just before going to sleep at night or just after waking up in the morning. If those are not practical times, any time during the day is fine. It is also best to do it at approximately the same time each day. Again, if that's not practical, ten minutes anytime during the day is fine.

If you find the process so beneficial that you want to spend more than ten minutes at it, two ten-minute periods a day are more powerful than one twenty-minute period. Three ten-minute periods—upon awakening, sometime in the middle of the day, and just before going to sleep—are ideal. But don't wait until you have time for "the ideal." Start at least one ten-minute period a day *now*.

Obviously, keep your notebook where curious eyes cannot see it. This is *your* process. You should feel free to write anything you want about anything in your life. Wondering who may read it or be looking over your shoulder may inhibit your spontaneity. If necessary, buy a strong box and keep your notebook under lock and key.

Please give this exercise a try. We're sure you'll find it so valuable that you'll continue doing it with pleasure.

You'll also probably find it eminently practical. The suggestions during the "listening period" alone are sure to save more than ten minutes each day—sometimes they save whole days or weeks.

Spend time on yourself. Spend time with yourself. You're worth it.

*Man always
travels along precipices.
His truest obligation
is to keep his balance.*

JOSÉ ORTEGA Y GASSET

PART FIVE

BALANCE

Next to loving, balance is probably the most important aspect of wealth.

This world doesn't just *seem* to be contradictory—it *is*. There are so few hard-and-fast rules. Everything seems to depend on circumstances.

Getting through any of it with a sense of wholeness takes a lot of loving—and balance.

I like work;
it fascinates me;
I can sit
and look at it for hours.

JEROME K. JEROME

A Question of Balance

Balance is a very personal thing. "One man's meat is another man's livestock." Life is full of extremes, an interplay of opposites. One person may like one extreme, another person may like the opposite. Most people find themselves on the continuum between the two.

The continuums are many. Some of the more important ones are work and play, activity and rest, togetherness and solitude. Let's take a closer look at each.

Work and Play. Some people enjoy setting goals and achieving them. Once a goal is achieved, they plant their flag upon it and move almost immediately to the next. They enjoy work.

Conversely, other people like to appreciate what they've got. They enjoy the moment so much they sometimes have difficulty at work. "Would you get back to work!" "Look at that big white cloud over there!"

Activity and Rest. Some people love being active. They consider sleep a waste of time and spend very little time doing it. The last time they took a hot bath was when they were eighteen months old. If they are not physically doing something, they're bored.

Other people enjoy rest. Exercise is an anathema to them. The only sit-ups they do are when they sit up in bed. They enjoy sleep, love dreams and always try to get five seats across on airplanes so they can lie down. The last time they perspired was when they took a hot bath—which was about two hours ago. The last time they perspired *outside* of a bathtub was in 1972, when the air conditioner broke in the middle of a heat wave.

Togetherness and Solitude. Some people want to be with at least one other person all the time. Sometimes it's the same person, sometimes it's different people, but people it must be. Cooking, eating, bathing, sleeping—they are never alone. In addition, they often have pets that score high in physical affection and tactile stimulation.

Food
is an important part
of a balanced diet.

FRAN LEBOWITZ

While watching a movie on television, if their partner says, "I'm going to the kitchen to get ice cream, do you want anything?" they say, "I'll join you."

Others enjoy solitude. They like their own company the best. They have trouble falling asleep if someone else is in the same house, much less the same bed. They are often employed as forest rangers, lighthouse keepers and writers.

Is one end of any continuum "right" and the other "wrong"? Of course not.

We like to think—in our more optimistic moments—that society is catching on to this idea. "It is suddenly all right to be a hairdresser," observed Tony Lang. "No one really knows how this happened."

What I dream of
is an art of balance,
of purity and serenity
devoid of troubling
or depressing subject matter...
a soothing,
calming influence
on the mind,
something like
a good armchair
which provides relaxation
from physical fatigue.

HENRI MATISSE

Getting What You Want vs. Enjoying What You've Got

Another important continuum—and, obviously, one of the major themes of this book—has at one end enjoying what you've got and, at the other, getting more of what you want.

Enjoying what you've got is like sitting inside your house during a winter storm. The room is snug, the fireplace is roaring, the cocoa is hot, the company is congenial (be it other people or a good book). Everything is perfect, just as it is.

Getting what you want is gathering whatever money you have, putting on your boots, parka, gloves, scarf, hat, and trudging through the snow, praying that by the time you get to the store it will still be open and that the money you have will be enough to buy the thing you want.

The two processes have nothing to do with each other.

What's the answer? Balance.

Sitting in front of the fire for days and weeks eventually gets boring. We develop cabin fever. The best of company becomes irritating.

"I'm going to run to the store to get something," we say, jumping up and putting on our parka.

"What are you going to get?"

"Some milk." Any excuse will do.

"But we have milk."

"Some egg nog, then."

"We have eggs. I can make you some egg nog."

"Oh, don't trouble yourself. The store's just a few miles away."

"Wait, I'll come with you."

*A man of courage
never needs weapons,
but he may need bail.*

ETHEL WATTS MUMFORD

"That's okay," we say, opening the door. "I'll be right back." We step outside, close the door, and are gone.

Ah, freedom! The smell of the cool, crisp air. The beauty of the snow. The cold wind blowing on our face. Refreshing.

We walk through the snow. It grows darker. The cold begins to feel, well, cold. The store is around the next bend—and just in time, too.

Alas, the store is closed. What? What's the purpose of a store if it's going to be closed?

It is now quite dark. The snow falls, gets blown around, and falls again. Our feet are no longer cold; they are *numb*. We remember those scenes from *Doctor Zhivago*—eyelashes and moustaches caked with ice. Although we don't have a moustache, there must certainly be ice crystals forming on our upper lip.

A car pulls up. It is our overly solicitous companion. "I called the store, and they were closed, so I thought you might need a ride."

"Yes! Yes!" we say, as the ice cracks and falls from our lips. We get in. The car is warm. "Thank you, thank you."

"I made some egg nog."

"You are so wonderful. Take me home. I just want to sit in front of the fire. I never want to leave. There's no place like home. There's no place like home."

How long, sweating before the fire, do you think we'll last before the call of store-bought egg nog becomes, once again, irresistible? An hour? A day? A week?

This is where knowing our personal balance point comes in. If we know, for example, that after three days we will want to stalk the wild egg nog, then we can plan for it. If we know that two hours of stalking is sufficient, then we can make productive use of the time. Every three days, for two hours, we can plan to get some exercise: take a walk, shovel the walk.

We can also let others know of our pattern.

If a man is in health,
he doesn't need
to take anybody else's temperature
to know where he is going.

ELWYN BROOKS WHITE

"I'm going out for my walk."

"Oh. Is it Tuesday?"

"Yes."

"Have a good time. See you when you get back."

We know that we want to spend about two hours alone and outdoors approximately every three days. That's our balance point.

The important thing to note is that's *our* balance point. Other people may want two hours inside for every three days outside. Still others may only need to *look* outside every three days.

Once you know *your* pattern (not the pattern you're *supposed* to have, or the pattern the average well-balanced person has, but *your* pattern), you can plan your life accordingly.

But how do we find our balance point?

*Flops
are a part
of life's menu
and I've never been a girl
to miss out
on any of the courses.*

ROSALIND RUSSELL

Finding Your Balance Point

There's only one way to find our balance point on any given continuum: trial and error. At first, when exploring a continuum, there will be lots of error.

Finding a balance point in life is like finding the balance point on a tightrope—at first, we do a lot more falling than we do walking. Gradually, gradually we find the points of balance within us. We learn to trust them. Our coordination improves, and what was haltering and faltering at first becomes, with enough trial and error, lithe and graceful.

The *trial* portion of trial and error doesn't just mean you need to try a lot of things. It also means you'll be *on trial*. There are any number of people who will think you should live your life the way they think you should live it. They are—all in one—judge, jury and executioner. Let them say what they will, but stay away from their execution grounds.

If these people are judging you based upon their interpretation of Christianity, here are three useful quotes to memorize. You can rattle them off—including chapter and verse citations—just before turning and going about your business.

The first two are from Jesus. "Do not judge, or you too will be judged" (Matthew 7:1). "Do not judge, and you will not be judged. Do not condemn, and you will not be condemned. Forgive, and you will be forgiven" (Luke 6:37).

St. Paul had this to say: "I care very little if I am judged by you or by any human court; indeed, I do not even judge myself" (1 Corinthians 4:3).

Along the way, of course, we'll have to deal with our judgment of ourselves. We are a product of our culture. We are trained not to take risks, not to explore new territory, not to try things, not to make our own conclusions. We are trained to toe the mark, fit in, and be normal.

*Money isn't everything
as long as
you have enough.*

MALCOLM FORBES

As we explore our balance points, the natural, predictable reaction will be guilt. Expect this. Be ready to forgive yourself not just seven times seventy, but seventy thousand times seventy thousand. (That's 4.9 billion.)

Once we find our balance point on a certain continuum, it's good to know where the people we relate with have their balance point on that continuum.

There is the story of the marriage counselor who was seeing a husband and wife in separate sessions. At the husband's session, the counselor asked, "How's your sex life?" The husband answered, "Terrible! She only wants it two or three times a week!" During the wife's session, the counselor again asked, "How's your sex life?" The wife answered, "Terrible! He wants it two or three times a week!"

When we find people whose balance points on various continuums are similar or complementary to ours, we say we are compatible.

When we say "complementary," it's important to realize that people don't have to have the same balance point as we do to complement us perfectly. People on the giving side of the giving/receiving continuum get along better with people on the receiving side than they do with people on the giving side. When two givers get together, too often it becomes, "After you," "Oh no, after you," "Oh no, after you, I insist," "Oh, no, no, after *you,* after *you.*"

Explore first the continuums that lead to your big dream. You will probably never find your balance point on every continuum. That's fine. Such is life. You may master the tightrope, but never tame the lions. Such is the circus.

Finding your balance points takes courage. Courage, you'll recall, means "from the heart." Don't discover your balance points in defiance. Look for them in love.

*You can convert
your style
into riches.*

QUENTIN CRISP

The Courage to Live a Balanced Life

That we each have different balance points along any continuum is not in and of itself a problem. It's a large world. There's lots of room for variation.

The problem arises when our culture tries to herd everyone to the middle of the continuum, saying, "Here. This is where you should be to live a balanced life. If you want to live anywhere else, you are abnormal."

We understand *why* this happens: the rules of society are made primarily by controllers, and—if all people fit into the same cookie-cutter pattern—they are easier to control.

We do not, however, have to listen—much less obey—the "normal" guidelines set forth by others. Some people throw away the best parts of themselves in a futile effort to be normal.

As the psychiatrist Harold H. Bloomfield, M.D., pointed out, "The only normal people are the ones we haven't gotten to know yet."

Normalcy is a myth. And yet the fear of being "abnormal" is so great that some people sacrifice their lives to it. (And we mean this quite literally—a large percentage of suicide notes refer to not "fitting in.")

Trying to live a balanced life by cultural standards, then, can throw one out of balance. Trying to live what is generally considered "a well-balanced life" can lead to being out of balance personally.

Find the courage (heart) to live *your* well-balanced life. Love yourself enough to live your life in balance.

*If you don't do it excellently,
don't do it at all.
Because if it's not excellent,
it won't be profitable or fun,
and if you're not in business
for fun or profit,
what the hell are you doing there?*

ROBERT TOWNSEND

EPILOGUE
Living in a Consciousness of Wealth

Wealth is more than just money—much more. Much of what we consider wealth, in fact, has nothing to do with money.

Wealth is health, happiness, abundance, prosperity, riches, loving, caring, sharing, learning, knowing what we want, opportunity, enjoying and balance.

We consider these attributes of wealth as *attitudes,* not things.

Wealth is a way of looking at life.

Do these words sound familiar? That's because they were taken from the first section of this book.

When you read them then, they might not have had the same meaning they have now. When you think of wealth now, you may not think of it as you did before.

Reading this book might have inspired you. It might even have gotten you "high." Inspirational books, well, inspire. The trouble is, all too soon, the inspiration fades. That's why this book is filled with techniques for *achieving* wealth.

Please do not just *read* this book.

Do this book.

Now that you've read all the way through *WEALTH 101,* we suggest you start again at the beginning. When you come to an exercise, stop and do it. Most people read a book like this without doing the exercises, just to see where the authors are coming from and where they are going. If you like where we're coming from—and especially where we are going—please take the time to explore your own experience of the book.

Experience comes from doing the exercises—saying the affirmations a thousand times each, discovering your purpose, choosing a big dream, building a sanctuary, meeting

*Lazy hands make a man poor,
but diligent hands
bring wealth.*

PROVERBS 10:4

your Master Teacher, learning to meditate, writing down the good, making a treasure map, seeding, tithing, putting together a notebook for the ten essential minutes a day, practicing the ten essential minutes a day, listening to the meditation tape, and all the rest.

What is there to experience? Why, yourself, of course. Along with health, happiness, abundance, prosperity, riches, loving, caring, sharing, learning, knowing what you want, opportunity, enjoying and balance.

You know, wealth.

For Further Study:
Organizations Founded by John-Roger

This is Peter, stepping out of my co-author character, to tell you about some of the organizations founded by John-Roger.

J-R must like founding organizations. I certainly *hope* he likes founding organizations—he's founded enough of them. It's probably more accurate to say that organizations formed *around* John-Roger; he stands still for a while and teaches, and the people listening to him form organizations by which these teachings can be shared with others.

The organizations range from the secular to the spiritual—that is, some are of The Gap, and some are not. I'll list them in approximate order of Gap-ness—starting with the purely secular.

Now that you've had a taste of J-R's teachings (through this book), you might want to explore some more. (In this book we have barely scratched the surface—he's been at it nonstop for the past 29 years.)

I'll be brief. You may want to ask your Master Teacher which, if any, of these you might like to pursue.

The Heartfelt Foundation is dedicated to service. They do various community projects, large and small, all over the world. If you'd like to take part—or organize a service project in your community—give them a call. 2101 Wilshire Blvd., Santa Monica, CA 90403; 310-828-0535.

Institute for Individual and World Peace. Just as it says. If you want to learn more about peace and how you can effect it—or if you have any ideas to contribute—drop them a line. 2101 Wilshire Blvd., Santa Monica, CA 90403; 310-828-0535.

University of Santa Monica. Offers a dynamic two-year M.A. degree program in Applied Psychology, in a monthly weekend format. This practical program is on the cutting edge where psychology meets spirituality, and is also available as a non-degree option. Approved by the State of California Dept. of Education. Write or call for a brochure. 2107 Wilshire Blvd., Santa Monica, CA 90403; 310-829-7402.

(Those organizations that would be classified as Gap-like begin here.)

Movement for Spiritual Inner Awareness (MSIA) is for those who want to live in a way that makes spirit and God a part of their lives. MSIA has no formal membership, dues, rules or dogma. It encourages people in their own experience of the divine, without restricting personal choices. The booklet "About MSIA" describes MSIA and its goals. You can also find out if J-R's TV show, "That Which Is," is available in your area. Write or call MSIA, Box 3935, Los Angeles, CA 90051; 213-737-4055.

Discourses. John-Roger's Soul Awareness Discourses are the most complete, effective and delightful course in Spirit I know. You simply read one a month at your own pace. Each Discourse contains about 30 pages of text and more than 60 blank pages for your own daily notes, reminders, dreams, discoveries, affirmations or anything else you'd like. They're $100 per year (12 Discourses), and I can't recommend them too highly. For more information, please contact MSIA.

Mandeville Press. Publishes J-R's earlier books, including *Relationships—The Art of Making Life Work, The Power Within You,* and *Wealth and Higher Consciousness.* On a more spiritual note, there's *Loving...Each Day, The Spiritual Promise, The Spiritual Family* and *The Way Out Book.* Other books are available. They also publish *The New Day Herald,* a bi-monthly newspaper of articles on, mostly, loving. A vast collection of John-Roger on audio and video tapes is available, looking at life from a spiritual yet practical point of view. A catalog is available from MSIA.

Other Books in THE *LIFE 101* SERIES
All by John-Roger and Peter McWilliams

Meditation on Wealth

A special meditation on wealth by John-Roger, with an introduction by John Morton. One cassette tape. $10.

WEALTH 101 Audio Tapes

The complete and unabridged text of this book, read by Academy Award nominee Sally Kirkland, David Warrilow, Christopher McMullen and Peter McWilliams. Includes John-Roger's *Meditation on Wealth* (described above). Six cassettes. $22.95.

LIFE 101:
Everything We Wish We Had Learned About Life
In School—But Didn't

The overview book of THE *LIFE 101* SERIES. The idea behind *LIFE 101* is that everything in life is for our upliftment, learning and growth—including (and, perhaps, especially) the "bad" stuff. "The title jolly well says it all," said the *Los Angeles Times*—jolly well saying it all. 400 pages. **Trade paperback, $9.95. Audio tapes** (complete and unabridged, five cassettes), $19.95. **Wristwatch** (Paul LeBus designed), $35.00.

You Can't Afford the Luxury
of a Negative Thought: A Book for People
with Any Life-Threatening Illness—Including Life

This is not just a book for people with life-threatening illnesses. It's a book for anyone afflicted with one of the primary diseases of our time: negative thinking. If, however, you have the symptoms of a life-threatening illness—be it AIDS, heart trouble, cancer, high blood pressure or any of the others—negative thinking is a luxury you can no longer afford. 622 pages. **Trade paperback, $14.95. Audio tapes** (complete and unabridged, eight cassettes), $22.95. **Workbook** $11.95. **Wristwatch, $35.00.**

Meditation for Loving Yourself

A beautiful meditation tape, it lasts a little over half an hour. John-Roger is "backed" by a musical score composed and performed by Scott Fitzgerald and Rob Whitesides-Woo. $10. This meditation is also included in the audio cassette package of *You Can't Afford the Luxury of a Negative Thought.*

DO IT!
Let's Get Off Our Buts

This is a book for those who want to discover—clearly and precisely—their dream; who choose to pursue that dream, even if it means learning (and—gasp!—practicing) some new behavior; who wouldn't mind having some fun along the way; and who are willing to expand their comfort zone enough to include their heart's desire. 500 pages. **Trade paperback,** $9.95. **Audio tapes** (complete and unabridged, six cassettes), $22.95.

If you were searching
for a word to describe
the conversations
that go on down the mine,
boring would spring to your lips.
Oh, God! They're very boring.
If you ever want to hear things like:
"Hello, I've found a bit of coal."
"Have you really?"
"Yes, no doubt about it,
this black substance
is coal all right."
"Jolly good, the very thing
we're looking for."
It's not enough to keep
the mind alive, is it?

PETER COOK

Index

A

Abell, Richard, 97
Ability suit practice area, 221, 227
Ability suits, 221, 227–229
Abundance, 18–21, 25, 127, 173
  affirmations, 487–488
  definition, 19
Acceptance, 322
  definition, 323
  of death, 326–329
Accomplishments
  recognizing, 287, 289, 291
Adam and Eve, 102–109
Adams, Franklin P., 197
"The Addams Family"
  Gomez Addams, 120
Addison, James, 189
Addison, Joseph, 197
Ade, George, 114, 321
Adversity
  See Problems
Affirmations, 183
  definition, 175
  examples, 176, 179
  money, 409
  negative, 183
  of appreciation, 189
  of goals, 315, 473
  of gratitude, 199
  of wealth, 382–383
  of worthiness, 183
  using, 177
  visual, 453
The Age of Anxiety, 96
Agreements
  See Trust
AIDS, 328
Alexander, Peter, 215
Allen, Fred, 73
Allen, Steve, 252
Allen, Woody, 218, 386
Ameneope, 321
"Amos 'n' Andy"
  Kingfish, 232
"The Andy Griffith Show"
  Floyd Lawson, 326
Anger, 101, 253, 255, 439
  See also Depression
Anxiety, 96–101
  antithesis of enjoyment, 95
  causes, 113
  definition, 97

Appreciation, 47, 129, 145, 184–189, 489
  definition, 47
  experiment, 185
  of adversity, 13, 140–143, 342, 349
  of blessings, 141, 143
  of excellence, 186
  of laughter, 347
  of life, 138–139, 143
  of nature, 32, 145, 194, 200, 228
  of self, 187, 189, 233, 379
  of tears, 347
Aristotle, 15, 23, 378, 446
Arlen, Michael, 117
Armstrong, Edith, 490
The Art of Love, 59
As You Like It, 126
Auden, W. H.
  The Age of Anxiety, 96
Aurelius, Marcus A., 15, 149, 204
Awareness, 77, 79–80
  lack of, 116
  of money, 417
  of wealth, 129
Azarias, 203

B

Bacon, Sir Francis, 11, 29, 43, 163, 450,
  468
Baker, Russell, 145
Balance, 25, 48–49, 69, 157–159, 173, 433,
  493
  activity vs. rest, 495
  definition, 49
  getting vs. enjoying, 499–503
  in caring, 35
  in life, 305, 509
  togetherness vs. solitude, 495–497
  work vs. play, 495
Baldry, W. Burton, 131
Baldwin, James, 66
Balfour, Lord, 274
Bangs, John Kendrick, 330
Banks, Harry F., 137
Barrie, James, 321
  Peter Pan, 17
Barry, Dave, 213
Barrymore, John, 484
Baudelaire, Charles, 117
Beauty, 364
Beecham, Sir Thomas, 210
Beecher, Henry Ward, 116, 159, 470
Beethoven, Ludwig van, 176

You mean you can
actually spend 70,000 dollars
at Woolworth's?

BOB KRASNOW
UPON SEEING THE INTERIOR
OF IKE AND TINA TURNER'S HOME

The man who is worthy of being
"a leader of men" will never complain
about the stupidity of his helpers,
the ingratitude of mankind nor
the inappreciation of the public.
These are all a part of the great game of life.
To meet them and overcome them
and not to go down before them in disgust,
discouragement or defeat—
that is the final proof of power.

WM. J. H. BOETCKER

*If you would like to receive
information about future
books, tapes, lectures, etc.
by John-Roger and
Peter McWilliams,
please send
your name and address
to*

*Prelude Press
8159 Santa Monica Boulevard
Los Angeles, California
90046*

*or call
1-800-LIFE-101*

Thank you.

If I am rich,
it is because
I have taken
my wages in people.
You are my reward.

QUENTIN CRISP

About the Authors

JOHN-ROGER, an educator, has been very busy during the past twenty-nine years. He has traveled the world, teaching, lecturing, writing and presenting seminars on just about every conceivable area of personal growth. He has founded several organizations dedicated to a broad range of projects including health, education, spirit, philosophy, service, integrity, corporate excellence and individual and world peace. He has written twenty-nine books, recorded hundreds of audio and video tapes, and has a nationally syndicated television show, "That Which Is."

PETER McWILLIAMS published his first book, a collection of poetry, at the age of seventeen. His series of poetry books went on to sell more than 3,000,000 copies. A book he co-authored on meditation was #1 on the *New York Times* bestseller list, as was *DO IT! Let's Get Off Our Buts*. He is the co-author of *How to Survive the Loss of a Love*. His *The Personal Computer Book* was a bestseller. He is a nationally syndicated columnist, teaches seminars, and has appeared on the "Oprah Winfrey Show," "Donahue," "Larry King" and "The Today Show."

*You have just
been listening to
that Chinese sage,
On Too Long.*

WILL ROGERS